Revolutionary Ireland, 1912–25

Revolutionary Ireland, 1912–25

Robert Lynch

Bloomsbury Academic
An imprint of Bloomsbury Publishing Plc

BLOOMSBURY

LONDON • NEW DELHI • NEW YORK • SYDNEY

Bloomsbury Academic

An imprint of Bloomsbury Publishing Plc

50 Bedford Square	1385 Broadway
London	New York
WC1B 3DP	NY 10018
UK	USA

www.bloomsbury.com

BLOOMSBURY and the Diana logo are trademarks of Bloomsbury Publishing Plc

First published 2015

British Library Cataloguing-in-Publication Data
A catalogue record for this book is available from the British Library.

ISBN: HB: 978-1-4411-5704-1
PB: 978-1-4411-5838-3
ePDF: 978-1-4411-8689-8
ePub: 978-1-4411-6861-0

Library of Congress Cataloging-in-Publication Data
A catalog record for this book is available from the Library of Congress.

Typeset by RefineCatch Limited, Bungay, Suffolk

To Yvonne, with thanks for all your endless love and support

CONTENTS

MAP OF IRELAND

Letterkenny •
• Derry
DERRY
Ballymena •

DONEGAL
ANTRIM

Donegal •
Omagh •
Belfast •

TYRONE
DOWN

Enniskillen •
Armagh •
Downpatrick •

FERMANAGH
ARMAGH

Sligo •
LEITRIM
Monaghan •
Newry •

SLIGO
MONAGHAN

MAYO
• Leitrim
• Cavan
Dundalk •

• Castlebar
CAVAN

LOUTH

ROSCOMMON
Longford •
Navan •

Roscommon •
LONGFORD
MEATH

Mullingar •

WESTMEATH

Ballinasloe •
DUBLIN

Galway •
KILDARE
Dublin

GALWAY
• Tullamore

OFFALY
Kildare •

Port Laoise •

Wicklow •

LAOIS
WICKLOW

CLARE
Ennis •
Carlow •

• Nenagh
Kilkenny •
CARLOW

Thurles •
KILKENNY

Limerick •

LIMERICK
TIPPERARY

WEXFORD

Clonmel •

KERRY
Wexford •

• Tralee
Waterford •

Killarney •
CORK
Mallow •
WATERFORD

Cork •

_____ Border between Republic of Ireland
and Northern ireland

-------- County boundaries

0 _____ 75 km

CHRONOLOGY

1884	November	Gaelic Athletic Association (GAA) formed by Michael Cusack
1886	June	First Home Rule Bill defeated in Westminster
1891	October	Death of Home Rule leader Charles Stewart Parnell
1892	November	Gaelic League founded by Douglas Hyde
1893	September	Second Home Rule Bill defeated in House of Lords
1900		Home Rule Party reunited under John Redmond
1902		Independent Orange Order formed
1903		Wyndham's Land Act
1905	March	Ulster Unionist Council (UUC) formed Arthur Griffith's Sinn Fein formed
1906		Liberal landslide general election victory
1910		Two general elections in January and December
1911	August	Parliament Act
1912	11 April	Third Home Rule Bill introduced in House of Commons
	28 September	Ulster's Solemn League and Covenant signed on 'Ulster Day'
1913	31 January	Ulster Volunteer Force (UVF) founded
	24 September	UUC calls for creation of Ulster Provisional Government if the Home Rule is enacted
	19 November	Irish Citizen Army founded in Dublin
	25 November	Irish Volunteers founded at Rotunda in Dublin
1914	20 March	Curragh 'mutiny'
	2 April	Cumann na mBan founded in Dublin
	24 April	Weapons landed at Larne to arm UVF
	25 May	Third Home Rule Bill passed for third time by the House of Commons
	26 July	Weapons landed at Howth for Irish Volunteers
	20 September	John Redmond makes Woodenbridge speech urging Irish Volunteers to enlist in the British Army
	15 September	Third Home Rule Act suspended for duration of the war pending an amendment for special treatment for Ulster
	24 September	Split in the Irish Volunteers

1915	May	Irish Republican Brotherhood (IRB) form Military Committee to plan insurrection
	7 August	10th (Irish) Division lands at Gallipoli
1916	21 April	Roger Casement arrested in Kerry and gunrunning ship *Aud* intercepted by Royal Navy
	22 April	MacNeill countermands order for Volunteer manoeuvres set for Easter Sunday
	24 April	Easter Rising begins in Dublin
	29 April	Easter rebels surrender; Martial Law extended to the rest of Ireland
	3–12 May	Fifteen rebels executed in Dublin
	1 July	36th (Ulster) Division decimated on the first day of the Somme offensive
	3 August	Roger Casement hanged at Pentonville gaol in London
	4 November	Martial Law ended, Maxwell replaced as army commander
	23 December	Remaining internees released from Frongoch internment camp and Reading Gaol
1917	5 February	Count Plunkett wins by-election victory in North Roscommon
	16 June	Remaining prisoners released from prison
	10 July	Eamon de Valera wins by-election in East Clare
	25 July	Irish Convention opens in Dublin
	26 October	De Valera elected President of Sinn Fein
1918	6 March	John Redmond dies, replaced by John Dillon as leader of the Home Rule Party
	9 April	Military Service Bill introduced clearing the way for possible extension of conscription to Ireland
	18 April	Anti-conscription conference held in Dublin
	18 May	'German Plot' arrests of republican leadership
	11 November	Armistice ends the Great War
	14 December	Sinn Fein win seventy-three Irish seats in general election
1919	21 January	Dáil Eireann convened at Mansion House in Dublin; Two Royal Irish Constabulary (RIC) constables shot dead in attack by Volunteers at Soloheadbeg in South Tipperary
	1 April	Eamon de Valera elected President of Dáil
	11 June	De Valera leaves for the United States
	28 June	Treaty of Versailles signed
	12 September	Dáil made illegal
	26 October	De Valera elected President of Sinn Fein

1920	2 January	Recruitment begins for 'Black and Tans'
	25 February	Government of Ireland Act introduced in House of Commons
	4 April	Irish Republican Army (IRA) launch attacks on over 300 unoccupied RIC barracks across Ireland
	June	Sinn Fein and Nationalists make substantial gains in local elections following on from victories in urban elections in mid-January
	21 July	'Shipyard Expulsions' in Belfast leads to three days of rioting
	27 July	Auxiliary Division formed
	6 August	Dáil instigate Belfast Boycott
	1 November	Recruitment started for new Ulster Special Constabulary
	21 November	'Bloody Sunday' in Dublin
	28 November	Kilmichael Ambush
	23 December	Government of Ireland Act becomes law
1921	13 May	Sinn Fein candidates victorious in elections, form Second Dáil
	24 May	Unionists win substantial victory in elections to new Northern Ireland parliament
	22 June	Northern Ireland parliament opened by King George V
	9–14 July	Sustained sectarian rioting in Belfast leading to twenty deaths
	11 July	Truce implemented ending War of Independence
	16 August	Second Dáil meets in Dublin
	26 August	Dáil elects Eamon de Valera as President of the Irish Republic
	11 October	Anglo-Irish negotiations begin in London
	22 November	Security and policing powers transferred to new Northern Ireland government
	6 December	Anglo-Irish Treaty signed
	14 December	Dáil Treaty debates begin
1922	7 January	Dáil approves Treaty
	21 January	First Craig-Collins Pact
	12 February	Violence erupts in Belfast after IRA shootings along the border, leading to almost thirty deaths in three days
	26 March	Army Convention establishes IRA Executive
	30 March	Second Craig-Collins Pact
	7 April	Northern Ireland government introduce the Civil Authorities (Special Powers) Act
	May	Ineffectual IRA offensive launched in Ulster

	23 May	Mass internment of hundreds of Republicans in Northern Ireland
	31 May	Royal Ulster Constabulary (RUC) established
	16 June	Pro-Treaty candidates win substantial majority in elections for constitutional assembly
	22 June	Sir Henry Wilson assassinated in London
	28 June	Provisional Government troops open fire on the Four Courts thus initiating Irish Civil War
	30 June	Four Courts garrison surrenders followed by sporadic fighting in Dublin
	12 August	Arthur Griffith dies
	22 August	Michael Collins killed in ambush in West Cork
	11 September	Proportional Representation for local government elections abolished in Northern Ireland
	28 September	Dáil votes to create special military courts
	10 October	Catholic Church issues pastoral excommunicating members of the anti-Treaty IRA
	17 November	First executions of Republican prisoners take place
	7 December	Northern Ireland parliament votes to opt out of the Irish Free State
1923	10 April	Liam Lynch killed in ambush in Knockmealdown mountains
	27 April	Suspension of IRA campaign, finalised on 24 May with Frank Aiken's 'Dump Arms' order
	15 August	De Valera arrested in Co. Clare and interned until July 1924
	27 August	Cumann na nGaedheal wins general election
	10 September	Irish Free State admitted to the League of Nations
1924	6 March	'Army Mutiny' in response to plans to reduce army numbers
	10 May	Northern Ireland government refuses to nominate candidate for Boundary Commission
	6 November	Boundary Commission convened following Labour government's legislation allowing the British Government to appoint a representative for the Northern Irish government
	24 December	Last internees released by Free State government
1925	7 November	Leaked Boundary Commission report published in *Morning Post*
	20 November	Eoin MacNeill resigns from the Boundary Commission
	3 December	Final settlement of boundary and financial arrangements between British and both Irish governments in London

WHO'S WHO OF THE IRISH REVOLUTION

Frank Aiken (1898–1983): IRA Commander from South Armagh. Became IRA Chief of Staff after the death of Liam Lynch in April 1923. Prominent later member of Fianna Fail and close ally of Eamon de Valera, later holding various ministerial posts including most notably Minster for External Affairs from 1957–69.

Tom Barry (1897–1980): Prominent IRA guerrilla leader. Led the West Cork Flying Column during the War of Independence which carried out the Kilmichael Ambush, the most successful guerrilla ambush carried out by Republicans during the conflict. Later published a book about his exploits, *Guerrilla Days in Ireland* (Mercier, 1955).

Richard Dawson Bates (1876–1949): Senior Ulster Unionist politician. Secretary of the UUC, elected MP for East Belfast in 1921. Became the first Minister of Home Affairs of Northern Ireland where he introduced the Civil Authorities (Special Powers) Act in 1922. He would remain in office until 1943.

Ernest Blythe (1889–1975): Leading pro-Treaty politician from Lisburn, County Antrim. Elected to First Dail in December 1918. Irish Free State Minister for Local Government and later Minister for Finance. Prominent in pushing for a 'peace policy' in regard to Northern Ireland in the autumn of 1922.

Dan Breen (1894–1969): IRA leader from South Tipperary who took part in the Soloheadbeg Ambush of January 1919, seen as the starting point of the War of Independence. Like Barry wrote a bestselling memoir, *My Fight for Irish Freedom* (Tralee, 1964).

Sir Edward Carson (1854–1935): A prominent Dublin lawyer who was leader of the Ulster Unionist Party from 1910–21. Prominent in Ulster Unionist protests during the Ulster Crisis and instrumental in the machinations at Westminster which led to the Government of Ireland Act in 1920.

Roger Casement (1864–1916): An Irish-born British diplomat who travelled to Germany to acquire guns for the Easter Rising. After the failure of his plan he was arrested and hanged in Pentonville prison in August 1916.

Robert Erskine Childers (1870–1922): British-born author and propagandist for Sinn Fein. Acted as secretary to the Sinn Fein Treaty delegation in London. Opposed the Treaty on return and helped launch the Republican propaganda efforts during the Irish Civil War. Later captured and executed by Provisional Government authorities in November 1922.

Thomas Clarke (1858–1916): Veteran IRB member and prominent leader of the Easter Rising after his release from prison. Executed in the aftermath of the Rising.

Michael Collins (1890–1922): Republican revolutionary from West Cork. After spending over a decade working in London, returned to take part in the Easter Rising. Rose to prominence while interned and emerged to become a leading member of the IRB, IRA and Sinn Fein. Appointed Minister of Finance, Director of Intelligence of the IRA, he was also head of the Supreme Council of the IRB. Later prominent signatory of the Anglo-Irish Treaty, becoming Chairman of the Provisional Government. Killed in an ambush in West Cork during the civil war in August 1922.

James Connolly (1868–1916): Irish Trade Unionist and Socialist activist who led his Irish Citizen Army alongside the Irish Volunteers during the Easter Rising. Executed in the aftermath of the Rising.

William Thomas (W. T.) Cosgrave (1880–1965): Sinn Fein leader who became Minister for Local Government in the revolutionary Dáil and later Chairman of the Provisional Government. Would remain leader of the new Irish Free State until 1932.

Sir James Craig (1871–1940): Ulster Unionist leader who played a prominent role alongside Carson in resistance to the Third Home Rule Bill. Later to be the first Prime Minister of Northern Ireland, a position he held until his death in 1940.

Joseph Devlin (1871–1934): Home Rule (later Nationalist) MP for the Falls Road area of West Belfast. Prominent leader of the Ancient Order of Hibernians and unrelenting critic of partition.

John Dillon (1851–1927): Key leader of the Home Rule Party becoming its leader after the death of John Redmond in March 1918.

Arthur Griffith (1871–1922): High-profile Dublin journalist and founder of Sinn Fein. Became prominent figurehead for the movement after its rebirth in the wake of the Easter Rising. Acted as President of the Dáil during de Valera's absence during the War of Independence and later became President after the Treaty split. Signatory of the Anglo-Irish Treaty.

Thomas Johnson (1872–1963): Dublin Trade Unionist, prominent in the Dublin lockout of 1913. Later drafted Sinn Fein's Democratic Programme. Emigrated to the USA.

Liam Lynch (1893–1923): Cork IRA commander of the 1st Southern Division during the War of Independence. Later became the Chief of Staff of the anti-Treaty IRA during the civil war before his death in an ambush in April 1923.

Sean MacDermott (1883–1916): Belfast-born IRB organiser and later signatory of the Easter proclamation. Executed in the aftermath of the Rising.

Eoin MacNeill (1867–1945): Academic and founder of the Irish Volunteers in 1913. Became Free State representative on the Boundary Commission of 1924–25.

Mary MacSwiney (1872–1942): Sister of Terence MacSwiney who became a Sinn Fein TD and later one of the strongest opponents of the Anglo-Irish Treaty. Member of the Republican government under Eamon de Valera during the civil war.

Terence MacSwiney (1879–1920): Sinn Fein Lord Mayor of Cork and IRA commander who died while on hunger strike in Brixton prison in October 1920.

Constance Markievicz (1868–1927): Countess, due to marriage to a Polish count, who took part in a number of radical suffragist, socialist and Irish nationalist organisations. Commander of a detachment of the Irish Citizen Army during the Easter Rising. Sinn Fein Teachta Dála (TD) and the first woman to be elected to Westminster although she never took her seat. Opponent of the Treaty and later supporter of Fianna Fail.

Richard Mulcahy (1886–1971): IRA commander from Waterford. Became Chief of Staff of the IRA during the War of Independence. Backed the Treaty and became Commander in Chief of the new Free State Army after the death of Michael Collins. Later to become leader of Fine Gael.

Rory O'Connor (1883–1922): Prominent leader of the anti-Treaty Executive IRA faction during the early stages of the Irish Civil War. Led the occupation of the Four Courts in March 1922. Captured during the battle for Dublin and later executed in December 1922.

Eoin O'Duffy (1892–1944): Monaghan IRA leader. Became pro-Treaty Chief of Staff of the IRA in 1922 and was prominent in organising a covert offensive against the Northern Irish government prior to the outbreak of the civil war. Served as Commissioner of the new Free State police force, the Garda Siochana. Later established the pseudo-Fascist 'Army Comrades Association' and 'League of Youth' (also known as the 'Blueshirts').

Kevin O'Higgins (1892–1927): Prominent pro-Treaty Sinn Fein and Cumann na nGaedheal politician. Elected Sinn Fein MP for Laois in 1918. Assistant Minister for Local Government to W. T. Cosgrave in the First Dáil. Vice-President of the Executive Council and Minister for Justice in the Irish Free State government where he oversaw policy of executions of Republican prisoners. Assassinated by the IRA in Dublin, 10 July 1927.

Patrick Pearse (1879–1916): Gaelic cultural activist, poet, teacher and IRB member. Nominal leader of the Easter Rising. Read the proclamation of the Irish Republic outside of the General Post Office on 24 April 1916. Later executed.

Count George Noble Plunkett (1851–1948): Dublin-born papal count, academic and father of Joseph Plunkett, one of the leaders of the Easter Rising. Became first Sinn Fein MP after victory in the North Roscommon by-election in 1917.

Joseph Plunkett (1887–1916): One of the signatories of the Easter proclamation. Prominent in the military planning for the Rising. Executed in its aftermath.

John Redmond (1856–1918): Leader of the minority Parnellite faction of the Irish Parliamentary Party and later leader of the reunified Home Rule Party. Allied with the Liberals in the wake of the 1910 elections and supported the passing of a Third Home Rule Bill for Ireland. Died in March 1918 to be replaced by his deputy John Dillon.

Eamon de Valera (1882–1975): Born in New York, returned to Ireland at the age of two after the death of his Spanish father. Brought up by relatives in County Limerick. Commander of a detachment of Irish Volunteers during the Easter Rising. Became leader of Sinn Fein in 1917 and President of Dáil Eireann from April 1919 and later President of the Irish Republic from August 1921. Prominent opponent of the Anglo-Irish Treaty. Later established Fianna Fail becoming President of the Executive Council in 1932 and later President of the Irish Republic after leading several Fianna Fail governments.

Sir Henry Wilson (1864–1922): Irish-born Field Marshall and former Chief of the Imperial General Staff of the British Army. Later appointed as Military Adviser to the Northern Irish government until his assassination in London in June 1922, an event which was key in precipitating the outbreak of the Irish Civil War.

Introduction

The Irish revolution remains not only the great foundation myth of the southern Irish state but also that of all shades of Irish Nationalist opinion, from moderate constitutionalists through to physical force Republicans. The events themselves have engendered an enormous amount of popular and scholarly interest producing best-selling memoirs by leading radicals, a whole host of biographical studies of leading political figures and numerous television documentaries and cinematic dramatisations.

Portrayals of modern Irish history have been dominated by a variety of what have been termed Nationalist narratives of the period. Such narratives have essentially told the Irish story as a deliverance tale where a subjugated and distinctive ethnic national group managed, after many attempts, to finally throw off the yoke of British colonial oppression to establish its own native government. That achievement was only partial in 1922, however, and it was only after many decades of further political struggle that a full Republic was declared in 1949. For many radical Nationalists the revolution remains unfinished due mainly to the continued existence of partition in the form of the six county state of Northern Ireland. In such perceptions it is only with the achievement of Irish unity under a fully separatist government that the Irish revolution will be complete. At the other end of the scale many Nationalists have also argued for a long revolution spanning many decades prior to the moment of independence, harking back to the Famine of the 1840s or even Wolfe Tone's rebellion of 1798 as a starting point. In such views the various political movements, both constitutional and militaristic, are linked together in one long unbroken liberation struggle.

Thus any description of what occurred in Ireland between 1912 and 1925 as a 'revolution' is by its very nature a contentious claim. However, despite such opposition there can be little doubt that, even if the term 'revolution' proves problematic for many, revolutionary change did occur in Ireland in between the years 1912 and 1925, most of its consequences largely unforeseen. For example, the Ulster Unionist threat to create its own provisional government in 1913 was, despite their professed loyalty to Britain, a revolutionary act. The transfer of power from Britain to two new Irish states was achieved through an unprecedented political mobilisation of the Irish population, evidenced in membership of mass political organisations, transformative election results, labour agitation and, perhaps most prominently, sustained political violence ranging from sectarian rioting to government authorised reprisals and widespread guerrilla warfare.

The study of this period has undergone its own historiographical revolution in recent years which has done much to challenge the predominant Nationalist paradigms. Dismissed by critics as 'revisionism', the reality was that a growing sophistication in terms of research methodology and the release of substantial new primary sources, led to a whole range of fresh historical perspectives. In the mid-1970s, amidst the re-emergence of Nationalist inspired violence in the shape of the Northern Irish 'Troubles', two groundbreaking studies in the shape of Charles Townshend's *The British Campaign in Ireland* and David Fitzpatrick's *Politics and Irish Life*, set the agenda for a whole new generation of scholars. In particular the violence of the revolution, so often glorified in popular histories of the period, has come under increasing academic scrutiny in recent years. Peter Hart's controversial book *The I.R.A. and its Enemies* sought to reveal the previously hidden reality of Irish Republican Army (IRA) violence in the provinces, arguing that far from having a symbiotic relationship with the people, the IRA were engaged in a campaign of terror, with their activities characterised largely by brutal reprisals and focused on soft targets within local communities, in particular Protestants who accounted for over a third of civilian deaths despite being only a small minority of the overall population in Cork, the area of his study.[1]

Hart's approach to the topic, studying the local realities of the revolution on the ground, away from the rhetoric of national politics, has been mirrored by the emergence of a whole host of local and county studies which seek to examine the reality of revolution in the Irish provinces by analysing the growth of advanced Nationalist sentiment in the south and west of Ireland and the process by which British authority collapsed or was made unworkable. What emerged was in effect a whole host of mini revolutions taking place under the umbrella of the national Sinn Fein revolution and driven by a heterogeneous series of local factors and priorities concerning what participants thought the revolution had set out to achieve.

The release of large numbers of new archival sources has managed to both broaden academic understandings of the period and also keep the subject fresh in the public mind with all manner of new revelations. Even now amidst the centenary celebrations of the revolutionary decade, substantial amounts of documents are still closed to researchers and major releases in the South, such as the hundreds of statements from IRA veterans in the shape of the Bureau of Military History collection and the newly opened pension applications from political activists to the southern government, have led to a whole host of new studies and reassessments. Similarly in Northern Ireland the opening of previously closed security files from the Ministry of Home Affairs has done much to enlighten understanding of how partition was achieved and how the new northern state managed to consolidate its position in the early years of its existence.

The aim of this book is to provide both students, and those studying Irish history for the first time, with a general introduction to the key events and contemporary debates within Irish revolutionary studies. Due to the often confused and complex flow of events a chronological, rather than thematic, structure has been favoured. While there are numerous very valid critiques of the periodisation of the revolution, the most widely used delineation of events has been employed.[2]

This book will largely look at the political revolution which saw the creation of two new partition states in Ireland which embodied the most extreme manifestations of Irish nationalism and unionism in the shape of Sinn Fein and Ulster Unionism. The reason for this is that the Irish revolution is notable by the fact that it was overwhelmingly a revolution about constitutional symbols and the origins of political authority. The social side of the revolution was minimal. It can be argued that Ireland's social revolution had already occurred long before the political revolution began. By the early twentieth century Irish land grievances, which had been the most prominent cause of mass political protest in the nineteenth century, had largely been met with the passing of a series of revolutionary Land Acts by the British Government which placed almost three-quarters of Irish land in the hands of native Catholic farmers. Indeed ironically while that class of farmers had been the most prominent component of the radical land agitation campaigns of the 1870s and 1880s, by 1912 they represented the backbone of the moderate conservative constitutional Home Rule party which would soon be swept away by the dynamic separatism of the Sinn Fein movement which emerged in the wake of the Easter Rising. The revolution would thus have little directly to do with social and economic change. As one prominent Sinn Fein member noted, this was a conservative revolution: 'Getting rid of foreign control rather than vast social and economic changes was our aim.'[3] Thus if one seeks to create a simple definition of the Irish revolution it would be almost wholly limited to struggles over the extent and nature of Irish independence.

Each chapter concludes with advice for further reading and a series of key questions about each topic which form the basis of popular essay questions and historical debate. Numerous web links have also been included to allow students to explore certain aspects of the various subjects in greater detail. At the end of the book a number of the most important documents have also been included. These, along with a select bibliography of the most significant works on the period, have been chosen to give students as broad a range of primary and secondary references as possible.

1

Background to the Revolution

The Ireland which was revolutionised adopted its particular form with the Act of Union of 1801. The Act abolished the Irish parliament which, while existing for several centuries, only since 1782 had achieved a significant level of independence. This short-lived body, known as 'Grattan's Parliament', after its most influential leader Henry Grattan, would become an idealised symbol for Nationalists of all shades throughout the following century of the nation's lost political autonomy.

The Union itself was neither complete nor did it abolish the remnants of the old pseudo-colonial system. The Irish population was decimated by the Great Famine of 1845–51. Between those years numbers fell from a high of 8.2 million down to 6.6 million due to a combination of death and emigration. This decline would continue throughout the rest of the nineteenth century meaning that, by 1901, Ireland had lost almost half of its population in fifty years falling to a low of 4.5 million. Politically this meant that by the time of the revolution Ireland, like Scotland, the other member of the Union, was over-represented at Westminster. This curious arrangement was reinforced by the fact that the state still had a Viceroy at its head administering from Dublin Castle and there remained a whole web of archaic Irish departments which retained a complex relationship with ministries in London, most of which merely added an Irish section to their administration, thus further convoluting the constitutional arrangement. Ireland was certainly treated differently from the rest of Britain with uniquely its own armed police force, the Royal Irish Constabulary (RIC), who would administer a series of colonial type coercion acts throughout the nineteenth century unheard of elsewhere in Britain. Similarly legislation passed at Westminster was not automatically applied to Ireland, being enacted in a piecemeal fashion through the political prism of Dublin Castle or shelved entirely in favour of specific Irish legislation. Such landmark legislation, generous as much of it was, would however largely be ad hoc responses to periods of political and social agitation on behalf of the majority Catholic population rather than part of a general trend towards modernisation and rationalisation of Ireland's constitutional position. As such by 1912, for both opponents and defenders of the Union it was equally plausible to paint Ireland as either a colony or a partner of the rest of the United Kingdom.

Irish Unionism

Organised Unionism in Ireland had grown up in response to the threat of home rule in the 1880s. The movement was driven by a number of interlocking fears about the consequences of a devolved Catholic-dominated government in Dublin. Forged from an alliance of southern Anglo-Irish landowners and business leaders in the north-east, traditional fears of religious persecution were added to by concerns that a home rule parliament would jeopardise the economic prosperity of the heavily Protestant areas of East Ulster.

By the turn of the century Belfast was the most important industrial and financial centre in Ireland. While Dublin remained the administrative and ceremonial capital of Irish life, Belfast was the powerhouse of the Irish economy. By 1907 two-thirds of all industrial exports originated in the Belfast region and Belfast banks held over 50 per cent of all deposits and over 80 per cent of business credit balances. This extraordinary industrial growth was matched by a process of urbanisation, with population growth rocketing from 75,000 in 1841 to 387,000 in 1911, by some measures bypassing the southern metropolis as the largest city in Ireland.

This extraordinary rise of Belfast from a small settlement to a major Imperial city was achieved by a combination of luck and dynamic innovation. Driven by the mechanisation of the native linen industry in the mid-nineteenth century the city became a burgeoning export centre. The extraordinary attributes of Belfast harbour made the city the ideal location for the establishment of a flourishing maritime economy. Shipbuilding, revolutionised in terms of both scale and technology after the 1850s, would along with its attendant industries, come to dominate the economy of East Ulster in the fifty years prior to partition. In 1858 Edward Harland took over a small yard in East Belfast and along with Gustav Wolff built one of the most profitable and innovative shipyards in the world churning out characteristically large iron hulled, barque rigged single screw steamers. Although they catered for a worldwide clientele their links with the British mainland, especially Merseyside, remained the mainstay of the business. Indeed it was orders from White Star (famously secured over a game of billiards in 1869) that would both increase these links and supply the 'Big Yard' with some of its most notable commissions. From the launch of the *Oceanic* in 1870 Harland and Wolff set new standards of quality and innovation culminating in 1909 with the launch of the triple screw liners in the shape of the *Olympic, Britannic* and *Titanic*. By 1914 the yard experienced continued success under the guidance of William Pirrie after Harland's death in 1895, and employed almost 15,000 men in East Belfast.

It was not however the only shipbuilding concern in the city. While Harland and Wolff stole the show with their massive creations, the much forgotten 'wee yard' of Workman and Clark established in 1879 turned out a more eclectic mix of products from sleek sailing ships to frozen meat carriers. While employing only half the workforce of its larger competitor Workman Clark turned out more gross tonnage of shipping than any other yard in the UK. Ancillary industries and commercial concerns also flourished in the Lagan Valley. Belfast ropeworks, opened in 1878 by none other than the son of the Victorian self-help guru Samuel Smiles, met the increasing demand for heavy rope for the shipbuilding industry. The 1880s also saw the growth of a native engineering sector replacing the earlier reliance on orders from Clydeside, making shipbuilding both self-sufficient and more economical. Along with this growth in mechanical and marine engineering dozens of medium-sized businesses flourished from food processing to tobacco and beverage manufacture, including the production of aerated water, and in the early years brewing which gave way eventually to whisky distilling. As a financial centre Belfast was unrivalled and banks such as the Ulster Banking Company, Belfast Banking Company and Northern Banking Company provided much of the early investment vital for the new industrial metropolis. While in the 1830s one could sensibly place an imagined Ulster parliament in Armagh and Londonderry there was little doubt on the eve of the partition decade that Belfast lay at the central nexus in not only Ulster but the entire Irish world.

The success of Belfast led this new East Ulster elite to two crucial conclusions that would have a profound effect in shaping the partitionist solution that would emerge in the aftermath of the Great War. The first was that Belfast prosperity was wholly reliant on Ireland remaining part of the British world and any loosening of this connection would have disastrous consequences for these industrial achievements. There was some truth in this. The development of close links between East Ulster and the north-west of England and the west of Scotland was crucial to the well-being of the Belfast economy. The crippling shortage of coal and iron in Ireland was offset by the import of these raw materials through Glasgow and Liverpool, the latter of which was also a crucial entrepôt for Ulster manufactures to be sent to worldwide markets. The resistance to home rule in the nineteenth century was thus backed up by genuine fears. There was real substance in Edward Harland's threat in 1886 that if home rule were enacted he would pack up and move to Glasgow.

The second conclusion drawn was to be more damaging to the future of Irish unity. Claims emerged that the success of the Ulster economy was down to an Ulster Protestant proclivity for hard work and entrepreneurship; that it was the Protestant people of Ulster, their culture and worldview which had given rise to this success. This perception was, if not wholly false, desperately exaggerated. There is no evidence for a higher level of entrepreneurial skill in East Ulster despite the lingering stereotypes. Most of the key movers and shakers came from outside Ireland and those that were successful benefited enormously from circumstance. Between 1860 and 1914 the values of merchant shipping in the United Kingdom rose from £375 million to £1,403 million and Belfast also benefited from a wider shift of shipbuilding and heavy engineering away from the south and east of England to the north and west with ports such as Newcastle, Glasgow, Birkenhead and Barrow all experiencing the same dynamic growth. It was also the case that this drive to industrialisation and urbanisation was a very local phenomenon peculiar to East Ulster rather than peculiar to Protestant Ulstermen. Most of Ulster remained overwhelmingly rural with two-thirds of the population working on the land. Outside of the small enclave of the Lagan Valley, Ulster remained an agricultural and impoverished economy, little different from other parts of Ireland outside of the major urban centres. Indeed it was Belfast peculiarity in the Irish context that allowed it to exploit some of the lowest labour costs in the UK leading to its burgeoning population. The option of migrating to Belfast and heterogeneous economy lessened the effect of agricultural depressions. In terms of partition these perceptions created a widening gulf between Belfast and, not just Dublin, but the rest of Ireland.

These business elites would play a key role in the anti-home rule campaigns of the later nineteenth century. The powerful Belfast Chamber of Commerce founded in 1883 had grown in size and influence along with the city it represented. From a mere 76 members in 1827 it had swelled to 260 in 1893, only 3 per cent of whom were Catholics. While the Chamber has been viewed as the middle ground between business and politics, increasingly this middle ground would disappear and the two elements become fused together. In the decade prior to partition Irish Unionism became dominated by East Ulster priorities in terms of both its ideology and its geographical focus.

As such, growing economic divisions in Ireland ran in parallel with a wider power shift within Irish Unionism itself. The decades prior to partition would see a shift from the previous heterogeneous all-Ireland Unionism of the late-nineteenth-century campaigns against home rule to a localised homogeneous Ulster Unionism dictated by the interests of the commercial classes of East Ulster. By 1918 there was only one landed southern Unionist MP in the House of Commons. The story of the Ulsterization of Irish Unionism is really the story of the breakdown in the relationship between landed southern Unionist elites and the commercial middle classes of Belfast and the Lagan Valley. The shift was also a shift towards the Presbyterians of Ulster. In 1911, 95 per cent of Irish Presbyterians lived in Ulster, 90 per cent of them in the future Northern Ireland, while almost half of all Church of Ireland Protestants lived in the twenty-six counties which made up the future southern state. The famed 'long retreat' of Irish Unionism out of Ireland was also a retreat into northern heartlands.

The growth of Belfast would define the eventual partition settlement in the most profound sense. Indeed so all-pervasive was the domination of East Ulster priorities that the partition settlement which would emerge in the shape of Northern Ireland amounted to Belfast and its own defined hinterland. This is demonstrated markedly by the decision to keep the cities of Newry and Derry within the Northern area despite their being cut off almost completely from their natural hinterlands. Indeed Northern Ireland remains almost unique amongst partitioned counties in having two of its major urban centres lying only a matter of a few miles from the border. Along with the cold jettisoning of the three 'outer Ulster' counties of Monaghan, Donegal and Cavan, the partition saw the maintenance of the heartlands in the east of the province and the symbolic and economically important cities at its eastern and western extremities being secured, the commercial Belfast leadership allowed Ulster to fray at the edges.

While the rise of Belfast was extraordinary, it was typical of many British cities during the late-nineteenth century. What is perhaps more salient is the failure of industrialisation and its attendant urbanisation to impact the south and west. Viewed in an Irish context the rise of Belfast was indeed extraordinary.

Irish nationalism

By contrast the new generation of Irish Nationalists who would dictate the political sentiments of the majority during the partition period looked west not north for their inspiration. The so-called 'new nationalism' which emerged to fill the void in Irish nationalism after the fall of Parnell was in reality an often confused creation of a very modern homogeneous national culture, despite its archaic pretensions, as heterogeneous and dynamic as the economic transformation which had gripped East Ulster. Based on a mixture of Gaelic revivalism and invented cultural pastimes, it both consciously and unconsciously articulated itself against everything that Belfast and East Ulster had come to represent. Douglas Hyde, the founder of the language movement the Gaelic League and future first President of Ireland, stated in 1906:

> A pious race is the Gaelic race. The Irish Gael is pious by nature. He sees the hand of God in every place, in every time, and in every thing. There is not an Irishman in a hundred in whom is the making of an unbeliever. The spirit and the things of the spirit affect him more powerfully than the body and the things of the body. In the things he does not see, he does not believe the less for not seeing them; and in the things he sees, he will see more than a man of any other race; what is invisible for other people is visible for him.[1]

The Irish Revolution can in many ways be defined as the story of an internal revolution within Irish Nationalist political culture. The Home Rule party, the voice of Nationalist Ireland since the 1870s which had called for a repeal of the Act of Union of 1801 and the creation of a devolved legislative assembly in Dublin, would be supplanted by radical separatists in the form of Sinn Fein and its attendant military organisations, the Irish Republican Brotherhood (IRB) and the Irish Volunteers. This was by any measure a staggering achievement. So dominant had been the Home Rule party that their removal as the spokesman for Irish Nationalists was a necessary but daunting first step for any separatist movement before moving on to tackle the British directly. However, this change remains complex and, despite the rhetoric, was less a revolution than an amalgamation of various strands of Irish nationalism. There was a great deal of continuity where the ideas, methods and indeed membership of the Home Rule party would continue to shape the political strategies of Irish nationalism.

Certainly prior to the Easter Rising of 1916, and for a time after, advanced forms of nationalism were firmly in the minority. Irish Nationalists were steeped in the political traditions and cultures of the constitutional nationalism. Since Charles Stewart Parnell, 'the uncrowned King of Ireland', had reinvented it in the mid-1880s the relentless political machine of the Irish Home Rule party dominated Irish Nationalist political life. Even with the split of 1890–1, and the disgrace and death of Parnell himself, the party still maintained its monolithic presence in Irish life. All patronage flowed from it, from its single authoritarian leader at the top down to its grass roots made up of a myriad affiliated organisations, most of whom the party had forcibly co-opted. The rigid discipline of its members allowed for the party to remain solid in difficult times. Dissent was quashed mercilessly, and at times physically, such as at the infamous 'baton convention' of 1909 where Nationalists with a differing vision from the leadership were attacked with clubs and thrown out of the meeting.

However, for all its strengths the Home Rule party also had some inherent weaknesses. The rigid structure of the organisation meant that a leadership clique soon began to form and solidified over the decades. The elites in charge rarely changed, passing their political influence down to the next generation from father to son or uncle to nephew. These family dynasties came to dominate leadership positions and it was increasingly difficult for a new generation to break in. Those few that did manage to affect fundamental change in the party, it can be argued, were often detrimental to the purity of the party's political vision. For example one of the most dynamic and charismatic new leaders to emerge, the West Belfast Catholic Joe Devlin, brought along a new tinge of sectarianism and pushed the party, whose first three leaders had been Protestants, in an even more conservative and Catholic direction.

Such conservatism was mirrored in the parliamentary party which was obedient, unimaginative and disciplined to the point of ossification. There was little dissent from the leadership policy line which meant that despite its size and domination of Nationalist Ireland the party began to rely more and more on a small, increasingly conservative elite to meet fresh challenges when they arose. After 1916 its inability to do this would prove fatal.

The party's growing conservatism was fed into by the constraints placed on the party by the Liberal alliance. Parnell's gamble to throw in his lot with Gladstone and the Liberals in the 1880s had not produced the desired result with the failure of the Home Rule Bill in 1886. Prior to this decision the Irish Party had remained outside of the structures of British political life and sold its votes to whichever party would best serve its interests. Irish votes in Westminster were very significant, amounting to some eighty-five seats. As such whichever of the main parties won the election still needed to have a very significant majority in order to form any kind of working majority government and far more than that to make it safe from the vagaries of by-elections and occasional defections. As such the decision in 1885 to side with the Liberals left the Tories little choice but to side with the opponents of home rule in the shape of Irish Unionists. This new dichotomy was to become an established truism of British politics. For good or ill the post-Parnellite Home Rule party was tied to the fate of the Liberals, having no other viable or credible political home now that the Tories had chosen the side of the Union.

In many ways the Irish question had done much to create this political dichotomy in British politics. The decision taken by Gladstone to support Irish home rule was to prove fateful for the future shape of British, and therefore Irish politics. The Liberal party itself fell apart over the issue with a large group of so-called Liberal Unionists crossing the floor of the house to join with the Tories. The Conservative party itself found in the Irish question an issue that could unite its various disparate elements and indeed the party managed to dominate British government for almost two decades in its aftermath, a period only punctuated by a short-lived Gladstonian administration in 1893 whose only major policy, a failed attempt at a second Home Rule Bill, also brought it to a quick end. Tory unity itself would hold until 1903 when the party split on the issue of Tariff Reform, allowing the Liberals to come back into power.

It is wrong though to think that the almost two decades of Unionist dominated Conservative government would be marked by a defensive or passive approach to the problem of Ireland. Indeed if anything the opposite was the case. With a visionary policy of meeting Irish grievances which many felt underpinned the desire for home rule, the Tories tried to push forward a radical reform agenda. This policy of 'Constructive Unionism' or 'Killing Home Rule with Kindness' as it has been called, was designed to address the sense of injustice which had driven the growth of organised Irish nationalism since the Famine of the 1840s. The most notable of these policies dealt with the land issue which had fired so much radicalism in the 1880s. Building on a series of earlier liberal land measures, the Wyndham Land Act of 1903 was so successful that it essentially ended the land issue as a force within Irish political life. The scheme which allowed Irish tenant farmers to buy their land with financial help from the government resulted in almost half of all Irish land changing hands from old Anglo-Irish elites to the hands of Catholic owners. These Land Acts were incredibly successful and represented a virtual social revolution for an agricultural economy like that in Ireland and were greeted as such at the time. Added to this was a raft of other constructive measures, the most notable of which were the Local Government Act of 1898 and the creation of a 'Catholic' university by the later Liberal government in 1908 in the shape of the National University of Ireland.

Underlying these policies was a hope that they would lead to the creation of a large pool of more conservative rural landowning farmers (exactly the type of people who had formed the backbone of the Land Agitation of the 1870s and 1880s) whose prosperity was largely reliant on British initiatives. In the end it was reasoned that by giving Irish farmers a stake in Irish agriculture they would be less likely to risk their new prosperity with calls for home rule. It was an imaginative scheme which attempted to provide Ireland with the material benefits that any imagined future home rule parliament might have done. While based on some rather prejudicial Unionist views of Irish nationalism as essentially shallow and self-serving it would mean that home rule would thus no longer be the key political issue. This certainly was of profound concern for the Home Rule party, with one of its leaders John Dillon fearing that home rule as an issue would be forgotten as Ireland became more bound up with broader political movements in Britain from where much of this renewed prosperity emanated.

Constructive Unionism was also a threat to the Home Rule party in another way. Even leaving aside its success in undermining support for the home rule, the policy certainly reinforced the lethargy that characterised Irish political life. The domination of the Home Rule party meant that large numbers of seats in the south and west were never contested (something that was also becoming the case for safe Unionist seats in heavily Protestant areas of East Ulster). Only during the election of 1892 was there any real semblance of a political contest between Irish Nationalists with eighty-three of the 103 seats in Ireland contested. However this had much to do with the split in the party engendered after the fall of Parnell, which lingered on long after his death, rather than any fundamental disagreement in terms of policy or political philosophy. This was demonstrated markedly by the fact that by the time the party had reunited under John Redmond, the general election of 1906 saw only twenty-one of Ireland's 103 seats facing contests. Overall therefore the static nature of Irish politics meant that very few MPs were ever replaced and aside from the odd by-election resulting largely from the death of the sitting representative there was little new blood entering the parliamentary party.

Ultimately therefore Irish politics was more imagined than real. The most obvious peculiarity was that the overwhelming majority of Irish voters had voted for home rule but never got it. The two Liberal home rule bills of 1886 and 1893 had both ended in failure, the first in the Commons and the second in the Lords. Even when the Liberals returned to power in 1906, so overwhelming was their majority they had no need for Irish votes in parliament and were also aware that the Tory-dominated Lords would reject any kind of attempt to introduce devolved power to Ireland, as had happened in 1893.

It is thus perhaps peculiar that so many Nationalists remained loyal to the party despite the fact it made little headway in meeting its defining political aspiration. Even during the bitter split over Parnell, most Irish people continued supporting them. One reason for their continued dominance was the party's ability to quash the formation of any kind of alternative political power base by a vigorous policy of taking control of almost all groups with a Nationalist political dimension and placing them under the umbrella of the Home Rule party. One example of this was United Irish League (UIL) which began life as an opposition group in County Mayo but was infiltrated by the Home Rule party, being tamed to such an extent that it soon formed the basis of the party's grass-roots organisation.

In order to incorporate so many disparate Nationalist movements therefore the party could not afford to be ideological but instead represented a giant bandwagon. With the main ambition of home rule yet to be achieved, the party relied on a very persuasive argument about the need for unity and the dangers of sectionalism and ideological struggle before the goal had been reached. This ability to maintain a heterogeneous membership all focused on a single political issue would be one of the chief political legacies inherited by Sinn Fein.

Also, while the party leadership grew increasingly remote and elitist, the average home rule MP retained closer links to his electors than those in British political parties. The party drew on the conservative Catholic farmer class as the backbone of its support. The average MP was more often than not a local notable with strong ties to his community. Paid around £400 per year by the party, home rule MPs were the first to receive a direct salary (something Sinn Fein would mercilessly criticise them for in 1918).

It is also the case that while home rule itself remained unachieved, in other areas the party could point to a progressive list of practical political achievements. The Land Acts, housing provision, local government, the Catholic university and the extension of the Liberal welfare reforms to Ireland were popular political achievements. Although the Home Rule party was not responsible for their introduction, and indeed many of the party were secretly opposed to many of the changes, they were able to take a great deal of credit for them arguing that their strong presence at Westminster had, if not impelled the British to enact them, certainly hastened their arrival.

Perhaps the most important legacy of the Home Rule party however was to provide Ireland with a strong tradition of democratic political engagement. This constitutional strand of Irish nationalism would endure a lot longer than the party itself and was to inspire the political side of the Republican movement at various key times during the turbulent revolution to come. While the militarist would dominate the movement for long periods, the democratic impulse endured. Indeed it can be argued the Irish civil war was effectively a long overdue showdown between these two strands of Irish nationalism. The victory of the pro-Treaty side of the movement was thus a victory for the central role of democracy in Ireland's future political culture. The fact that Ireland, unlike so many post-colonial states, was able to introduce and sustain a liberal democracy at the first time of asking was a tribute to the unyielding constitutionalism of the Home Rule party.

Advanced nationalism

Those Nationalists which would come to replace the Home Rule party were largely a political irrelevance in the first decade of the twentieth century. One of the key questions of the period is how a small minority of radical separatists came to dominate the agenda of Irish nationalism winning the support of the vast majority of the population and sustaining it despite its confrontational and violent revolutionary campaign. Politically these radicals were made up of a wide range of inchoate groupings and individuals, running from Republican militarists in the shape of the IRB, through Gaelicist cultural activists to ill-defined pseudo-political bodies such as Sinn Fein.

The catalyst for this new mood was the so-called 'new nationalism' which emerged after the failure of the second Home Rule Bill. With the campaign for devolution foundering the Irish party fell into a bitter internecine struggle between supporters and opponents of the disgraced Irish leader which continued for almost a decade after his death in 1891. This period from the 1890s would see the rise of a whole host of Irish cultural movements which sought to stem what they saw as creeping Anglicisation. The most popular movement was the Gaelic Athletic Association (GAA), formed in 1884 by Michael Cusack, which sought to appeal to Irish youth with the creation of a number of what it defined as native Irish sports including Gaelic football, handball and hurling. With over 800 branches in 1908 and tens of thousands of members, the organisation affirmed its nativist credentials with campaigns against foreign or 'garrison' games such as cricket and football, defining the association with a more stringent form of Irish identity. The other major success story was the Gaelic League formed in 1893. Although less popular than the GAA its activists sought to protect and promote the Irish language with calls for its compulsory inclusion on the Irish school syllabus. The 'new nationalism' was incredibly diverse. For some it offered merely the chance to play Irish games to relieve the boredom of small town Irish life whilst for others it was an attempt to uncover an imagined authentic Ireland. Many found that cultural heartland in the west and made numerous summer pilgrimages to Irish-speaking areas to study their traditions, record folk memories, wear traditional costume or sketch the landscape and its people. Overall though this campaign for an Irish Ireland was an attempt to explore and define the essence of Irishness and distil it into a more exclusivist homogeneous national identity. It was this identity which would underpin and inspire the later revolutionary generation. Broadly speaking these nebulous organisations who allied themselves to this new identity shared a worldview which can best be described as advanced nationalism and a tendency to be more separatist and idealistic than the more pragmatic Home Rule party. While many professed themselves to be apolitical they shared a reverence for Irish culture and a broad political impulse which rejected the conservatism and all-pervasive dominance of the Home Rule party.

The key figure around whom many of these radicals gathered and the most adept at articulating this advanced Nationalist outlook was Arthur Griffith. Typical of this outlook, Griffith was a journalist and polemicist but was not active in any formal political sense. One of the most controversial figures of his age, he gave voice to a whole variety of strong views and opinions, united only in their constant and withering criticism of the home rule orthodoxy. His views themselves were a confused mix of conservatism and radicalism. For example he was a bitter critic of J. M. Synge's controversial play *The Playboy of the Western World* which sparked riots in Dublin in 1907. He was also vocal in his criticism of the labour leader Jim Larkin, who led the radical trade union protests during the Dublin Lockout of 1913. At the same time however his writings, a strange combination of the impractical and the visionary, were avidly supported by those who sought political separation from Britain. Personally however he had no overt political ambitions and little seeming interest in money or personal glory. Despite his role as a figurehead, at various key times in his career he would step aside and allow other more adept political leaders to take his place at the head of the movement, whether that be Eamon de Valera in 1917 or Michael Collins in 1922.

His key contribution to Irish political life and chief love was journalism, contributing and editing various publications from 1899. His own newspapers included the very influential *Nationality, United Irishman* and most notably *Sinn Fein.* During the Great War he would beat the censor by his innovative creation of *Scissors and Paste,* a collage of a newspaper made up from various other published news reports juxtaposed and cut in various ways so as to subvert the censor and present a more critical Nationalist message. The paper itself would only last for a few weeks at a time before being banned but did show up Griffith's innate genius as a publicist. As a writer he was incisive and punchy in his analysis and presented original ideas in an appealing way. His arguments were carefully crafted offering a mixture of madcap visions of an imagined Irish future and some carefully argued pieces on economic nationalism using vast amounts of statistics and debates about tariffs and the creation of native industries.

If one signature political idea of Griffith can be discerned, it was his view that the Act of Union of 1800 was illegal and should therefore be ignored. He argued that the Irish parliament of 1800 had no right to dissolve itself and should therefore be resurrected by current Irish parliamentarians who sat at Westminster. Even though the parliament he wished to resurrect,

Grattan's parliament (1782–1800), named after its leader Henry Grattan, was in no way a Nationalist body, being rather an elitist and profoundly corrupt institution, this idea involved a key later political principle of Irish separatists in the form of abstention. His broader vision was again rather quirky arguing in his 1904 publication, *The Resurrection of Hungary*, not for full separation but the creation of a dual monarchy along the lines of the Ausgleich of 1867 which saw the creation of the Austro-Hungarian empire with two equal parliaments, one in Vienna and one in Budapest. He felt that this idea was key to winning over Irish Unionists by maintaining the King as the link with Britain whilst also offering Nationalists full legislative independence. The comparison with Hungary and Ireland however was an unfortunate one considering the brutal record of the Hungarians in putting down internal dissent and crushing its own minority populations. Griffith certainly felt his idea would offer a solution to the Irish question that would appeal to separatists, moderate Nationalists and Unionists. While he had been a Republican as a young man, he had rejected it as an unrealistic and potentially dangerous and counterproductive ideology. His commitment to the Dual Monarchy idea however was not ideological but rather what he saw as the only practical solution to heal the divisions within Irish political culture.

Griffith's commitment to overt political activity was therefore reluctant and half-hearted. However, in the political culture of advanced nationalism at the time his lack of precision and dogma made him an ideal if unlikely rallying point. Oddly his main pastime had been arguing with other radical factions rather than marshalling them but the sheer preponderance of advanced Nationalist groups led him to the idea of creating a closer federation of organisations who could better stand up to the dominance of the Home Rule party. To this end he became involved in the formation of Cumann na nGaedheal in 1900 (a name later used by the governing party of the Free State between 1922 and 1932) under the old Fenian John O'Leary and Maud Gonne. Three years later Griffith struck out on his own with the creation of a National Council which had emerged out of a group formed to protest against the visit of the King to Dublin in 1903. Added to these groups were the newly emerging Dungannon Clubs, a network of Republican debating societies, which emerged in the north under the control of Bulmer Hobson, an energetic IRB member and Quaker from Belfast, in 1905. To this broad front would be added the myriad other Irish cultural groups such as the Gaelic League.

The creation of Sinn Fein (translated as 'we ourselves'), the party whose name would soon resound around the world as the main representative of advanced nationalism in Ireland, took place in 1907 after a decision to run a number of candidates in the local elections to the Dublin Corporation. The group only became a national one when two sitting home rule MPs joined Griffith's radical group, both resigning their seats and one of them deciding to run again under the Sinn Fein banner as an Abstentionist. In the resulting by-election however the Sinn Fein candidate was defeated and Griffith drifted away from the project to return to his journalism. After reaching a highpoint in 1909 of 1,200 members spread over 100 branches across Ireland, the new leadership allowed the party to drift and fall into decline to such an extent that there was only one branch in existence by 1914.

Griffith's first foray into politics had been a failure and he had shown himself to be an ineffective political leader. In the two general elections of 1910, when home rule was once again back on the agenda of British politics, Griffith's Sinn Fein stood aside to allow the Home Rule party a clear run. While Griffith claimed this decision was to give the home rule leader, John Redmond, a final chance to do their best for Ireland, the reality was that he had failed to provide a cohesive and viable advanced Nationalist alternative. Tellingly he could not even provide a rallying point for those disillusioned with the Home Rulers during the Ulster Crisis, many of whom would choose instead to join a new body in the shape of the paramilitary Irish Volunteers. However, Griffith's reversion to his old role as an instigator and polemicist on the radical wing of Irish nationalism continued. Most important was his very public profile which contrasted markedly with the secretive underground workings of the IRB. Due to this visibility Sinn Fein and Griffith would become symbols to attach to the Irish Volunteer movement and understandably, if erroneously, Sinn Fein would become the label attached to the group and its supporters who would carry out the Easter Rising in 1916. Ironically Griffith himself played no part in the Rising and disagreed strongly with the idea of physical force enterprises as doomed to failure. However, his arrest and imprisonment in its aftermath sealed his radical reputation and that of his party as a prominent symbol for the newly emerging separatist grouping which emerged in the aftermath of the Rising, giving him and his party a prominence that they had neither desired nor deserved.

The Irish Republican Brotherhood

Those that did launch the Rising held a far more militant vision than Griffith's Sinn Fein and a much longer history. While not being openly hostile to Griffith and his supporters, Irish Republicans rejected the methods and ideology of constitutional politics. Even though much of their tradition was imagined, they saw themselves as the inheritors of a much longer tradition of physical force rebellion flowing from Wolfe Tone in the 1790s, through Robert Emmet in 1803, down through the Young Irelanders of the 1840s to the Fenian movement of the 1860s and beyond. The core of their beliefs was the creation of an Irish Republic won by physical force means. They shared a romanticised view of Celtic mythology which, in typical European late-nineteenth-century fashion, recalled an imagined golden age before Ireland's subjugation under British colonial oppression. As such they saw their job as to rid Ireland not only of the British influence politically but also culturally to rediscover the authentic Ireland which had been smothered under oppression and creeping Anglicisation. They also shared a profound contempt for the current generation who they saw as too moderate and happy to benefit from the Land Acts and the economic benefits of British rule to the detriment of higher national ideals. They knew well, and at times wore it as a badge of pride, that the vast majority of Irish people saw them as dangerous fanatics and shared none of their political ideas. However, for them their legitimacy was not dependent on contemporary support, drawing instead on older imagined ideas of dead generations, less tainted by the pollution of colonial rule. In the Republican imaginarium Ireland was an eternal idea which could not be destroyed or altered by the vagaries of contemporary political fashions. Their romantic ultra-Nationalist ideas were thus emotional and sentimental. The 'Republic' was less an alternative form of practical political organisation but an ideal utopian vision whose creation would fulfil Ireland's national destiny. They looked back to an imagined past and forward to an idealised future Ireland and were therefore something different from the people who currently resided there and as such there was little need to consult them politically or otherwise. Many of the leaders of the Easter Rising of 1916, most notably Patrick Pearse, would take this utopian idealism into the realm of the spiritual, ironically he himself becoming part of that vision after his execution in 1916.

Republicans certainly believed the notion of creating British rule with a human face in the shape of home rule to be a delusion. For them it was British rule itself which was the fundamental problem, not the form in which it was applied. As such they rejected politics because it was tainted and compromised by definition. By contrast their notions of separatism and militarism were pure and unambiguous. They were not in their view to be gifted independence by the British but rather must struggle to win it if it were to have any real meaning. Even during the bloodshed of the First World War, they retained their faith and belief in militarism and personal sacrifice, Patrick Pearse writing of the war that it was to be welcomed as 'the old heart of the earth needed to be warmed by the red wine of the battlefield'.[2] For many, such images would shape their approach to the revolutionary struggle which was soon to engulf Ireland and would inspire generations of Republicans in the decades afterwards.

The group who would come to define this outlook, the IRB, was founded in 1858. Emerging out of the chaos of the token 'Rising' of 1848 this new group, created by one of its veterans, the peculiar James Stephens, would be a secret conspiratorial organisation controlled through an elaborate cell-like structure of 'circles'. Drawing on expatriate support in the United States, in 1867 this group, known pejoratively as the Fenians, was able to lead an uprising of its own. However, due to shambolic planning and the fact that the organisation was infiltrated by spies and informers, the rising collapsed into farce. So devastating was their defeat in 1867 that the IRB amended its constitution to state that there would be no further rebellions until the people of Ireland expressed their clear support. This peculiar decision to rely on a vague democratic principle reflected more the isolation of the organisation from mainstream Irish political life. Despite a decision to collaborate with the constitutional Nationalists and the rural agitation of the Land League in the 1880s in the so-called 'New Departure', it was clear the IRB was beginning to unravel. Certainly by the turn of the century the IRB was a heavily compromised organisation, with an ageing membership for whom the local pub often became increasingly the forum for its ostensibly secret meetings. Its image as an old man's drinking club by the end of the nineteenth century may be overdone but does communicate its moribund nature and lack of dynamism. Indeed so little were the IRB considered a threat that the Liberal government actually cut funding for its web of spies and informers soon after coming to power in 1906. However, it was exactly at this time that a new generation of radical violent separatists, schooled in Gaelic radicalism, would emerge to reinvigorate the movement which would be prepared only a decade later to launch its own insurrection which, although as much a failure as that of 1867, would finally push Ireland into open revolution.

Sample essay and examination questions

What was meant by 'killing home rule by kindness', and was it doomed to failure as a policy?
Was the 'new nationalism' inevitably separatist in its politics?
Analyse the reasons behind the rise of Ulster Unionism between 1885 and 1910.
How did southern Unionists differ from northern Unionists?
What were the strengths and weaknesses of the Home Rule party between 1890 and 1910?

Further reading

P. Bew, *The Politics of Enmity 1789–2006* (Oxford, 2007)
R. V. Comerford, *The Fenians in Context* (Dublin, 1985)
D. Ferriter, *The Transformation of Ireland 1900–2000* (London, 2004)
R. F. Foster, *Modern Ireland* (London, 1988)
A. Jackson, *Ireland 1798–1998* (Oxford, 1999)
A. Jackson, *Home Rule: An Irish History, 1800–2000* (Oxford, 2003)
J. Lee, *The Modernisation of Irish Society, 1848–1918* (Dublin, 1989)
F. S. L. Lyons, *Ireland since the Famine* (London, 1973)

2

The Ulster Crisis, 1912–14

The 'New' Liberals and home rule

When the Liberals returned to power in 1906 the problems of the Home Rule party became apparent. Their massive landslide victory meant that the Liberals could rule without Irish support and there was little sign of home rule re-emerging on to the national political agenda. Herbert Asquith, who took office after the death of Henry Campbell Bannerman would remain Prime Minster for almost the next decade, was keen to sidestep the issue of home rule for Ireland, seeing the policy as a threat to Liberal unity having already caused a split in the party in the 1880s from which they were only now recovering. A half-hearted attempt to introduce a watered down Irish assembly in the shape of the Irish Council Bill in 1907 drew little support and quickly collapsed. Instead the Liberals would focus on a massive programme of social welfare reform introducing unemployment benefits, old age pensions and a programme of national insurance. With such a momentous series of legislation to pilot through parliament, the issue of home rule was seen as time consuming and divisive and with no need to rely on Irish votes, due to their enormous majority, the prospects for a new home rule bill seemed poor.

However all this was about to change. In 1909 the Conservative-dominated House of Lords began to act in a deliberately partisan way. While the Lords had the power to veto any legislation coming from the Commons, they rarely did so, at most proposing a series of amendments which would then be opened to negotiation in the lower house. However, the radicalism of the New Liberals upset the equilibrium of British politics and the Lords responded to its new legislation with a series of delays and amendments. In 1909, in an unprecedented move, the Lords rejected the Liberal budget. In response Asquith called a general election set for January 1910. The Liberals expected to register a clear victory due to popular public support for its 'People's Budget'. However, the result was inconclusive with the Liberals winning 274 seats, only two more than their Conservative opponents. It was at this point that the Irish question would once again move to the centre stage of British politics.

Redmond was now holding the balance of power. Negotiations dragged on for almost a year until finally a deal was struck with the introduction of a third Home Rule Bill being the price for continued Irish support. Another election in December 1910 ended with almost the same result as that in January. However, with Irish support, Asquith brought forward a Parliament Bill the following year. The bill proposed a series of profound changes to the British Constitution. It reduced the maximum length of the parliament from seven years to five and created salaried MPs. Most notable however was its attack on the power of the veto of the House of Lords whereby the upper house could only delay the passing of legislation, meaning that any bill that passed through the Commons in identical form three times would become law no matter how the Lords voted. The House of Lords was forced to accept this suspensive veto when Asquith threatened to create hundreds of new Liberal peers to force through the legislation. Now the Liberals could move on to fulfil the promise they had made to Redmond with the introduction of a new home rule bill for Ireland. Introduced in April 1912, in the context of the new Parliament Act it meant that even with its inevitable rejection by the Lords, the bill would become law in the summer of 1914.

For all of the trouble that the Third Home Rule Bill was to cause it was hardly a revolutionary piece of legislation. Virtually identical to its two nineteenth-century precedents, it offered a moderate form of devolution with a large number of areas reserved for the Westminster parliament. These included foreign policy, military affairs, trade and constitutional matters. Alongside these issues were a variety of other reserved areas which dealt with the plethora of new social welfare reforms, especially those of the Liberal government after 1906, which had been introduced since the previous Home Rule Bill almost twenty years earlier. Most notable however was that no part of the Bill made any provision for special treatment of Ulster, despite its key role in opposition to the previous two home rule bills and its growing domination of the agenda of Irish Unionism.

For the Presbyterian business elites of East Ulster, home rule threatened to distance Belfast from the prosperous markets of the British Empire, tying the region to an impoverished south and west which it would inevitably have to subsidise through the imposition of draconian taxes and tariffs. The Union thus became a byword for wealth and security for many Protestants who suspected that Nationalist calls for devolution were merely the first step toward inevitable separation. While managing to defeat the threat of home rule in 1886 and 1893, Irish Unionism continued to change and develop. The declining influence of southern landed elites in the wake of Tory land reforms along with the growing importance of mass political movements meant that organised Unionism increasingly became focused on the province of Ulster where as many as a quarter of Irish Protestants lived. This process of so-called 'Ulsterization' was as much a reaction against the increasing perception that in the midst of the cultural revival movement the character of Irish nationalism was becoming increasingly Gaelic and Catholic. In 1905 an Ulster Unionist Council (UUC) was created and Nationalist mythologies were met with a renewed interest in the history and cultural traditions of Ulster Protestantism typified by the revival of the Orange Order and rejection of Gaelic cultural forms and language.

While the definitive split in Irish Unionism occurred after 1912 there were a number of longer-term developments which precipitated its demise. The first of these was the decline in the power and influence of the old landed Unionist elites reflecting both the growing confidence of the commercial classes of East Ulster and also the wider European shift in power from landed to industrial capital. Across Europe the old landed elites were on the wane. In Ireland itself there was a gradual lessening in intensity of land grievances which had done so much to define debates over the Irish question in the second half of the nineteenth century. The Irish Land Acts of 1870 and 1881 twinned with the subsequent Land Purchase Acts of 1885 and 1903 transferred vast tracts of lands from landlords to small tenant farmers. This change overwhelmingly favoured smaller farmers at the expense of the Unionist landlord class. This was particularly marked in Ulster where by 1912 almost three-quarters of farmers were tenant owners, higher than in any of the other three provinces.

The heterogeneous nature of Irish Unionism, while a strength in the era of late-Victorian high politics, was to become a crippling weakness in the new populist politics of the partition era. Politically, southern Unionism was divided far more severely by the threat of home rule than Ulster Unionism. It was caught between adapting a strategy of outright opposition and a more moderate acceptance of its inevitability and attempts to win concession nd shape the nature of home rule to their advantage, a strand of southern Unionism that would continue throughout the partition period articulated by Lord Midleton and his Anti-Partition League. It is possible to argue that the decline of the landed southern elites averted an inevitable showdown between the two brands of Irish Unionism. However, it is wrong to judge the relationship between Ulster and southern Unionism as one of outright hostility. Many southern Unionists remained keen advocates of Ulster Unionist strategy viewing Ulster resistance to the Third Home Rule Bill as a way of wrecking the whole home rule project. The later partitionist shifts of Carson subsequently completely undermined this strategy. Those landed elites who remained within the fold of an increasingly Ulsterized Unionism such as Basil Brooke in Fermanagh and Oliver Nugent in Cavan, were forced to dance to Belfast's tune. The replacement of Carson by the Presbyterian Craig in 1921 was the final symbolic act in this shift northwards. It is possible to see the demise of landed class influence as a victory for Ulster Unionists, allowing them to codify a more populist and homogeneous identity. However, it did not appear so at the time, robbing this embryonic Ulster of political influence, financial support, a heterogeneous culture, and a more defensible and logical all-Ireland focus.

Reactions to the Third Home Rule Bill

While Irish Unionism had undergone huge changes since its emergence in the 1880s, this could not be said for the British approach to the issue of home rule which took no account of such subtleties. The Third Home Rule Bill had largely echoed the solution which had been made in the 1880s, demonstrating something of the lack of interest or dynamism within the Liberal party about the issue. The days of home rule for Ireland being a moral Liberal crusade, as it was during the premiership of Gladstone, appeared to be long gone. Many leading figures in the Liberal party, such as Winston Churchill, had little time for the Irish Party and most treated the issue as a necessary evil or at best unfinished business, the passing of which would allow them to get on and deal with what they perceived to be more pressing issues such as the social reform programme or foreign policy.

However, unlike the Liberals the Conservative opposition was anything but lethargic in its response, offering a vociferous rejection of the Bill from the moment it was promulgated. It is certainly possible to argue that the strident Conservative opposition was an attempt to exploit the Unionist cause in Ireland in order to shore up the Tories' own ailing political aspirations. Indeed by 1912 things were looking increasingly bad for the party, having lost three general elections in a row and, with the passing of the Parliament Act, the sweeping away of a large amount of its institutional power. The fact that the Home Rule Bill would be the first significant test of the new laws also made it an ideal battleground for the Conservatives with Tory hopes hinging on the possibility of using the Irish question as a way of undermining the new laws leading to a reassertion of the power and prestige of the House of Lords.

Nonetheless there can be little doubt about the sincerity and passionate commitment of many Conservative members in their decision to avert the threat of home rule. Under Andrew Bonar Law from November 1911, himself of Scottish Presbyterian stock, the party moved in a radical direction in opposition to home rule. In the Commons Bonar Law constantly sought to place the Bill in a broader context presenting it as a nefarious conspiracy by a Liberal cabal bent on undermining the very foundations of the British Constitution. At a meeting of Unionists held at Blenheim Palace on 27 July 1912 he made a notorious speech in which he promised that 'if the attempt [to introduce home rule] be made under present conditions, I can imagine no length of resistance to which Ulster will go, in which I shall not be ready to support them, and in which they will not be supported by the overwhelming majority of the British people', adding darkly that 'there were things stronger than parliamentary majorities'. Implicit in such statements for many was the threat of civil war.

Ulster was chosen as the battleground for this confrontation. Of the eighteen Unionist MPs in Ireland, sixteen were based in Ulster. The province contained 96 per cent of all Irish Presbyterians and 60 per cent of all Church of Ireland members. By contrast the three southern provinces were overwhelmingly Catholic in their make-up with a Protestant population of little over 9 per cent. Certainly if Unionists wished to base their campaign around the perceived injustice of home rule and the existence of popular opposition to the scheme on the ground then Ulster was the obvious choice. However, the Ulster issue was not a clear cut one. While having by far the largest concentration of Protestants in Ireland, the province as a whole was almost equally split between Protestants and Catholics, a fact reflected in the number of seats held by both parties in the province at Westminster. Five of the nine counties of Ulster (Donegal, Cavan, Monaghan, Tyrone and Fermanagh) had Catholic majorities and as such the notion of demanding special treatment for Ulster or its exclusion from the Bill was a difficult proposition. Even so, it was clear that demanding such a radical step as exclusion was far from the minds of the Unionist leadership. Indeed the principal goal of the opposition movement was to defeat home rule in its entirety. The focus on the injustice such a policy would be to Ulster was largely a political tactic. As Carson himself was to plainly state: 'If Ulster succeeds, home rule is dead'.

With the Conservative opposition making increasingly confrontational noises in elite parliamentary circles, on the ground grass-roots Ulster Unionism began to mobilise with a sustained and aggressive campaign of their own utilising all manner of protest and propaganda. These methods ranged from the more traditional forms of protest such as: mass petitions and demonstrations; the dissemination of an enormous amount of anti-home rule propaganda through the medium of books, pamphlets, newspapers and film; through to a series of headline-grabbing publicity stunts. The most notable of these occurred in September 1912 when almost 500,000 Unionists including almost all politicians, church leaders and industrialists signed a 'Solemn League and Covenant' (Documents 1 and 2) pledging to resist home rule, some of the protesters allegedly signing in their own blood. More ominously across Ulster groups of men, particularly in provincial border areas, began to drill in a variety of pseudo-military organisations. So prevalent did this paramilitarism prove that the following year the Unionist leadership was forced to respond, drawing the various ad hoc units under one single Ulster-wide organisation with the creation of an Ulster Volunteer Force (UVF). This new body would be a far more professional outfit; organised along British military lines and staffed by a large number of ex-army officers and NCOs, the UVF boasted its own cavalry, engineering and medical corps. Despite never being very well armed, largely with wooden replica guns and at most one rifle for every fifty men, it would attract almost 100,000 recruits by the summer of 1914. Despite Nationalists' constant mocking of the new force as a 'sham' and a 'circus', its grass-roots membership was belligerent and committed. Crucially its existence would allow Unionist politicians to use the threat of violence if any attempt were made to force Ulster into a home rule parliament against her will.

The response of the Home Rule party to this seeming radicalisation of Ulster Unionism was restrained and largely dismissive. John Redmond, who now found himself as the leader of an Irish Nationalist party at Westminster in the odd position of standing with the government against the now rebellious Tory establishment, was convinced that Unionist threats were largely empty. He saved his most forthright speeches for the Liberals, concerned that the government would get cold feet, constantly moving to reassure them that Unionists were engaged in a giant game of bluff.

Other more advanced Nationalists however saw in Unionist mobilisation genuine signs of Irish militancy. Although the radical violent separatism of the IRB had never been popular, with the organisation, even after its recent revival, numbering at most 2,000 largely ageing and ineffective members, the creation of the UVF would prove to be inspirational. Hard as it may be to believe, many advanced Nationalists believed, in Patrick Pearse's words, that the most important thing was 'to see arms in Irish hands', regardless of the political aspirations of the holders. For radical Nationalists the advent of a new spirit of popular militarism in Ireland appeared to trump any sectional concerns; Pearse concluding that 'the Orangeman with a rifle was a much less ridiculous figure than the Nationalist without a rifle'. As such moves began in the south for the creation of a similar organisation. After the publication of an influential article by Eoin MacNeill, academic and Gaelic League enthusiast, entitled 'The North Began' which called for Nationalists to emulate northern Unionists, a public meeting was held at the Rotunda in Dublin where on 25 November 1913 the Irish Volunteers were formally created. Their explicit aim, of 'protecting Irish liberties' and defending Ireland's right to home rule, mirrored the defensive language of the UVF. It was also moderate enough to attract high levels of recruitment from across the south and west of the country with the organisation peaking at some 180,000 in the summer of 1914. However, from early on the leadership of the organisation of the new movement was strongly linked with the IRB who saw in the Volunteers the popular mass military movement that would enable them to further their long-held plans to establish an Irish Republic won by force of arms.

The search for a solution

With two paramilitary forces now formed in Ireland many felt there was a pressing need to find some form of compromise agreement. Although Asquith made it clear that the Liberals had no intention of changing the bill or offering concessions to the Unionists, whom he rightly suspected of wishing to use the Ulster issue to wreck the bill in its entirety, this had little effect in discouraging various parties from putting forward a whole range of speculative solutions. The main idea to emerge was that of excluding all or part of the Ulster province from the operation of the Home Rule Bill.

Originally presented by a Liberal backbench MP, Thomas Agar-Robartes, in June 1912, the idea would form the basis of the partitionist solution later to be enshrined in the Government of Ireland Act of 1920. Carson himself was one of the first to offer tentative encouragement to the exclusion plan although he remained for the most part committed to defeating home rule in any form. In Ulster itself the UUC made public its plans for the creation of a provisional government should the bill be enacted and elaborate military plans were made to mobilise the UVF to defend the province in the event.

While Redmond encouraged the Liberal government to hold firm, the notion of exclusion, albeit on a temporary basis, became an obvious way out of the impasse. In November 1913 the Cabinet agreed in principle to support an amendment allowing for the counties to vote themselves out of the Home Rule Bill for a defined period. Redmond's reaction to this was furious, arguing that such a move would paint the government as giving in to Unionist threats. He also found the idea of partition objectionable and expressed concern at the fate of the northern Catholic minority who would be placed under the effective control of an artificial Protestant majority. However, by March 1914 with pressure continuing to build and civil war appearing a distinct possibility Asquith managed to convince Redmond that the exclusion of all or part of Ulster was the only workable solution. The offer he made in a speech in the Commons was that each Ulster county if it so chose could be excluded from the bill for a period of six years. While Carson rejected the temporary nature of the exclusion with the memorable line that it was little more than 'a sentence of death with a stay of execution for six years', the time limit itself was something of a red herring. There was an acknowledgement that at least two general elections would be held in the interim and Bonar Law made it clear if he were returned to power he would make temporary exclusion permanent. Also, even if the Liberals were to stay in power there was little thought given to what to do in the likely event that the rebel Ulster counties would refuse to place themselves under a Dublin government in 1920 as they had done in 1914.

However, in the end the solution was rejected vehemently by the Unionists, leading a frustrated Asquith to try and pass the unamended bill as written with no special treatment for Ulster. During the early summer of 1914, with the failure of the compromise, the situation polarised dramatically. Bonar Law took the unprecedented step of threatening to use the Tory Lords to hold up the military budget unless he received an explicit promise that British troops would not be used to coerce Ulster unless a general election were called on the future of the Home Rule Bill.

In the end Bonar Law did not follow through on his plan due to serious concern in the Conservative party that such a move would be unpopular in the country. However, events on the ground in Ireland soon appeared to demonstrate that the army itself was now becoming politicised. On 20 March 1914 it was reported that a number of army officers had refused to follow orders to reinforce British garrisons in Ulster, a move many saw as the first step towards an all-out attack on the province. In reality this so-called 'Curragh Mutiny' was a confused series of blunders, misunderstandings and poorly communicated orders. Aware that many army officers in Ireland lived in Ulster and were thus reluctant to take part in any future coercion of the province, the War Office offered them the chance to absent themselves during any future operations. However, by the time this order reached Ireland through the incompetent hands of General Arthur Paget, this offer had become an ultimatum to officers residing outside Ulster that they had to either obey orders or face dismissal including the loss of their army pensions. Painted into a corner, around fifty officers declared their preference not to take part in a pre-emptive strike against Ulster and to choose dismissal if it came to the bit, although they would be prepared to take part in a more neutral peacekeeping role. Worse still, the Secretary of State for War, J. E. B. Seely, in a ham-fisted attempt to defuse the situation implied that the government, while it maintained the right to use force, had no intention of doing so against Ulster. The publicity surrounding the incident was to prove very damaging to the government with the press generally painting a sympathetic portrait of the Ulster Protestants. For Asquith the incident reinforced his own long-held concerns about the potential political dangers of using the army to coerce Unionists and effectively ended any realistic option of overcoming Unionist opposition by military means.

The Liberal government's increasing sense of powerlessness was dealt another public blow a month later when over 30,000 German rifles were landed in East Ulster to arm the Ulster Volunteers. In a well organised operation the so-called Larne gunrunning of 24 April 1914 further showed up the ineffectiveness of government control in the province, whilst at the same time reinforcing the perception of the UVF as a viable and now well armed organisation. Worryingly in response the Irish Volunteers in the south followed suit, smuggling 1,500 rifles in through Howth in late July. Unlike in Ulster however the plans for the Volunteers were discovered and, although the guns were kept out of the hands of the authorities, three people were shot dead and scores injured when the army fired on a crowd on Bachelors Walk who were trying to block the military's route to the landing site.

The growing radicalisation of the situation in Ireland placed the Liberals under enormous pressure. The Ulster Unionist demand, articulated by none other than King George V himself, was for the now permanent exclusion of not only the four Protestant counties (Londonderry, Antrim, Down and Armagh) but also Fermanagh and Tyrone where Catholics held a slim majority. On 23 May 1914 the Home Rule Bill finally passed its third reading in the Commons, placing it only one step, that of royal assent, away from becoming law. An amending bill offering once again county option and temporary six-year exclusion was rejected by the Lords who called for the exclusion of all Ulster. In a desperate move the King invited the leaders of all parties to a series of meetings at Buckingham Palace to thrash out a settlement. Over three days, between 21–24 July, Carson and Redmond sought to thrash out a compromise agreement. However, their attempts foundered in the face of Ulster's notoriously complex demographics; a view shared by Asquith who blamed 'that most damnable creation of the perverted ingenuity of man—the County of Tyrone.' The meeting eventually broke up without a resolution. leading Asquith to conclude: 'Nothing could have been more amicable in tone or more desperately fruitless in result.'[1]

The desperate need to find some kind of solution was now a race against time. Parliament was due to break up at the end of August with the Home Rule Bill needing to be fully enacted, completely abandoned or made to start its long two-year journey through parliament all over again. Asquith now decided to make one last offer. He renewed his earlier offer of county option but this time with no fixed time limit. In the end this offer was never made, although it was unlikely to have succeeded anyhow considering Carson's recent pronouncements. The worsening situation in Europe, where the Austrians were already moving troops into Serbia, prompted Bonar Law to contact Asquith suggesting that in the interests of national unity to face the growing crisis in the Balkans, the Irish issue be shelved and the matter of home rule postponed until the approaching continental conflict was resolved. Asquith accepted the offer as did Redmond. In only a matter of weeks Britain would be at war and the vexing issue of Ireland would be placed in suspended animation. In the end the bill would become law in September 1914, although as a concession to Unionists its operation was suspended until after the end of the war, whenever that might be, and with an amendment promising that it would not be fully enacted until the passing of additional legislation dealing with the position of Ulster, although no specific proposals or principles for this were spelled out.

In the end it could be argued that the outbreak of the Great War had saved Ireland from civil war as both Nationalists and Unionists would outdo one another in displays of loyalty to the Crown and throw themselves into the war effort. Certainly Asquith would later note how the Irish question had appeared so insoluble that the distracting arrival of war was one of the best strokes of luck he had in his political life. It was Winston Churchill however who best summed up the weariness with home rule which pervaded senior government circles, noting that 'the parishes of Fermanagh and Tyrone faded back into the mists and squalls of Ireland, and a strange light began to fall upon the map of Europe.' For Irish Nationalists the fact that the Home Rule Bill was now on the statute book was an event of major historic significance. Even though the issue of Ulster was still to be resolved, there was no disguising the relief that after decades of struggle and frustration the long-held aspiration of home rule had been met. With the war expected to last only a matter of months, there was widespread celebration in the south as everyone looked forward to the creation of a devolved government in Dublin. However, such a hope was to prove illusory. The war dragged on for four bitter years and by the time it was finally over in November 1918, both British and Irish politics had been transformed in radical new directions and the battle over home rule appeared as little more than a quaint irrelevance from a bygone age.

Sample essay and examination questions

How much of a threat did the UVF pose to peace in Ireland?
Was Ulster Unionist resistance to home rule anything more than one giant bluff?
Why was the opposition by Ulster Unionists to the Third Home Rule Bill so successful?
Assess the long-term impact of the Ulster Crisis on the character of Irish politics.

Further reading

P. Bew, *Ideology and the Irish Question: Ulster Unionism and Irish Nationalism, 1912–1916* (Oxford, 1994)
P. Bew, *John Redmond* (Dublin, 1996)
A. Jackson, *Sir Edward Carson* (Dundalk, 1993)
A. Jackson, 'Unionist Myths 1912–1985', *Past & Present*, no. 136 (August 1992)
P. Jalland, *The Liberals and Ireland: The Ulster Question in British Politics to 1914* (Brighton, 1980)
K. Jeffery, *Ireland and the Great War* (Cambridge, 2000)
M. Laffan, *The Partition of Ireland, 1911–1925* (Dublin, 1983)
A. O'Day, *Irish Home Rule, 1887–1921* (Manchester, 1998)
J. Smith, *The Tories and Ireland, 1910–14* (Dublin, 2000)
A. T. Q. Stewart, *The Ulster Crisis, 1912–14* (London, 1967)

Useful web links

A selection of fascinating documents and background information relating to the Ulster covenant are available at the website of the Public Record Office of Northern Ireland (PRONI) http://www.proni.gov.uk/index/search_the_archives/ulster_covenant.htm [accessed 2 June 2014].

A copy of a 1912 anthology entitled *Against Home Rule* containing Unionist articles by some of the most prominent political figures of the period including Bonar Law, Edward Carson and Austen Chamberlain, Walter Long and Leo Amery is available at http://www.gutenberg.org/files/15450/15450-h/15450-h.htm [accessed 2 June 2014].

3

The Easter Rising, 1916

The Easter Rising remains the great iconic event of modern Irish history. For many it is the crucial turning point which would tip Ireland into open revolution. Despite its long history, it remains the key ideological myth of modern Irish Republicanism, an event which links the physical force ideologies of the nineteenth century with those of the present. There is no doubt it changed Ireland irrevocably, leading to the destruction of the until then dominant moderate Nationalist Home Rule party and its replacement by a more advanced and radical separatist ideology.

Ireland and the Great War

As we have seen, with the outbreak of the Great War the threat of civil war in Ireland melted away while the contentious Home Rule Bill itself remained in a strange form of suspended animation. Indeed, despite the convulsions to come, the European war drew enormous support from Ireland as both Unionists and Nationalists threw their weight behind it in an effort to outdo one another in demonstrations of loyalty.

Around 250,000 Irishmen were to serve in the British armed forces during the course of the war. Although conscription was never introduced in Ireland, volunteering was widespread and continued right up until the end of the war. Around a third of all young men under the age of thirty-five volunteered to fight, a very high proportion. Protestants were more likely to volunteer in proportion to their share of the Irish population as a whole with a quarter of the Protestant population making up just less than a half of all recruits. However, if the figures are examined in a provincial setting then three-quarters of all Protestant recruits came from Ulster, where they formed just 53 per cent of the population. With Ulster removed, the religious difference of volunteers was less pronounced with Catholic recruits predominating. In general though the Irish contingent was formed around a solid minority of Ulster Protestant recruits. Significantly in Ireland, recruitment, although diminished, continued throughout the war after the initial mass enrolments of the summer of 1914. It must not be forgotten that something like 35,000 Irishmen died fighting in the Great War, far more than those in all the other conflicts of the revolutionary period combined.

As in the rest of Britain the reasons for enlistment were multifarious. A sense of adventure and a chance to escape the dullness of small town Irish life was an important motivation for some while for others it was a last resort to escape financial distress, especially with a recent downturn in Irish industrial employment and a recession in the Ulster linen industry. In the Irish case the appeal to patriotism was important, especially the impact of John Redmond's famous Woodenbridge speech to Irish Volunteers on 20 September 1914 (Document 3), cannot be underestimated. In the speech Redmond argued that 'the interests of Ireland, of the whole of Ireland, are at stake in this war'. After this appeal to Irish national sentiment, he drew out the high moral purpose of the struggle against the dangers of Germans and Prussian militarism:

> This war is undertaken in defence of the highest principles of religion, morality and right, and it would be a disgrace for ever to our country, a reproach to her manhood, and a denial of the lessons of her history, if young Irishmen confined their efforts to remaining at home to defend the shores of Ireland from an unlikely invasion and shrinking from the duty of proving upon the field of battle that gallantry and courage which have distinguished your race all through its history.[1]

For Unionists the reasons were perhaps more clear cut with their loyalty to the Crown and the Union being a strong motivator. However, although Ireland may have had its own particular set of circumstances the reasons people joined up were multifaceted, complex and interwoven, and differed little in essence from those of so many men across Britain and the rest of Europe.

Irishmen were recruited mainly into three divisions, the 36th (Ulster) Division, representing effectively the UVF in arms, who were allowed to keep their distinctive insignia and the 10th (Irish) and 16th (Irish) divisions representing the other three provinces. They were to serve in all theatres of the war. The 10th Division served mostly in the east from Gallipoli to Greece and Palestine while the 36th and 16th Divisions served largely on the western front. The most harrowing losses were suffered by the Ulster Division who, during the first two days of the Battle of the Somme in July 1916, would lose over 5,000 men killed or wounded, a sacrifice commemorated to this day and one which would do much to shape Ulster Unionist identity.

With the end of the war, Irish veterans returned to an Ireland unrecognisable to the one they had left. While in Ulster returning servicemen were greeted as heroes, in Nationalist Ireland they were greeted largely with suspicion, abuse and violence. While some, most notably Tom Barry, were able to shed their previous wartime allegiances, and become leading members of the IRA offering invaluable military experience, most kept their heads down and their role in the war remained hidden. Unemployment levels amongst veterans were notably high in the south and west with over 30,000 ex-soldiers claiming benefit. Even as the economy recovered they faced discrimination in their attempts to find work from Republicans and members of the labour movement. While in Ulster the opposite was the case, where service in the war became a key rite of passage and a badge of honour for the new generation who would shape Northern Ireland, in Nationalist Ireland it became a source of shame.[2]

The Irish Volunteers

Perhaps the most significant outcome of the Ulster Crisis, and certainly one that would appear ever more important as the war progressed, was the creation of the Irish Volunteers in November 1913. Created in direct imitation of the UVF, the Irish Volunteers numbering some 180,000, pledged themselves rather vaguely to maintain Irish liberties by preventing the Liberal government from going back on its commitment to support Irish national aspirations.

While the vast majority of Volunteers would answer Redmond's call at Woodenbridge to go 'wherever the firing line extended' a small group of around 11,000 within the movement refused the home rule leader's call to disband and enlist. Retaining the name the Irish Volunteers (as distinct from Redmond's Irish 'National' Volunteers) this rump of advanced Nationalists determined to stay out of the conflict. It was this small group that would be responsible for the launching of an armed Rising at Easter 1916 and as such became not only the driving force behind the Irish revolution but would also shape the political culture of independent Ireland for the next century.

The Irish Volunteers would be joined by two other distinctive paramilitary organisations with very different ideologies and histories. Indeed aside from their co-operation during the Rising the various groups shared little in common. Even within the small leadership clique there were profound divisions over the aims of the Rising.

The prime movers in the conspiracy were the IRB. Since the heady days of the Land War in the 1870s the organisation had begun to fade. With an ageing membership, declining organisation and facing a rejuvenated constitutional Nationalist movement the IRB had become little more than an old man's drinking club by the turn of the century. However, in the context of the rise of cultural nationalism, a new breed of young radical leader had risen to the fore. For them their growing sense of Irishness meant more than just the chance to play Irish games or learn the language, it was an ideal for living and merely a stepping stone to the creation of an independent Irish Republic. This group of new IRB leaders, led by Sean McDermott, Patrick Pearse and Tom Clarke, inspired by the old Fenian dictum 'England's difficulty was Ireland's opportunity', saw the war as a singular chance to make a bid for Irish freedom by force of arms. With the imminent arrival of the Home Rule Act, such a Rising was also perhaps their final chance to implement their radical separatist agenda before they became a complete political irrelevance. For the IRB therefore the decision to launch a revolt was a last resort, a demonstration of the weakness rather than the strength of advanced nationalism.

While the creation of the Irish Volunteers in 1913 as a mass paramilitary organisation was a profoundly encouraging development for the radicals within the IRB, in reality, even after the split of September 1914, the organisation was under the control of cautious conservatives such as Eoin MacNeill and Bulmer Hobson. Certainly there was very little clarity in what the Irish Volunteers stood for and many, joining the organisation for a variety of reasons, carried along in a nebulous cloud of advanced nationalism Gaelic revivalism and resistance to the threat of conscription.

Certainly the Irish Volunteers, the organisation which was to provide the manpower to carry out the Rising, was hardly a body wedded to the idea of insurrection. While its members were certainly well to the left of the larger National Volunteers the leadership were moderate and politic. The leading lights, Bulmer Hobson – a journalist and Quaker from County Down – and academic professor Eoin MacNeill, who was Chief of Staff of the organisation, saw any kind of unprovoked rising as pointless, doomed to failure and almost bound to alienate support from the Irish population. Only in the case of a radical measure from the British Government such as a decision to introduce conscription in Ireland or to move against the Volunteers would a Rising be justified.

Organising the Rising

The idea for a Rising emerged with the IRB who barely one month into the war decided to stage an armed rebellion before the war ended. Key radicals managed to secure positions on a new executive committee of the Irish Volunteers and this was followed in May 1915 with the creation of a secret Military Council within the IRB itself to draw up detailed plans for the Rising. Both Eoin MacNeill and Denis McCullough, President of the Supreme Council of the IRB, while not against a Rising per se wanted the move to have either widespread public support or the harshest British provocation. The shadowy role of the Military Council and the presence of its members in key positions on the Volunteer Executive including Patrick Pearse, as Director of Military Organisation and Joseph Plunkett as Director of Military Operations, meant that the support of the nominal leaders of both the Volunteers and the IRB was neither needed nor sought.

Perhaps the most curious of these select individuals and the man who has come to be most closely associated with the Rising was Patrick Pearse. Pearse has been seen as the chief ideologue of the revolution. This was mainly due to his place as the nominal and rather fanciful head of the Republican government established by the Rising and his role in formulating and presenting the fateful Easter Proclamation (Document 5). Pearse, an earnest Gaelic enthusiast with a passion for education, came to extremism late on, slowly moving from a constitutional Nationalist view to a more radical form of romantic separatism, ending in a spiritual and heavily Catholicised idealism, full of messianic and self-sacrificial images. This Gaelic romanticism would also be a key feature of the ideology of other leaders of the Rising including Thomas MacDonagh and Joseph Plunkett.

While the IRB Military Council continued its planning and consolidated its position within both the Volunteers and the IRB, attempts were made to recruit support from outside of Ireland. The main source of this help would be Germany. Roger Casement, a member of the British consulate radicalised by his experience witnessing British concentration camps in the Boer War, managed to make contact with German intelligence proposing they should send a force to land on the west coast of Ireland in support of the planned Rising. He also proposed the idea of recruiting an 'Irish Brigade' from Irish prisoners of war held in Germany. With the Germans committing themselves to at least the supply of equipment and weaponry, attention turned to recruiting the only other notable paramilitary force in Ireland in the shape of the trade union leader James Connolly's Irish Citizen Army. Set up in the wake of the Dublin Lockout to protect future labour strikes, this socialist paramilitary group had pledged themselves to launch their own uprising, but after meeting with the IRB, Connolly was persuaded to throw in his lot with the Volunteers and the IRB in their endeavour.

Connolly, a native of Edinburgh, the son of Irish emigrant parents, was by far the best known and most intellectually able of all the leaders of the Rising, having become the dominant face of Irish socialism – especially after trade union leader James Larkin left Ireland for the United States after the collapse of the Dublin Lockout in 1913. Connolly's decision to join such a conservative and Catholic Nationalist enterprise as the Rising remains a subject of much bemusement amongst historians. For himself he seems to have been able to square the circle of nationalism and socialism with, much like Pearse, an idealised view of an imagined pre-conquest Ireland where communal living and equity predominated before the arrival of the capitalist Saxon. In the face of European war he also saw Ireland as some kind of potential rallying point for the European proletariat. Certainly Connolly's ideological issues and challenges were not enough to stop the other conspirators from realising that his 200 well armed and trained men in the Irish Citizen Army were vital to the enterprise. The Rising was thus an uneasy, curious alliance, a marriage of convenience where the rebels shared if anything a sense of desperation as they witnessed the rather sleepy contentment of the Irish population two years into a world war.

Plans

The plan for the Rising, devised by Joseph Plunkett whose only experience of military matters appeared to be playing with toy soldiers as a child, was for a nationwide rebellion supported by German arms and, it was hoped, military personnel. In order to deflect both the British authorities and his own colleagues within the Irish Volunteers Pearse, as Director of Organisation, called for three days of parades around Easter Sunday which were to provide a cover for the Rising. The major force to carry out the attacks in the shape of the Irish Volunteers were to be engaged in large-scale manoeuvres for the Easter holiday as a front for a general mobilisation, where they would be told only at the last minute of the intention to stage an insurrection. A risky strategy, provoking possible mass desertions, it was hoped that any initial shock might give way to more active support once the Rising in Dublin had taken place.

However, despite attempts at the utmost secrecy, MacNeill managed to hear about the plans and immediately threatened to call off the Volunteer manoeuvres. However, he was unsure how to proceed, especially when informed of the intended landing of 20,000 German guns off the west coast under the supervision of Casement. The capture of Casement on his return to Ireland in a German U-boat and the loss of the German arms, after the ship carrying them *The Aud* was discovered by the Royal Navy, made up MacNeill's mind and along with other moderates such as Bulmer Hobson, he sent out a countermanding order calling off the planned manoeuvres for Easter Sunday. Certainly with MacNeill now actively against the Rising and the British themselves on the verge of mass arrests, the leadership faced a stark choice of going ahead or cancelling their plans and going into hiding. They chose the former and the Rising, compromised, shorn of foreign, and as it turned out domestic, support, was launched on the morning of 24 April 1916.

The prelude to the Rising

For all the later criticism which has been heaped upon the plan for the Easter Rising it is possible to view the event as something of a notable achievement. In the midst of a war, the rebels had managed to plan a covert and extensive nationwide Rising involving thousands of well armed Volunteers across the country. They had also managed in the shape of the IRB Military Council to convince the moderate leader of the Volunteers, Eoin MacNeill, that the idea of a rebellion was at least a possibility. In the end McNeill's opposition was based less on the principle of the Rising but more on how workable it was with the loss of the intended German weapons and the lack of any definite provocation from the British.

MacNeill himself, while viewed as a moderate who countermanded the Rising, in fact dithered more than condemned the events. He was certainly concerned by the arrest of Casement and shocked when the sheer extent of the IRB's deception was revealed. Certainly MacNeill's order to stand down from the manoeuvres planned for Easter Sunday did appear to make a big difference. While the Rising would last almost a week it seems fair to think that those who had been stood down would have joined in later. However, this was not to happen. Certainly far more Volunteers had turned out on Easter Sunday even after the countermanding order than did on the following day when the Rising got fully underway. As such provincial Ireland was largely quiescent. The plans for the rest of the country had themselves been amateurish and unworkable and there was little evidence to predict that within three years there would be an outbreak of widespread guerrilla warfare in provincial areas. Such a move was only hinted at by the small-scale operations which occurred in Meath around Ashbourne under the command of IRB leader Thomas Ashe and later Chief of Staff of the IRA and Minister for Defence, Richard Mulcahy, who acted as his second in command. With a small company of Volunteers they managed to take over a number of police barracks, launching a major attack at Ashtown. In the ensuing fire fight, which lasted many hours, eight policemen were killed before Ashe and Mulcahy withdrew their column into the hills before being ordered to surrender when the Rising collapsed in Dublin. In Louth another unit tried to march to Dublin but failed to make it into the city before the surrender. In Wexford a unit of almost 100 Volunteers occupied the town of Enniscorthy for three days before surrendering in the face of approaching British troops. Otherwise it was only in Galway that there was any notable attempt at insurrection. Here Liam Mellows led a large group of 500 Volunteers in a series of token attacks on RIC stations in a number of coastal villages. However, when British reinforcements arrived by land and sea his men were forced to disperse, many of them being rounded up in the coming days. The lack of weapons was to be the biggest problem with many of Mellows' men arming themselves with shotguns and improvised pikes.[3]

The Rising then was confined almost wholly to Dublin, a place where the IRB Military Council still retained some control, and crucially access to the weapons imported during the Howth gunrunning of 1914. The original plan was to seize the heart of the city as a central point which would be then reinforced by a general rising across the country supported with German arms. In the event the original plan had to be scaled down with only the Dublin part of the plan remaining in place. Several prominent buildings were occupied in the centre of the city in a rough ring on both sides of the river around the headquarters at the General Post Office (GPO) in Sackville Street. The plan, if one can be discerned, was to hold the centre of the city against the inevitable British Army onslaught for as long as possible. The idea of urban warfare was quite a new one but the inspiration may have come from the Paris Commune of 1871 or perhaps more recently the Siege of Sidney Street in London in January 1911 where a motley group of anarchists and burglars managed to hold out against overwhelming numbers of police and army.

Whatever the precedents there was little or no chance of the Rising succeeding once it had started. In order to explain this seeming incompetence there has been a wide-ranging debate over the ultimate motivation of the rebels. Perhaps the strategy was so poor, it is argued, because there it was never meant to be a serious military action but rather an act of martyrdom. Was the Rising a genuine attempt at a coup or was it really just a blood sacrifice? The original idea, while ambitious, may have had some chance of success but the static nature of the Dublin occupation, barring a woeful and unimaginably poor performance from the British Army, was doomed to failure. Certainly the intended aim of the Rising right up until the last 48 hours was for a nationwide coup. While much focus has been placed on the chief ideologues of the event and their morbid mindsets and of self-sacrificial poetry, there seems little evidence that the vast majority of those outside of the small handful of propagandists on the Military Council sought martyrdom. Certainly the Rising was taken seriously by those who planned it and it seems unfeasible that hardened IRB men such as Tom Clarke and Sean McDermott would go along with a plan that was hard wired to fail.

It was in reality a case of the Rising becoming a self-sacrifice due to circumstance because any hope of real success was already gone. The Rising was for a few a blood sacrifice, for others a realistic attempt at a coup, while for many it was simply a show of force which few seem to have thought much beyond. It is true of course that apart from the leaders of the Rising all of the others would survive and live to fight again so the Rising was far from an exercise in futility apart from for those who had most to lose at the top of the organisation. However, the Rising became a blood sacrifice when failures, most notably that of Roger Casement to deliver German help, became clear. It was only at this late stage that the more romantic Nationalist figures of Pearse, MacDonagh and Plunkett rose to the fore.

It was also clear that British intelligence had itself uncovered the extent of the plot and was on the verge of making mass arrests after the Easter break. This delay had been caused by a perception that the loss of the German arms and the effectiveness of MacNeill's countermanding order had already severely compromised the Rising which would now be called off. Viewed in this light the rebels were left with a stark choice between probable arrest on Tuesday or the staging of at least some form of armed challenge on Monday. They chose the latter.

Even if all of the most optimistic schemes behind the planning of the Rising had come to fruition the rebels still faced a formidable challenge.

Whatever the intentions of those who took part in the Rising their woeful inexperience was evident throughout. Almost all of the Volunteers lacked military training of any sort. The generation who took part in the Rising were not those who fought in the Great War and so lacked the necessary experience which would be put to such devastating effect by certain members of the IRA, such as Tom Barry, who had fought for the British Army in Mesopotamia, in the War of Independence. The only leader who had any notable military experience was James Connolly who had been a member of the British Army but kept his involvement a secret from his allies for understandable reasons. The other leaders were divided between propagandists and idealists such as Pearse and Plunkett and IRB conspirators in the shape of McDermott and Clarke. On the ground their inexperience reached at times absurd proportions. For example the garrison at Stephen's Green, believing that the epitome of modern warfare was to be found in trench fortifications such as those being constructed in France at the time, dug trenches in the park allowing the British troops to occupy the buildings surrounding the area and fire down on them with impunity. There followed a hasty retreat to the College of Surgeons where the garrison remained for the rest of the week.

One interesting fact about the Stephen's Green garrison was that it was placed under the command of a woman, in the shape of the exotic figure of Constance Markievicz. However, she was very much the exception rather than the rule. The women's organisation Cumann na mBan did not figure in the strategic calculations for the Rising and only joined late on the first day, with many female relatives of the leaders, including James Connolly's daughter, being denied their requests to join the fighting itself. Even then they were denied a frontline role in the fighting, instead being given the role of providing nursing care and supplies to the various commands. They were also used to carry messages to the various commands, a job which they shared with a number of children who were members of the Republican Boy Scout organisation Fianna Eireann and the boys' corps of the Citizen Army. Many of these would go on to become prominent members of the IRA during the War of Independence including Vinnie Byrne, one of Michael Collins' key assassins, who was only fifteen years old at the time of the Rising.

Other locations chosen were just as hopeless in strategic terms. Jacob's Biscuit Factory, under the command of Thomas MacDonagh, was tucked away from main thoroughfares and protected nothing. As such the British were able to merely cordon it off and ignore it; meaning it saw little or no fighting throughout the Rising. The GPO itself was certainly an impressive and strong building but was on the wrong side of the river to work effectively as a headquarters, meaning the various commands were effectively split in two even before a shot had been fired. Such a blunder was unforgivable especially as there was no real symbolism behind the choice of the GPO as a headquarters. Indeed the biggest criticism of rebel strategy was their failure to take over Dublin Castle, the administrative centre of British rule in Ireland and a profoundly symbolic target. The castle itself was defended by a small garrison who would have been easily overwhelmed and the potential sight of the Republican tricolour flying over the building would have made a profound impact. Even the possibility of destroying records or arresting senior staff as hostages were all lost. In the event a token scouting mission to the castle was the most that was achieved and any full-scale attack was called off.

In other practical ways the rebels made poor choices in terms of the buildings they chose to occupy. Despite its obvious strategic value, the telephone exchange was not taken. Also they failed to take Trinity College which, with its thick walls, offered an excellent defensible position and strategic control of the major river crossings over the Liffey. Connolly, despite his military experience, was insistent that occupying the main shopping areas of the city would be safe as capitalist store owners would never allow their shops to be destroyed in the fighting. The garrison of Eamon de Valera at Boland's Bakery, which was to prove the most efficient in terms of inflicting casualties on British soldiers advancing to the centre of the city along Northumberland Road, also saw some farcical episodes with a number of sentries abandoning their posts to join in with prayers and the saying of the Rosary. In the GPO a British soldier who had been in the post office buying stamps at the time of the attack, was arrested but somehow managed to procure a bottle of brandy and got very drunk while two Swedish sailors on leave in the city agreed to join in on the rebel side only as long as they received assurances it would all be over by Thursday before their ship sailed. Others in the GPO designed postage stamps for a future Irish state while many dwelt on their own personal political visions, most of which bore little relation to the Republic that Patrick Pearse had just declared on the steps outside the building to a small crowd of bemused Dublin shoppers. All in all the Rising was a confused affair carried out by confused people for ambiguous and multifariously different imagined futures.

The people who suffered most by the Rising, the Dublin citizenry, were largely apathetic to the whole event. Most had little notion of the deeper ideas that lay behind the Rising. Most members of the public neither actively supported nor condemned the Rising, but rather took advantage of it with widespread looting and even at times removing those goods being used by the rebels to form their barricades! Indeed looting became such a problem within the rebel cordon that Pearse himself made the uncharacteristic declaration that any looters would be arrested and shot. Typically his words never went beyond rhetoric and no shootings were ever carried out.

The chaos within the city centre was short-lived as everyone awaited the inevitable British backlash. The number of rebels had risen from 800 on the first day to almost twice that number by the middle of the week as various individuals drifted in from around the country to take part. However, despite this the strategy to sit and hold out in fortified positions remained the same.

Indeed once the shock factor of the Rising had abated, the initiative passed from the rebels to the British. The British moved eventually with efficiency and skill to cordon off the rebel strongholds, surrounding each one in turn and closing the net on the GPO in the centre. Reinforcements were brought in from Belfast, the Curragh and Britain (some of whom thought they had landed in France once the bullets started firing!) After only three days the British already felt strong enough to launch attacks on rebel positions although the focus remained on the GPO. The whole area of Sackville Street was mercilessly bombarded with guns fired from a gunboat brought up the Liffey river. Under this intense bombardment, the rebels tunnelled out of the building where, after Pearse witnessed the shooting of Dublin civilians in the crossfire, the decision was taken, despite protestations from Tom Clarke, to surrender. Pearse ordered that:

> In order to prevent the further slaughter of Dublin citizens, and in the hope of saving the lives of our followers now surrounded and hopelessly outnumbered, the members of the Provisional Government present at headquarters have agreed to an unconditional surrender, and the commandants of the various districts in the City and County will order their commands to lay down arms.[4]

Ironically the other garrisons on the periphery were still holding firm and many of them had seen very little fighting when the order came to surrender. There is little doubt they could have fought on for a significant time themselves and none of them had been taken or seriously threatened by the British. In total the Rising had lasted six days. The centre of Dublin was in ruins and over 450 people had been killed, 300 of them civilians, with 2,500 injured, again the vast majority of them civilians. While shambolic and farcical in many respects, the Rising did manage to achieve its main objectives. It had seen the proclamation of a Republic and however short-lived had lasted for a significant enough period of time as some form of insurrectionary regime.

Aftermath of the Rising

When the dust settled eyes turned to what the British reaction would be. Things looked ominous from the start when any pretence at civilian government was abandoned and a military governor in the shape of the austere General Sir John Maxwell was sent over to take command. Maxwell was a tough minded, no nonsense soldier with little knowledge or appreciation for the complexities and subtleties of Irish Nationalist political culture. In the aftermath there was a huge deal of confusion. While the initial reaction of the Dublin public was intensely hostile to the rebels with many women, whose husbands and sons were fighting in France, coming out on the street to jeer and berate the prisoners. However, the imposition of martial law by Maxwell would turn that hostility into fear and then growing resentment at the authorities. Thousands of Nationalist activists of all kinds including Gaelic enthusiasts and the more outspoken members of the Home Rule party were rounded up across Ireland while open displays of nationalism in both the cultural and political sense were banned.

The most damaging element of the British backlash however was undoubtedly their handling of the trial and execution of the ringleaders. It was not the fact that executions were carried out which proved to be the problem. Public opinion in Britain would have settled for little else especially with the reference to links with 'gallant allies in Europe' contained in the widely published proclamation. The main issue was the manner of the shootings. Dragged out over a number of weeks, the executions grew increasingly unpopular. On 3 May, only three days after the surrender, Pearse, Clarke and Thomas MacDonagh were executed. The next day they were followed by another four, another one the next day. After a brief pause, after appeals for clemency were heard, the executions resumed on 8 May when four more were shot, the following day another one. By this time there was widespread denunciation of the policy with both Redmond and Dillon making speeches in the Commons calling for the executions to end. Asquith was certainly very concerned about how the shootings were being perceived, warning Maxwell not to execute Countess Markievicz or any other of the female participants fearing that British complaints about the immorality of the German's execution of the British nurse Edith Cavell in Belgium the previous October would be heavily compromised. Fudging the issue, he instructed Maxwell to execute captives in exceptional circumstances only, at which Maxwell ordered the deaths of two further prisoners. The two men killed however, Sean McDermott and James Connolly, were exceptional as they had both been leaders of the Rising and were both signatories of the proclamation. Connolly's execution in particular caused widespread protest. Having been wounded in the ankle during the fighting he was brought to Kilmainham Gaol on a stretcher before being tied to a chair and shot. While the idea of nursing him back to health before his execution appeared like an absurd idea to the British military authorities, in the sensitive atmosphere surrounding the shootings such a decision seemed remarkably tactless, one observer famously comparing the process to 'watching blood seep from behind a closed door'.[5] The fact that two high profile prisoners such as Connolly and McDermott were killed last highlighted the major problem with the executions, namely the failure to try individuals in order of their importance. Indeed the targeting of individuals who had little real leadership role was to be heavily criticised later. These included most notoriously Willie Pearse, brother of the rebel leader, who after talking up his own role in the Rising was also condemned to death. In reality he had little actual power and seems only to have join the Rising so he could emulate his older brother who he idolised.

In total fifteen prisoners were executed. Considering the fact that ninety death sentences had actually been passed, viewed overall the policy was very restrained. Later the number would rise to sixteen with the execution of Roger Casement, hanged for treason in August to much consternation. In the case of Casement his homosexuality, as revealed in the so-called Black Diaries, stopped many public figures in the establishment from stepping forward to defend him.

In the end the Rising would have a profound impact on the future shape of Irish nationalism and a series of outcomes which could hardly have been imagined by its perpetrators. Almost in spite of itself the Rising would prove more successful than even its most optimistic leaders could have hoped. Less than a year after it ended the Home Rule party was already beginning to crumble under the political onslaught of a new advanced Nationalist movement in the shape of Sinn Fein which associated itself wholeheartedly with the ideals and methods of those who launched the Rising. It is indeed ironic that such an ideologically confused and ambiguous event would be presented as the key foundation myth of Irish nationalism. However, the crude mixture of idealism, political extremism and the dominant place of violence which had characterised the Rising would prove difficult to emulate when faced with the same challenges which had confounded Irish national aspirations for decades. As the next few turbulent years would show those who now had to turn that singular political vision into a real earthly reality, they would discover the legacies and implications of the Rising were both an inspiration and a curse.

Sample essay and examination questions

What expectations did those who participated in the Rising have for its outcome?
Was the 1916 Rising a coup or a blood sacrifice?
Was there any great need for a Rising?

Further reading

J. Augusteijn, *Patrick Pearse: The Making of a Revolutionary* (Basingstoke, 2010)

P. Bew, 'The Easter Rising: Lost Leaders and Lost Opportunities', *The Irish Review*, no. 11 (Winter 1991/1992)

D. G. Boyce, '1916: Interpreting the Rising', in Boyce and O'Day (eds.) *The Making of Modern Irish History: Revisionism and the Revisionist Controversy* (London, 1996)

R. D. Edwards, *Patrick Pearse: The Triumph of Failure* (London, 1977)

M. Foy and B. Barton, *The Easter Rising* (Gloucester, 1999)

F. McGarry, *The Rising, Ireland: Easter 1916* (Oxford, 2010)

F. McGarry, *Rebels: Voices from the Easter Rising* (Harmondsworth, 2011)

C. Townshend, *Easter 1916: The Irish Rebellion* (Harmondsworth, 2005)
M. Ward, *Unmanageable Revolutionaries* (London, 1995)

Useful web links

One of the best sources for the Easter Rising is the large number of Volunteer statements in the Bureau of Military History, all now available online at http://www.bureauofmilitaryhistory.ie [accessed 2 June 2014].
An interesting online exhibition about the Easter Rising produced by the National Library of Ireland is available at http://www.nli.ie/1916/ [accessed 2 June 2014].

4

The Rise of Sinn Fein, 1916–18

With the collapse of the Rising any new movement which would emerge to claim its dubious legacy faced an almost impossible task. The leaders of the Rising, from its chief ideologues to its men of action, were dead. The curious and unlikely coalition of physical force IRB men, Irish Irelanders and trade unionists, which had carried out the Rising was unlikely to hold together in any circumstance outside of the heat of battle. Indeed the reversion to the crude methods of physical force reflected the frustrating fact that no coherent organisation existed prior to the Rising to articulate an alternative advanced Nationalist political message, which can be best summed up as a stand against the Anglicisation of Irish culture and politics which the Home Rule party represented; Redmond himself summing up the Rising as being motivated principally by a 'hatred of Home Rule'.

In practical terms too, advanced Nationalists were very much on the defensive. Thousands of activists had been interned, local organisations had been broken up and their principal propaganda weapon – the press – which Griffith had used so skilfully was banned. Even the very real, if rather nebulous sympathy, which existed for those who had taken part in the Rising did not easily translate to the world of practical politics. Certainly if one thing can be discerned about the Rising, it was that it was a militarist solution to a political problem, led by people who demonstrated a distinct distaste for politics. Ironically, had the Rising itself been successful it might have caused even more conflict and confusion than was engendered by its failure. As such those who were left to make sense of the bequest of the Rising were stuck with the enormous challenge of transforming idealism, more often expressed in poetry than polemic, into a pragmatic political movement. The fact that this was achieved in barely two and a half years, and that this new movement went on to become the predominant voice in Irish nationalism was a remarkable, if not unprecedented, achievement in modern political history.

Initial reactions to the Rising

Considering the sea change which was about to occur in Irish Nationalist political culture, it is notable that the immediate post-Rising period itself was quiet and largely uneventful. Those radicals not yet under arrest went underground while those who retained some kind of a voice in public life immediately began to try and make sense of the ideological implications of the Rising. Most groups who were rightly or wrongly connected to the Rising by the British suffered a campaign of widespread repression from the authorities. The IRB and Irish Volunteers had lost their key leaders and while the latter experienced a rise in membership at the local level, their martial pretensions were directionless and little more than bravado. The effectiveness of the trade union movement in Ireland as an alternative political vehicle for advanced Nationalist protest was crippled by the loss of the Transport Union's headquarters at Liberty Hall in Dublin, which had been destroyed during the fighting, and rising tensions with unions in Belfast outraged by the involvement of Connolly and his attempt to link the Irish left to militant Irish nationalism. The GAA whose grass-roots cultural activism had been a crucial surrogate for the Volunteer movement suffered a similar containment of their public displays at meetings and sporting events. While open organisation proved impossible, the later discernible shift in public opinion towards sympathy for the leaders of the Rising was difficult to gauge and had no real forum in which to express itself. All in all, for what remained of the year 1916, the Rising engendered a kind of political inertia and a collective shell-shock. Only slowly would this impulse lead to a reassessment of where loyalties lay in the new political landscape.

Indeed the first public organisation expressing anything even close to support for those who took part in the Rising stood on the safer and more morally neutral ground of humanitarianism. As had happened with the Fenians in the aftermath of their own failed insurrection, the focus was on the sufferings of the interned prisoners rather than the political ideals they had fought for. Prominent female relatives of the leaders of the Rising, such as the wife of Tom Clarke, Kathleen Clarke, and the mother of Patrick Pearse, became the figureheads for a new committee, the Irish National Aid and Volunteers' Dependents Fund, whose principal aim was to offer financial assistance to the families of dead or imprisoned rebels. Clarke himself, along with other leaders, had foreseen this eventuality, allotting significant sums of money to look after the inevitable dependents and widows of those who would fall victim during the fighting. The presence of these prominent women, appearing in public in dignified mourning, maintained a symbolic focal point for the otherwise diffuse advanced Nationalist movement. Only later would the organisation take the more politically charged step of calling publicly for an amnesty for internees and prisoners.

Around half of those interned in the immediate aftermath of the Rising were released after only a week. While it was unlikely that this short experience radicalised many, this was certainly the outcome for those who remained incarcerated. Kept in various British prisons, the majority were interned at an ex-prisoner-of-war camp in Frongoch in North Wales. The prisoners in Frongoch would form the hard core of radical activists upon their release. Known euphemistically as the 'university of revolution', the camp had a notoriously relaxed atmosphere where internees were allowed to associate together freely, drilling, playing Gaelic games and attending education classes. Far from quelling the spirit of rebellion, this environment allowed for a previously diverse group of advanced Nationalists to gather under one roof, hone their rhetoric, make contacts and connect the diverse elements of advanced nationalism to create a new radical ideology. A new elite to articulate and lead this new movement soon emerged within the prisons. Joe Sweeney, later IRA commander in Donegal, noted of Frongoch that the Volunteers 'set up our university there, both education and revolutionary . . . and from that camp came the hard core of the subsequent guerrilla war in Ireland'.[1]

While some such as Eamon de Valera were afforded prominence due to the senior role they had played in the Rising, others came to the fore in a new revolutionary meritocracy. Most significant in this regard was Michael Collins, a native of West Cork who had thrown in his job in London, where he had lived for over a decade, to return to Dublin to take part in the fighting. Although only a lowly foot soldier during the Rising it was while he was imprisoned in Frongoch that Collins first began to show his remarkable abilities for leadership and organisation. Many men broke under the strain but Collins seemed to thrive. A big bulking, often crude and violent man, he seemed to enjoy the masculine rough and tumble of camp life. His famous physical size and love of a scrap meant he almost literally fought his way to the top of the group. Certainly as a man Collins was viewed as a big-hearted bully. He was bursting with energy, organised sports matches, drilled the men, bribed guards (some of whom even said that Collins was the real commandant of the camp), and organised money for the dependents of prisoners. He also displayed a remarkable ability for organisation and an overbearing and strict leadership style. Throughout his life Collins was a contradiction to those who knew him: 'He could be a warm, friendly, passionate, boisterous, fun loving and generous individual with a moderate and rational outlook, but he could just as easily be a cold, dour, unreasonable and utterly ruthless person – an arrogant bully with a ferocious temper and a mean vindictive streak.'[2] His experience in Frongoch allowed him to set up a whole network of contacts and embryonic organisations, including a revived IRB, that he would exploit vigorously over the following years in the cause of separatist militancy. Critical of the dreamy idealism of heroic failure which had characterised the Rising, Collins and the new brand of leaders would redirect the revolutionary struggle in a new and devastatingly pragmatic direction.

There was little doubt that the kind of fluid, heterogeneous, approach to the furtherance of Nationalist goals which Collins came to personify symbolised a new trend which was occurring more generally within Irish Nationalist culture. The confused legacy of the Rising gave advanced nationalism a chance to breathe, while the Home Rule party was increasingly suffocated by its lack of flexibility. Indeed its own response to the Rising had been confused and conveyed an ambiguous message. Both Redmond and Dillon, as the spokesmen of popular Nationalist sentiment, were quick to condemn the Rising. However, in the context of the seemingly interminable executions they increasingly turned their criticisms onto the severity of British Government policy. On 11 May, Dillon made a famous speech calling on Asquith to halt the executions, a speech which almost inevitably involved presenting a more positive message about the actions of the rebels, who had in Dillon's words 'fought a clean fight, a brave fight, however misguided, and it would have been a damned good thing for you if your soldiers were able to put up as good a fight as did these men in Dublin'. The fact that the executions scheduled for the next day went ahead further highlighted the Irish Parliamentary Party's (IPP) seeming impotence in affecting government policy at Westminster.

The ambiguity of the Home Rule party's response to the Rising was understandable and to a large extent reflected that of the Nationalist constituency it claimed to represent. The old certainties evaporated as new organisations and initiatives rose to populate the new political landscape. Many saw the chance to reflect this nebulous sense of advanced nationalism in a variety of new ways. One example of this was the Irish Nation League which while having the defined goal of representing those border counties which were to be excluded from the home rule remit, demonstrated a concrete example of a different and more advanced Nationalist political vision. The fact that this party would soon crumble and be subsumed within the Home Rule party machine did little to restore faith that the troublemakers were now inside the tent. In a thousand similar ways of personal and organisational initiative the old certainties of the monolithic Home Rule party began to crumble. Although eventually these early challengers would succumb to the dominance of the Home Rule party they would offer a chance for many people to dip their toe into the previously marginalised and discredited waters of advanced nationalism and even republicanism, presenting a bridge over which so many people would flock once the new Sinn Fein movement emerged and offered an alternative destination. In short it was clear that disillusionment with the 'old politics' of the Home Rule party long preceded the existence of a political alternative to articulate it.

The birth of Sinn Fein

While the Home Rule party was finding it difficult to exploit the new flexibility which had gripped Irish nationalism, the movement that would soon come to replace it and dominate Irish politics was faring little better in adapting to the new fluid situation. Sinn Fein, less a political party than a half-mocking label for any Nationalist left of the Home Rule party, came to be associated with the Rising as the only credible catch-all name which was associated with advanced nationalism and crucially the only open organisation which had any set of articulate, if rather quirky, political demands. With Griffith, the key personification of these ideas, in gaol other figures began to try and build a movement utilising the Sinn Fein brand name. The beginnings of the new movement were not auspicious. In Griffith's absence, Hubert Moore-Pym was left in temporary charge. Pym, who hailed from an Orange Protestant background, did a great deal to upset his colleagues and potential allies with his abrasive style and peculiar ideas, eventually leaving to resume his career as an unreconstructed Ulster Unionist. Even without Pym, the ideological base of the party was out of kilter with that of the Easter rebels, still running on a dual monarchist platform and an idealisation of the Austro-Hungarian Empire, which was ironically falling to pieces under the pressures of war and the impact of ethnic nationalism. However, in Griffith's absence the new activists did at least cement the link that Sinn Fein had in the popular imagination with the Rising. Through the publication of a newspaper they also encouraged, or at least did not discourage, those who were disillusioned with more traditional forms of constitutional nationalism to find a home in the party by painting it as the only coherent alternative. Even so the aftermath of the Rising presented far more confusion and ambiguity than political coherence. While it may be argued that a sea change was taking place within Irish nationalism amongst its supporters in favour of a more advanced alternative, there was little tangible evidence of this in the shape of new practical political outcomes.

Indeed it was in London, rather than Dublin, that any momentous political power shift was first to occur. In late 1916, with the traditional values of Asquith's Liberalism proving wholly unsuitable to the waging of total war, Lloyd George took over as Prime Minister at the head of a new Conservative-dominated coalition. Energetic and proactive, Lloyd George began a process of modernising the government of Britain with a series of bold new initiatives aimed at revolutionising the war effort. He also turned his energies to the pacification of Ireland. Inspired by the intervention of John Redmond, he arranged for the release of the vast majority of internees leaving only 150 prominent figures such as Eamon de Valera and Eoin MacNeill still in prison. Redmond had argued that such a show of clemency would take the sting out of the growing prisoners' relief campaigns and prevent the internees from becoming rallying symbols for extremists on the outside.

However, in reality almost exactly the opposite happened. Released as a gesture in time for Christmas, the internees received heroes' welcomes as they returned to their local areas where they immediately set about reinvigorating the Volunteer movement and other advanced Nationalist organisations. By the middle of 1918 Cork alone would have twenty Volunteer battalions made up of over 8,000 men.[3] Notable figures such as Griffith and Collins were also freed along with hundreds of other lowly foot soldiers who had taken part in the Rising but would now emerge as a readymade revolutionary elite to lead the new movement. This new group of radicals did not have long to wait for a forum within which to focus their activities. By pure coincidence the releases occurred in the midst of a by-election for the seat of North Roscommon and a decision was taken to run a candidate on the advanced Nationalist ticket. Although there had been a previous contest in West Cork this had been a confused and inconclusive affair where the Home Rule party had retained the seat against a more radical Nationalist opponent. However, the choice by advanced Nationalists to field a candidate from East Cork pricked local prejudices and the local man was victorious.

The North Roscommon by-election would be a completely different affair. The Home Rule candidate, James O'Kelly, had never had to face an election before and so the local political organisation was weak. Advanced Nationalists scouted around for a suitable candidate and having tried and failed to persuade Michael Davitt Jnr to run, they settled on the Papal Count Plunkett, whose son had been one of the leaders of the Rising. Plunkett was in many ways an odd character to represent the new generation of advanced Nationalists. Conservative, elderly and with a huge property portfolio he was in no way a radical. However, the fact that Plunkett remained interned during most of the campaign, having chosen the dreamy spires of Oxford for his imprisonment, meant he had little chance to make any public pronouncements which would have jeopardised the radical campaign. Instead he was portrayed largely as a grieving father of one of the martyrs of the Rising. Epitomising the fluidity of advanced nationalism in the wake of the Rising, he was backed by a curious coalition of trade unionists, Griffith's Sinn Feiners, members of other radical groups such as the Irish Nation League, and the usual motley assortment of Gaelic enthusiasts. More a movement than a political party, Sinn Fein became a repository for all kinds of political and cultural aspirations. Made up of socialists, militant Republicans, Gaelic revivalists and political opportunists, smaller parties were swallowed up and local and regional particularism shaded under the umbrella of Sinn Fein. This unlikely alliance, with the wealthy and conservative Count Plunkett at its head, represented a peculiar if not bizarre political bandwagon.[4]

Perhaps the most notable group to actively support Plunkett was the remnants of the Irish Volunteers. Although many of those who had been released from internment had set about organising and drilling in their local areas, with few supplies and no one to direct them there was little likelihood of any military venture succeeding. Florence O'Donoghue, a Cork IRA leader, recalled that the men who remained were 'a handful of the population . . . poor, untrained, almost unarmed, a lot of frothy patriotic sentiment . . . apparently futile and without a policy'.[5] As a purely martial organisation many within the Volunteers expressed a profound revulsion for politics. However, in their chastened condition, with little chance of continuing the fight, they chose instead to support the political efforts of those who would seek to displace the Home Rule party from its prominent position in Irish Nationalist politics. Throughout the next two years up to the triumphant election of December 1918 the Volunteers were to fulfil the role of a grass-roots political organisation for Sinn Fein, mobilising support, distributing propaganda and most importantly representing and keeping alive the direct link between the advanced Nationalist candidate and the legacy of the Rising. The election in Roscommon, held on 3 February 1917, saw a convincing victory for Plunkett who managed to win 3,077 votes compared to only 1,708 for the Home Rule party. Against all odds the triumph of this radical Nationalist alliance demonstrated the potency of this new political vision.

Plunkett's victory led to, if anything, more confusion in advanced Nationalist ranks. While it had demonstrated dramatically that radical elements could work together to achieve limited political goals, converting this impulse into some form of cohesive political alternative was another challenge. Protest voting would only go so far. Plunkett himself was emboldened by his victory, and along with his surviving sons, called for the new movement to convene at the Mansion House in Dublin to hammer out a new orthodoxy. His vision was an unexpectedly radical one, calling for the new organisation to declare itself both Republican and Abstentionist. He argued for a rejection of the moderation and ambiguities which characterised the heterogeneous organisations who formed the new alliance in favour of a set of clear and straightforward political demands. As such Griffith's policy of Dual Monarchy, which had been the cornerstone of the old Sinn Fein party, was denounced mercilessly by Plunkett as muddled and unworkable. By way of retaliation Griffith argued that such a dogmatic stance would unnecessarily hamper the new movement in its pursuit of its primary goal of replacing the Home Rule party as the majority voice of Irish nationalism, an already gargantuan task.

Plunkett's radical cry drew support from more advanced elements including the increasingly prominent figure of Michael Collins, whose mistrust of Griffith's moderation would continue unchecked in spite of their later alliance at the heart of the new pro-Treaty government which would emerge in 1922. After an underwhelming return to his native West Cork on his release, Collins had based himself at the heart of the new movement in Dublin. He was to show an incredible ability as an organiser and networker becoming at first secretary of the Prisoners' Aid Society providing him, through their families, with direct links to those who had been imprisoned, the men who would form the radical hardcore of the new movement. What is perhaps most important is that Collins controlled the purse strings of the movement; he was the man who signed the cheques. His was to be a very assiduous revolution. He collected everyone's expenses and gave everyone a receipt. He used this money also to set up a lucrative arms-smuggling operation and to invest in new forms of propaganda such as film cameras. Heaped on to his shoulders however was a further role, that of Director of Intelligence. Indeed despite his role as a fundraiser and administrator, there is little doubt that Collins fully intended on continuing the war against Britain.

The divisions which marked the new movement's tentative first steps towards finding out what they stood for, rather than what they simply stood against, was still a live issue when a second by-election was called in South Longford for April 1917. Despite the novelty of choosing a candidate who was still a prisoner, it demonstrated how the new movement remained wedded to the orthodox policy of exploiting its direct links with the Rising. Collins himself was instrumental in recruiting his friend and fellow IRB man Thomas Ashe to convince the incarcerated leadership that a prisoners' candidate was the safest alternative. Inside the prisons, those who remained, including Eamon de Valera, remained sceptical of placing their faith in the hands of the Irish people, many of them retaining bitter memories of the hostility they had received from the Dublin public in the immediate aftermath of the Rising.

The candidate chosen, very much against his own wishes, was Joseph McGuiness who despite his protestations was paraded under the wonderful slogan 'put him in to get him out'. Although McGuiness was a local man, the leadership in the prisons were perhaps right to be concerned about Longford as the place for the new movement to make such a stand. Unlike Roscommon, South Longford had a strong Home Rule party organisation and the candidate (chosen from a list of three by Redmond himself) would be well supplied with money, publicity and grass-roots organisation. John Dillon, the deputy leader of the Home Rule party, appeared to well understand the significance of the by-election, writing to Redmond: 'We have the Bishop, the great majority of the priests, and the mob – and four fifths of the traders of Longford. And if in the face of that we are beaten, I do not see how you can hope to hold the party in existence.'[6] The election campaign itself was very hard fought with hundreds of Volunteers from all over the country arriving in the area to support the candidacy of McGuiness. In the end it was a close run thing with McGuiness securing the victory by the slim majority of only thirty-seven votes. Indeed in the first vote the Home Rule candidate Patrick McKenna had actually been declared the winner after the first count. It was only after the discovery of a bundle of uncounted ballot papers that Sinn Fein managed to take the seat. Despite later mythical claims that the result was achieved only when an armed Volunteer placed a revolver at the head of the returning officer, the victory had far more to do with the late intervention of the Catholic Archbishop of Dublin William Walsh. Long supportive of advanced nationalism, he wrote a public letter which, while not directly supporting McGuiness, condemned the Home Rule party for its failure to stand up to the threat of partition, an issue which clearly resonated with a north midland county such as Longford.

The victory in South Longford marked a turning point for the new Sinn Fein party. Griffith was once again writing for his rejuvenated newspaper *Nationality* and by the spring of 1917 the party had over 100 clubs. The schism with Plunkett was soon addressed when Plunkett's overconfidence led him to take the drastic step of forming his own political party 'The

Liberty League' which would collapse and be subsumed under the umbrella of Sinn Fein. As Griffith had argued, Sinn Fein remained a loose coalition, becoming more of a movement than a political party, with membership defined more by a radical political instinct than Plunkett's dogmatic orthodoxy. One year after the Rising Sinn Fein had become the key brand label for advanced nationalism and, much like the Home Rule party had done for decades, it would now move to subsume and embrace all challengers to its title as the alternative voice for those disillusioned with the old politics. Radical nationalism now had a definite home under the accommodating umbrella of Sinn Fein. Flexible enough to have an avowed dual monarchist as its leader, it offered a home to both disillusioned conservative Home Rulers and radical Gaelicists, and physical force Republicans and all those who lay in between these two extremes.

Once again though it was from Britain that new impetus for the Sinn Fein bandwagon would come. Lloyd George, keen to consolidate US commitment to the war effort after their entry in April 1917, and well aware of the hostility of Irish-America, decided to release those high profile figures who were still being detained at Lewes Prison. These included de Valera and Thomas Ashe, who returned to a tumultuous welcome from the Dublin public on 18 June. The sheer exuberance of their welcome signified just how far advanced Nationalist sentiment had spread across the south and west of Ireland. Lloyd George's decision to release all remaining prisoners was, he hoped, the first step in a move towards reconciliation and the achievement of a final political settlement. This new sense of conciliation and harmony was to be expressed in a new forum to decide on the future of Ireland in the shape of a new Irish Convention. In a shrewd move Lloyd George effectively threw the problem back into Irish hands by inviting all shades of Irish political opinion to attend the new body whose decision he promised would be implemented by the British Government in new legislation no matter what its conclusion. While a clever move in terms of publicity, the convention, which sat from July 1917 right through until March 1918, achieved almost nothing. Boycotted by the new Sinn Fein movement it instead merely highlighted the fact that the issues which had spawned the pre-war Ulster Crisis were still proving insoluble. The one notable outcome for Irish politics was the final split between northern and southern Unionists, with Ulster Unionists moving closer to hardening their demands for permanent territorial exclusion from the Home Rule scheme. For John Redmond it would prove to be a final futile coda with him dying exhausted and in his own words 'a broken hearted man' on 6 March 1918.

Perhaps the most significant outcome of Lloyd George's futile political initiatives would be the release of the man who would replace Redmond as the leader of the Nationalist movement in Ireland in the shape of Eamon de Valera. De Valera, an American-born schoolteacher raised in Limerick, was the last surviving and most successful senior commander of the Rising, an image which would serve him well throughout the rest of his long political life. De Valera would become the Sinn Fein party's next candidate for a by-election to be held in East Clare, which was caused by the death of John Redmond's younger brother when fighting in France. East Clare was, much like Roscommon, a safe Home Rule seat which had not been contested since 1885. There was little dynamism in the local party and little time to prepare following the sudden death of the relatively youthful and healthy sitting MP. Despite the fact that the Home Rule candidate Patrick Lynch was a popular local notable, the result was a dramatic walkover for de Valera who won the seat with 5,010 votes compared to Lynch's 2,035. Due to his military credentials he benefited in particular from the support of a large contingent of Volunteers and his role in the Easter Rising played a prominent part in Sinn Fein propaganda. As in all their previous campaigns the new party concentrated largely on the failures and corruption of their opponents with little presented by way of constructive policy initiatives While there were later claims of intimidation from the Volunteers, the violent nature of the campaign was nothing new in Irish politics, having been employed liberally by the Home Rule party in the past. De Valera's victory set the Sinn Fein bandwagon rolling and would be confirmed shortly after with the election of W. T. Cosgrave, later the first President of the Executive Council of the independent Irish Free State and de Valera's later nemesis, in another by-election in Kilkenny City in August.

The by-election opportunities had done much to prepare the new Sinn Fein movement in becoming a significant nationwide challenger to the Home Rule party. They had offered a testing ground for a whole new generation of political leaders, spurred on the creation of local political clubs and given the reinvigorated Volunteer movement a much needed focus for its activities. What the party lacked however was the final piece of the jigsaw in terms of a distinct and identifiable political credo. This would be achieved at the party convention (Ard Fheis) held in October 1917 where the various strands of advanced nationalism who had supported the alternative movement came together to hammer out an orthodox party line. The convention made the headline decision to abandon the old Sinn Fein idea of Dual Monarchy and commit itself to an independent Republic.

However, the reality was that the many ideas which had informed the new movement would be subsumed under the separatist umbrella and put on hold until independence was achieved when amongst other things a referendum would be held to decide exactly what form of government the people wanted. The decision was also taken to make an appeal to the anticipated peace conference which would convene after the war with much hope pinned on the universality of Woodrow Wilson's fourteen point plan to respect the self-determination of small nations in any future settlement of the European peace. In another symbolic move de Valera replaced Griffith as President of Sinn Fein, the latter becoming deputy leader. Many, none more so than the British, had expected that when the new party finally sat down to hammer out a series of practical principles, its inherent contradictions would come to the fore and it would quickly splinter. This did not happen, although the internal contradictions would remain and certainly underpinned the split in the movement which would lead to civil war in late June 1922.

The ability of this new Sinn Fein movement to sustain its challenge led the British Government to once again turn toward a policy of coercion. In August, in the wake of the Cosgrave victory, a number of prominent radicals were arrested. Amongst these was the recently released Thomas Ashe who was arrested for giving a seditious speech at Ballinalee in County Longford. Demanding the status of political prisoners, Ashe and a number of other prominent Volunteers went on hunger strike. The authorities, fearful of the effects a new wave of martyrs would have on Irish opinion, opted to force-feed the prisoners. This crude and invasive procedure was both controversial and dangerous. On 25 September Ashe was force-fed, dying shortly afterward as a result. Ashe's death led to a profound level of sympathy amongst Irish Nationalists with over 40,000 people attending his funeral in Dublin. Symbolising his new prominence in the new movement, Michael Collins gave the graveside oration. After the Volunteers fired a volley into the air he said: 'Nothing additional remains to be said. That volley which we have just heard is the only speech which it is proper to make above the grave of a dead Fenian.'[7] The starkness of the speech contrasted sharply with that given by Pearse at the funeral of O'Donovan Rossa in 1915 (Document 4) and hinted at Collins' hard-headed pragmatism that would shape his approach to the revolution.

The death of Ashe once again provided a boost to the new movement. By the following month there were estimated to be over 1,200 Sinn Fein political clubs now in existence (around the same as the Home Rule party) with 200,000 members drilled into a dynamic national organisation. With its new, if rather vague policy, it was led by de Valera, who not only maintained his unimpeachable identity as the last surviving leader of the Easter Rising, an image that never stopped selling, and also had proved himself to be a studiously able and sophisticated modern politician.

The conscription crisis

While the new movement had overcome seemingly insurmountable challenges it faced in the aftermath of the Rising there was little doubt that it needed to sustain its momentum or risk losing its way and falling into faction. The momentum for the movement would come not from within but from without with a series of profoundly counterproductive moves from the British authorities. With a growing realisation of the increasing strength of the new separatist movement and the need to make conciliatory gestures to world opinion no longer necessary as American commitment to the war intensified, the government once again turned towards a policy of confrontation. In May 1918 the decision was taken to once again bring the leadership of the party into custody. With a series of blatantly trumped up charges concerning an alleged plot with the Germans to launch another rising in Ireland (which few even in the ruling elite believed), de Valera, Griffith, and almost the entire national leadership of the party were arrested and thrown into prison.

The second, and far more important, government initiative which garnered increasing support for the new Sinn Fein movement was the threatened introduction of conscription to Ireland in the spring of 1918 to meet the German offensive along the western front. While the Home Rule party had early on identified itself with the war effort, Sinn Fein had long advocated an anti-war stance. The threat of conscription turned the steady flow of disenchanted Nationalists into the Sinn Fein movement into a flood. Taking the lead at the head of a Nationalist coalition which included prominent members of the Home Rule party, the party energetically launched a series of mass rallies, protest marches and petitions complemented with passionate polemics crudely linking the threat of conscription with the need for separatism. So unpopular was the threat of conscription that even some members of the UVF found a home in the movement. For many, involvement in the anti-conscription campaign would be their first engagement with radical political action and it is doubtful that the large majority of new recruits understood exactly what the party stood for, most seeing it as some kind of anti-conscription party that would protect them with militant action or passive resistance.

The breadth of opposition to the threat of conscription was demonstrated by the prominent role played by the Catholic Church in the campaign. While Cardinal Logue remained cautious about publicly backing the movement, the Catholic Bishops showed little reticence in making their feelings known. After a meeting at Maynooth they issued a statement which backed the right of the Irish to resist the measure 'by all means that are consonant with the law of God.' The prominent role played by the church in the anti-conscription campaign did a great deal to promote Sinn Fein as a respectable political alternative to the Home Rule establishment. The Sinn Fein leadership, and de Valera in particular, realised how important clerical support would be in the coming struggle and moved to reassure the hierarchy about their intentions, distancing themselves from rumours that they held sympathies with Bolshevism and presenting themselves as Irish patriots with little intention of revolutionising the established social order or instigating any form of anti-clerical policy.

The impact of the conscription crisis was crucial in bringing Sinn Fein to a wider audience and giving people at least some sense of the movement as a viable and trustworthy political alternative. While it is an overstatement to say that the conscription crisis and its exploitation by Sinn Fein explains the later electoral popularity of the party, there can be little doubt of its significance in turning the party into an articulate spokesman for a genuinely popular cause. The fact that Sinn Fein had lost three by-elections in a row prior to the passing of the Military Service Bill in April demonstrated the difficulties the party had in maintaining active support without a popular and confrontational issue to galvanise Irish Nationalists. Donegal IRA leader Peadar O'Donnell would later claim: 'I don't believe that the executions of 1916 would have passed into ballads like '98 only that the threat of conscription came on its heels and that it was the threat of conscription that forced people onto their feet.'[8] The most damaging factor for the British Government was their failure in the end to actually introduce conscription. The idea itself had been shelved by May 1918, but when no definitive announcement to that effect was forthcoming – leaving the threat hanging over the heads of the Irish – Sinn Fein was able to continue using it as a source of populist support during what would prove to be the final months of the war, keeping both the issue and the party firmly at the centre of contemporary events in Irish political life.

The British response to the campaign was to turn once again to confrontation, appointing Lord French as the new Viceroy committed to crippling the new movement with a hard-line approach. On the evening of 17 May, seventy-three members of the Sinn Fein leadership, aside from Collins and the uncompromising figure of Cathal Brugha, were arrested in a series of early morning raids. They were charged with conspiring with the Germans in a plot to seize control of the country. The charges were almost wholly fabricated and a further wave of sympathy broke out across Ireland. In the midst of the crisis a further by-election was due to be held in East Cavan. The growing popularity and confidence of the party was shown by its decision to abandon the pan-Nationalist truce of the conscription campaign in its choice of Arthur Griffith as its candidate for the seat. Griffith, viewed largely as a moderate political figure when compared to more doctrinaire Republicans, was not viewed so by the Home Rule party. They saw Griffith as a long time political enemy who had spent over a decade pouring vitriol on the Home Rule party. The choice of Griffith, again as an imprisoned candidate after the German Plot arrests, was a profoundly provocative and symbolic move as was the Sinn Fein decision not to reciprocate the Home Rule party's decision to stand aside in an earlier by-election in King's County. Griffith's candidacy and eventual victory demonstrated that any hopes for some form of Nationalist alliance, if such had ever existed, was dead and there was now to be a bitter fight for the soul of Irish nationalism.

The 1918 general election

The events of 1918 had taken place under the cloud of a potential general election. With the war continuing, few knew when such an election would be held. Many military commanders expected the war to drag on for at least another year, while others felt that the end might come as late as 1920.

However, with the defeat of the German offensive in the summer of 1918, the end of the war came relatively quickly, surprising many political planners in both Britain and Ireland who had expected at least a year's grace before the calling of a general election. While the UK as a whole had waited eight years for an election, in Ireland the election would be the first offering any real competition for well over a generation. Aside from the odd radical or political adventurer challenging the dominant Unionist or Nationalist party machines, this would be the first three-way election in modern Irish political history. Perhaps even more significantly it was to be an election played by completely different rules. The Representation of the People Act meant that the Irish electorate more than doubled in size from 700,000 to almost 2 million. A whole new generation of young men over the age of twenty-one would be voting for the first time, a group far more likely to vote for Sinn Fein in large numbers, especially considering the election was to be held for the first time ever on a single day. More noteworthy was the fact that for the first time women aged thirty or over could also vote, a previously unknown quantity in Irish political life. Also in terms of the distribution of seats the election would be a huge step into modern democracy witnessing a radical redrawing of constituency boundaries to better reflect the population, increasing the number of seats in the urban centres of Dublin and Belfast and lessening those in smaller and depopulated areas.

Sinn Fein's tactics during the election campaign built on those which had been so successful in the various by-elections over the previous two years. They offered a radical Republican alternative to the Home Rule party which they painted as staid and conservative, in hock to British political interests and prepared to acquiesce in their partition of the country. The Sinn Fein manifesto (Document 6) called for an appeal to the Paris Peace Conference, abstention and the setting up of a new assembly in Dublin. They moved to rally support over emotive appeals to economic issues to create a simple popular message ('the path to national salvation'). The British were blamed for everything: 'The enforced exodus of millions of our people, the decay of our industrial life, the ever-increasing financial plunder of our country'. Sinn Fein used the Home Rule party's acquiescence in a scheme for temporary Ulster exclusion to batter their opponents mercilessly. In their manifesto they attacked the Home Rule party for contemplating the 'mutilation of our country by partition', a policy that will lead to 'national ruin'.

Amidst much romantic Nationalist bombast they also threatened uncompromisingly to resist any attempt to continue to subjugate Ireland by force. The rhetoric of violence constantly lurked beneath the surface. Arthur Griffith challenged that Unionists in Ulster 'must make up their minds to throw in their lot with the Irish nation or stand out as the English garrison. If they did the latter the Irish nation must deal with them.'[9] De Valera stated that 'Ulster must be coerced if she stood in the way.'[10] Unionists were an 'alien garrison',[11] and that Unionists in Ulster were akin to 'a robber coming into another man's house and claiming a room as his own.'[12]

The Easter rebels were much in evidence as was their rhetoric. The continued imprisonment of the leading political figures after the German Plot arrests gave the political side of the movement irresistible kudos during the campaign whereas the more militarist elements in the IRB or Volunteers, who had largely remained outside of prison, could orchestrate the campaign on the ground with their customary vigour. In comparison the Home Rule party placed its emphasis on its history and its record of steady practical achievements in terms of education, social welfare and land reform. The election, they argued, marked the chance to finally finish the project they had embarked on decades before, while the Sinn Fein party risked the whole Nationalist enterprise with their cavalier tactics and unrealistic aspirations.

It soon became clear also that the election was to be fought almost solely on the issue of Ireland's constitutional relationship with the rest of Britain. Social and economic initiatives were to play little role in the campaign. Much of the reason rests with the decision of the Labour party to stand aside. The threat of the Labour party, which had played a prominent role in the anti-conscription campaign with the Irish Trades Union Congress holding a very successful one day strike during the crisis, had presented a genuine challenge to Sinn Fein. In September the party conference had voted to stand in the elections, leading to a vociferous campaign from Sinn Fein that they were threatening to break the Nationalist consensus. While there were some abortive talks concerning an electoral pact, in November the Labour party, under increasing pressure from all manner of advanced Nationalist organisations, took the momentous decision not to contest the election. The decision led to condemnation from the Home Rule party who would now stand virtually alone against the new movement.

The election itself was less passionate and turbulent than may have been expected. The Home Rule party having been on the defensive for the past two years were in a demoralised state. Their decision not to contest a quarter of Irish seats was a sign of their negative state of mind and Sinn Fein was able to claim twenty-five seats in Munster without even having to take part in a contest. The Sinn Fein party was certainly vigorous and ruthless in areas where there were contests but claims that plural voting and personation played a decisive part in deciding the elections are unsustainable as, much like the culture of violence and intimidation, such practices had long been part of the Irish political scene.

The results of the election showed there had been a dramatic sea change in Ireland's political character. Sinn Fein won a staggering seventy-three seats compared to only six for the Home Rule party. Much has been made of the fact that the Sinn Fein share of the popular vote amounted to only 47 per cent with the Home Rule party achieving a respectable 22 per cent. However, this disparity can be explained largely by the failure of the Home Rule party to force a vote in areas where it anticipated heavy losses. There can be little doubt that had such elections taken place Sinn Fein's share of the vote would have been much larger, representing a clear majority of votes cast. In the end Sinn Fein won every seat in Munster, Connaught and Leinster apart from Waterford where John Redmond's son hung on doggedly, Louth on the Ulster border and fashionable Rathmines in Dublin where a Unionist managed to win the seat. The short reign of the party's new leader, John Dillon, was brought to an end after he lost his own seat in East Mayo to de Valera and resigned.

It was only in Ulster that the Sinn Fein bandwagon was brought to a halt and the Home Rule party managed to hold on as a significant political force. With all but one of the twenty-five victorious Unionist candidates winning their seats in Ulster, it was notable that four of the Home Rule party's six seats would also be located in the province. However, this was due in no small part to an electoral pact agreed with Sinn Fein, amidst fears of a split in the Nationalist vote, which divided Ulster's eight most vulnerable seats up between the two Nationalist parties. In all the Home Rule party won only two seats where they faced direct opposition from Sinn Fein. Nevertheless Ulster did represent a place where constitutional nationalism remained a force to be reckoned with. Even during 1918 when the Sinn Fein movement carried all before them, the party had suffered two significant by-election losses to the Home Rule party in South Armagh and East Tyrone. In a broader sense the continued existence of moderate nationalism in Ulster symbolised a more profound division between northern and southern Nationalists, a division that would prove significant in dictating Nationalist responses to the increasing threat of partition over the coming years.

Sample essay and examination questions

Account for the victory of Sinn Fein in the 1918 election.
Were the rise of Sinn Fein and the decline of the Irish Parliamentary Party traceable to the same causes?
Does the extension of the franchise under the 1918 Representation of the People Act adequately explain the triumph of Sinn Fein in the ensuing election?

Further reading

D. Ferriter, *The Transformation of Ireland, 1900–2000* (London, 2004), Chapter 2
T. Garvin, 'The Rising and Irish democracy', in M. Ni Dhonnchada and T. Dorgan, *Revising the Rising* (Dublin, 1991)
K. Jeffrey, *Ireland and the Great War* (Cambridge, 2000), Chapter 1
M. Laffan, 'The Unification of Sinn Fein in 1917', *Irish Historical Studies* (1970–1)
M. Laffan, *The Resurrection of Ireland: The Sinn Fein Party, 1916–1923* (Cambridge, 1999)

5

The War of Independence, 1919–21

The formation of Dáil Eireann

With its huge electoral mandate, attention now focused on how Sinn Fein planned on turning their radical rhetoric into a workable political reality. The first move, in line with Griffith's long cherished strategy of abstention, was to refuse to take seats in the Imperial Parliament at Westminster. Gathering instead at the Mansion House in Dublin on 21 January 1919, the Sinn Fein group took the momentous step of forming their own national assembly, Dáil Eireann, claiming direct authority over all of Ireland. The event itself threw up all kinds of ambiguities. Despite invitations being sent to the other elected Irish MPs, both Unionist and the remnants of the Home Rule party, only the Sinn Fein members chose to attend. Furthermore a full forty-two of these new members were absent, thirty-four of them languishing in British prisons. As such the first meeting of this new Dáil, lasting barely two hours, was attended by a mere twenty-seven members, barely a quarter of all Irish MPs.

Despite this the first meeting would see a number of significant declarations. The first was the creation of a new Irish government consisting of a prime minister and a cabinet answerable to the Dáil who controlled all legislative and financial functions. More important however was the Dáil's ratification of three pre-prepared documents which marked a historic shift in the relationship between Britain and Ireland.

The first of these was a full declaration of independence (Document 7) essentially ratifying the Republic as declared in 1916. This was followed by a 'Democratic Programme' (Document 9) which was similarly an attempt to build on the legacy of 1916 by marrying up the rather vague social ideas of Patrick Pearse and the Marxism of James Connolly, although the latter was significantly not mentioned by name in the document itself. Certainly the document was included largely to assuage leftist opinion within Sinn Fein and also appeal to those attending the imminent meeting of the first Socialist

International in Switzerland, rather than to define the Irish revolution as a socialist enterprise. It was itself a much watered down version of the original written by the labour leader Thomas Johnson, whose socialist rhetoric shocked many within the conservative Nationalist leadership of Sinn Fein, who feared that the coming struggle for independence would be deflected by forays into convoluted ideological debates at such an early stage.

In the end such concerns proved unfounded. The document, fiddled with and amended by Sean T. O'Kelly, the newly appointed Ceann Comhairle (chairman) of the new Dáil, up to only a few hours before its promulgation at the Mansion House, while retaining much of its egalitarian spirit of the original with the pledge that 'all right to private property must be subordinated to public right and welfare', would have little impact on the future direction of the revolution. Indeed the threat of profound ideological divisions tearing the new Sinn Fein movement apart was overwhelmed by the intensity of events over the next two years and relegated well behind the basic demand of self-determination. Any attempt to try and divert the revolution in a leftwards direction, as would happen with socialist-inclined Republicans such as Peadar O'Donnell in Derry, would be condemned as subverting the singular Nationalist goal of separatism and weakening the movement's resolve. As the writer Seán Ó Faoláin ably summarised the simple Irish Republican message during the revolution, 'Freedom first, everything else after.'

Thirdly came a more pragmatic political initiative. Beginning with a typically lofty 'message to the free nations of the world' (Document 8) it also called for the Irish right to self-determination to be recognised by the upcoming Paris Peace Conference, details of which had been announced only three days prior to the first Dáil's meeting. This appeal, along with abstention, was the one major political initiative which Sinn Fein had spelled out prior to its election victory. A number of Irish delegates were chosen and headed off to Paris 'in order that the civilised world . . . may guarantee to Ireland its permanent support for the maintenance of her national independence'. It was however an ultimately futile idea. There was little chance that the victorious allied powers would apply the principles of self-determination to their own national or ethnic minorities. In the end the Irish delegation was largely ignored, their concerns dwarfed by the bigger issues of carving up Eastern Europe and punishing Germany and her allies. A combination of the British veto and American indifference assured their failure, which would be sealed when the Treaty of Versailles was finally ratified in late June with no mention of Ireland.

The failure of the appeal to the Paris Conference was not wholly unexpected by Sinn Fein leaders and in the context of Woodrow Wilson's fourteen points over the rights of small nations their appeal was an absolute necessity no matter how futile in terms of results. It also characterised what would be Sinn Fein's main weapon in the struggle for independence, a reliance on grand gesture and propaganda. The appeal to the Versailles conference was aimed to resonate less with those in Paris than Irish-America who, although having a diminishing role in determining US elections, remained the major source of funding for all strands of Irish nationalism from the Home Rule party right through to the hardliners of the IRB.

Much as had been the tradition for Nationalists of all shades since the 1880s, Irish-America, along with other exile groups particularly in Britain and the Dominions, would be the principal audience for Sinn Fein's strategy of saturation propaganda. The key forum for the appeals of Nationalists and their opponents during the revolutionary period would remain the United States where generations of Irish immigration had led to powerful Irish-American political and cultural lobby groups. The British Government, especially Lloyd George, were extremely sensitive to the possibility of the Irish question compromising Anglo-American relations both during and after the Great War and this fear would play in the background of the various attempts made to reach a satisfactory settlement which would appease opinion in the US. Demonstrating the importance of American opinion, Eamon de Valera, the leader of the revolutionary Dáil, based himself in the United States during almost the entire period of the War of Independence. Prior to the revolution Irish-American aid to Nationalist organisations was predominantly financial although during the war such support had begun to wane largely due to the pro-German leanings of the leaders of the Easter Rising and the strong military and financial links which developed between Washington and London. However, with the end of the war and in the context of Woodrow Wilson's principles of self-determination and the rights of small nations, Irish-America once again began to mobilise. The Sinn Fein movement reciprocated with a sophisticated campaign of propaganda aimed at leading opinion-formers within the Irish-American community whose major focus was the refusal of Irish self-determination in the context of the Versailles principles. De Valera's visit to the United States was a spirited if ultimately futile effort to gain recognition of the Irish Republic from Washington. With a presidential election due in 1920 such a strategy was not an unreasonable one and certainly de Valera was to visit both national conventions of the two major political parties in an effort to put Irish issues on the agenda. However, with Wilson's declining health, his interventionist international initiatives were rejected by the Republican victor Warren Harding, who campaigned on a policy of 'return to normalcy' and an isolationist foreign policy. While failing to gain political recognition, de Valera did manage to reinvigorate a number of Irish-American organisations and, through a breathless round of lectures and fund raising dinners, raise almost $6 million, much of which would find its way back to Ireland to support the Dáil government's efforts to establish a functioning revolutionary government and extend its already substantial propaganda efforts.

Although placing a whole web of grandiosely titled embassies, ambassadors and officials in numerous countries, their roles were largely to co-ordinate and disseminate the Sinn Fein propaganda message. This propaganda, brilliantly imaginative and vast in scale, was honed under a new Ministry of Propaganda with Desmond Fitzgerald and later Erskine Childers taking charge. Pamphlets, speeches, film and newspapers such as the all-pervasive *Irish Bulletin* were translated into numerous languages and proved by far the most successful enterprise engaged in by Irish Republicans. Demonstrating perhaps the increasing conservatism and wealth of Irish-America, the major response to such efforts was more financial than political with de Valera spending almost eighteen months in the United States raising funds for the new Republic, most of which would be ploughed back into the propaganda mill from whence it came. Indeed the hoped for political pressure resulting from these campaigns would only have a real impact in the British Isles. The 'war', which was to follow the establishment of the Dáil, was thus a heterogeneous campaign with military confrontation as only one component. Indeed so marked was this feature of Irish Republicanism that the war effort has been described succinctly as 'armed propaganda'.

The role of the Volunteers

It is thus doubly ironic that on the very same day that the Dáil sat for the first time and issued the first of its propaganda statements, the military side of the movement also made its first aggressive move. In one of the most curious coincidences in modern Irish history, 21 January 1919 also saw an incident in South Tipperary where a group of radical Irish Volunteers which included Dan Breen and Sean Treacy, shot dead two RIC men escorting a cart of commercial gelignite, in a botched attempt to steal weapons. The attack, more the result of incompetence and frustration, had no sanction from the Volunteer or political leadership and was wholly down to the initiative of the small group in Tipperary.

The coincidental timing of these two events, although not linked in any direct way, has led historians to declare 21 January 1919 as the first day of the Irish War of Independence. The conflict itself, which would drag on for two and a half years until the summer of 1921, has undergone many changes of name and re-imaginings in recent times. Referred to variously as the 'Tan War', 'Anglo-Irish War' or the 'Troubles', all of these labels have proved unsatisfactory in encompassing a conflict which has been painted variously as both a war of colonial liberation and a squalid civil war tinged with sectarianism. The start date also creates a deceptive clarity in the post-Rising period where none existed. Since the release of the Volunteers in late 1916 attempts to reinvigorate the movement had led inevitably to confrontation in local areas. As early as February 1918 for example, the British had placed County Clare under martial law. The Volunteers, eager for arms, carried out small-scale raids on various properties, from isolated farms to small police barracks, to secure weapons with some kind of violent confrontation being the inevitable end result. After 21 January 1919 despite the shock of the Soloheadbeg killings, the violence and disorder would continue much as it had in the period that preceded it.

Since the Rising the Volunteers, despite being drawn into supporting political campaigns, had remained an unreconstructed militarist movement. Most believed that their role was simply to prepare and train for the inevitable renewal of hostilities in a second and this time more extensive Rising across Ireland. As such they took little notice of the new subtleties which the shift in the political dynamics implied. There had been little coherent development of the military side of the movement as had occurred with the political side. The headquarters in Dublin, while nominally in charge of the Volunteers, never managed to develop control over provincial units despite its countless efforts at reorganisation at the county and regional level. As had been the case prior to the Rising the Volunteer units consisted of groups of young men from close-knit communities with strong personal and familial links. Officers were elected, more often than not due to their local status in Gaelic sporting or cultural organisations, rather than appointed by a central authority. Florence O'Donoghue recalled that these elections tended to put 'the plausible talker rather than the capable worker' in positions of authority.[1] As such the rise in militancy within the movement was an organic process, a product of revolutionary meritocracy rather than bureaucratic initiative, where those prepared to take action quickly rose to prominence in their local areas.

In this sense Soloheadbeg was as much a sign of frustration from militarists as it was the starting gun for a full outbreak of hostilities. Indeed many had grown increasingly suspicious of the political side of the movement, seeing their dominance as both a diversion from the militaristic legacy of the Rising and also leading to inevitable compromise with the British and a dilution of the sacred purity of the separatist demand. In the minds of these radicals the Rising was a military endeavour pure and simple which in many ways was set up in direct antithesis to the political dynamics of the period. As in 1916 it would take a radical and visionary vanguard to lead the way in the struggle. It would be these radicals who would push the movement into violent confrontation and eventually into a full-scale guerrilla war in many parts of the country. Increasingly it would be the initiatives of the kind of men who carried out the shootings in South Tipperary rather than those who spoke to the world's press in the Mansion House which would define the direction of the revolution.

The conflict itself would begin slowly and was barely worthy of the name war for its first eighteen months. Had Soloheadbeg not happened when it did, historians might have plumped for a war which began in mid-1920 rather than early 1919 and indeed the shootings in South Tipperary did not affect the general trend of the escalation from the summer of 1917. The first phase of the conflict was a continuation of low-level small-scale acts of violence mainly occurring during raids for arms on isolated farms or homes in rural Ireland. There was certainly more direct confrontation, explicable by an increased boldness on the part of the Volunteers or alternatively an increased willingness to resist such raids by their victims. Shootings also began, with six policemen being killed in the first six months of the year with activity focused largely on South Tipperary, although Mayo and Limerick also saw some fatalities. In the whole of 1919 however only sixteen members of the crown forces (police and army) were killed. This was to rise as the conflict proceeded with forty-four fatalities in the first six months of 1920, 171 for the second half of the year and then rising sharply to 324 in the first six months prior to the Truce in July 1921. The number of IRA casualties showed a similar pattern of escalation, although slightly lower in number overall, rising from thirty-two in the first half of 1920, 226 for the second half of the year and 182 up to the end of the war in July 1921. The official number of civilian casualties totalled almost 200 although three-quarters of these were to die in the final six months of the war as the conflict became increasingly bitter with both sides turning their focus on soft targets. However, these 1,200 or so fatalities only tell part of the story with the conflict increasingly characterised by a low level campaign of woundings, punishment beatings, arson attacks, looting and expulsion and forced exile.

While the war in the early stages amounted to little more than unruly scuffles, where raids for arms were punctuated by the very rare shooting, the British response to the increase in disorder was to prove heavy-handed and deeply counterproductive. With the appointment of the hard-line Iain Macpherson, the government was to follow a policy of confrontation with the maintenance of the wartime Defence of the Realm Act. Soon after the conflict began, and especially after a British soldier was killed in an ambush in Cork, the town of Fermoy in the east of the county was raided and looted by the military. The British authorities outlawed the Dáil in mid-September and proclaimed large areas in the south and west of the country. All Nationalist organisations, including the Volunteers, Cumann na mBan and even the Gaelic League were proclaimed in November, after a series of bans in the most disturbed counties had proved ineffective. The crackdown was notable for its crude application and its effect on everyday civilian life. Local businesses were closed; parades and public gatherings banned; activists of all kinds arrested and small town markets, often the lifeblood of the local economy, were banned. In short, in many proscribed areas the effects of martial law were felt at every level of Irish society with some experiencing at worst violence and intimidation but more usually the demoralising effects of restrictions on travel, leisure pursuits and limitations on individual economic opportunity. It became obvious that the crackdown led to a distinct growth in sympathy for the Volunteers, which had been almost entirely lacking prior to the increased military presence. Despite the breadth of Sinn Fein's victory in the December election, it was clear that few people voted for the party as a way of supporting the resumption of violence or the instigation of an all-out war.

Despite the British crackdown the main focus of the war remained intensely local. The main targets of the Volunteers, or the IRA as they were beginning to be known, were the RIC who were convenient targets representing state authority at the local level. The RIC had been targeted by an IRA-enforced boycott which saw local policemen and their families shunned by the local community as they went about their everyday business. Such a policy did much to undermine state authority at the local level by distancing these policemen from the communities which they were meant to be policing.

Due to their local knowledge the RIC remained the principal target for the Volunteers throughout the conflict. The constant threat of violence and the demoralising effects of community ostracism forced the RIC to abandoned hundreds of small isolated village barracks to concentrate in the larger towns. This move in particular would be key to pushing the conflict into a more intense second phase. With so many abandoned barracks, often little more than small terraced houses, the local IRA moved in to burn them in a wide-ranging series of arson attacks in the spring of 1920. This was both a show of force and a practical wish to prevent their reoccupation at a later date. The strategy of the Volunteers was much changed from that of previous Republican risings in that idealism was tempered with a large dose of pragmatism. In August 1920 the IRA journal *An t-Oglach* spelled out the new priorities:

> [W]e are carrying out a well-considered plan of campaign in which the object is to harass and demoralize the enemy without giving them an opportunity to strike back effectively. We realize that it is far more profitable to kill for Ireland than to die for her. In short we are turning to account one lesson of Irish history – the mistakes of '98.[2]

The war itself retained a piecemeal and patchy presence. The most violent part of the country was the city of Belfast where over 550 people lost their lives in two years of sporadic sectarian rioting. However, the fighting in the north-east was atypical and the IRA played little part in defining the direction of the conflict which must be seen in the context of partition and a longer tradition of sectarian tension in Ulster. Outside of Belfast while every county had some form of Volunteer organisation, the majority of counties saw very little in the way of violence with the war largely confined to the province of Munster. Only in a few counties outside of Dublin, most notably Cork, could there be said to have been anything resembling a sustained and widespread guerrilla war. Other counties such as Longford, Mayo and Donegal experienced short and often intense periods of violence, their length being determined by intensely local factors such as the dynamism of the IRA leadership or the socio-economic status of the Volunteers themselves. Much of this had to do with the lack of control exerted by the Volunteer General Headquarters (GHQ) in Dublin which, despite its Napoleonic rhetoric, never managed to dictate to provincial IRA units.

The question as to why the war raged in some counties and not in others continues to vex historians. This is mainly due to the fact that there are always exceptions to any rule put forward as a universal explanation. There are a variety of theories used to explain the 'geography of revolution' ranging from the suitability of the local terrain for guerrilla fighting; the county's history of a radical political activity; the effectiveness of local leadership; and the ready supply of recruits, weaponry and suitable enemies. It is certainly clear that those areas which stood at both ends of the socio-economic scale, running from the affluent farming class to impoverished areas of the west, were unlikely to see a great deal of IRA activity. It is also the case that areas developed at different speeds, with counties such as Sligo only in a position to begin an effective campaign at the time of the Truce. If any conclusions can be drawn it is that diverse factors were decisive in different areas strongly reflecting local circumstances: leadership in Longford; terrain in Kerry; and a strong tradition of radical activity in Cork. Indeed the lack of uniformity in the campaign itself was thus mirrored in the heterogeneous reasons which affected the effectiveness of the IRA in provincial areas.

Collins and the intelligence war

In Dublin, the other major centre of the war, the conflict revolved around the activities of Michael Collins and his small band of elite hand-picked Volunteers. Along with the vigorous urban warfare of the Dublin Brigade, Collins instigated a covert intelligence war against the British security forces. A skilled organiser and administrator, he sought to undermine the notoriously well co-ordinated intelligence gathering capabilities of the crown forces which, through a combination of paid informers and assiduously compiled police reports from the provinces, had been instrumental in crushing rebel moves in the past. Moving to recruit large numbers of informers and paid spies from within the Castle authorities including two detectives, David Neligan and Ned Broy, Collins was able to intercept orders to military units in the countryside, thus allowing provincial IRA units to avoid capture or plan more effective operations.

In order to carry out these attacks Collins created a dedicated group of paid full-time assassins to carry out these killings. His immediate focus was on secrecy and strict discipline. The Volunteers who were busy reorganising upon their release were still organised along British military lines with companies and battalions containing hundreds of men – most of whom it has to be said were unwilling to engage in further violence. It was really only a hardcore of men, people who were prepared to take action that could be relied on. It was quality not quantity that mattered. Bringing other people into the organisation who were less committed was asking for trouble and leaving all kinds of opportunities for the organisation to be penetrated by the British. Collins understood this implicitly and throughout his life would rely on a very small number of hardened assassins and confidants.

His small group, all of them volunteers, came to be known as 'The Squad'. Most of them were single men in their early twenties from inner city Dublin with no family or work commitments. Originally of only five members, the group eventually grew to around a dozen coming to be known pejoratively as the 'Twelve Apostles'. The Squad members were all full-time assassins, paid £4 10s per week. They took orders directly and unquestioningly from Collins and no one else and were forbidden from discussing their activities with anyone including other members of the IRA. He ruled them with a rod of iron. Many testify they were more scared of coming back to Collins with an assassination not done than they were over the job itself. When the time came they were assembled in the basements of various hotels and boarding houses in north Dublin. They used in particular a hotel in Parnell Square called *Vaughan's*. In these anonymous buildings they were given a name and address, sometimes a photograph, often at the last minute, and then sent off to do their grisly work. They were never told who they were killing or why – it was all kept in Collins' own head. This group would grow in number as the war progressed, often co-opting various individuals from the Dublin Brigade to carry out its larger operations.[3]

Collins' organisation did not set out to kill as many British personnel as possible, unlike in the provinces, where the IRA would target any member of the crown forces as the chance arose. In fact Collins was restrained, every attack ordered had a purpose and, as with his financial dealings, he hated waste of any kind. He would carefully weigh the propaganda implications of the attacks and establish dossiers on targets, having them followed home, getting to know their routines.

However, when he had made the decision to kill, Collins never wavered and was utterly ruthless. The first targets were the Dublin 'G' Men, members of the political division of the Dublin Metropolitan Police (DMP), who were virtually wiped out by the beginning of 1920. After issuing a letter warning them to desist from their political activity, a threat that was largely ignored, Collins sent out his Squad to accost, beat up and threaten certain key 'G' Men. If this strategy failed to scare them off it then became a matter of executing them. District Inspector (D/I) Patrick Smith was the first to be killed by Squad men at the end of July 1919 in Drumcondra, and on 12 September D/I Daniel Hoey was shot dead near police headquarters in Brunswick Street in the city centre. As a consequence of this shattering blow to the morale of the Dublin police, D/I William Redmond was summoned from Belfast to reorganise the intelligence unit and with a specific brief to find Collins. Within a few weeks of his arrival in Dublin, he was assassinated in Harcourt Street.

The Squad were the blunt weapon in Collins' armoury but the real strength of his activities lay in an audacious intelligence gathering operation run from an innocent-looking city centre office in Crowe Street which lay close to Dublin Castle. While having numerous safe houses and front businesses across the city, the office at Crowe Street was the centre of operations. Masquerading as a normal city centre office, members of Collins' intelligence department maintained the pretence by arriving for work at 9.00 a.m. dressed in business suits and kept regular office hours. Under the guiding hand of 24-year-old Cork man Liam Tobin, a staff was assembled to create files on all of the key members of the British establishment and military. The nature of their work was incredibly mundane, trawling through society directories to find out the names and addresses of key people, where they ate, where they stayed and their daily routines. They also collected the names of all people employed as part of the bureaucracy in Ireland, especially inside Dublin Castle, and would work on turning them to the Republican side. According to Tobin they had dozens and dozens of officials at every level of the civil service working for them. All these techniques were very revolutionary for their time. Thus in the midst of the War of Independence Collins was developing a new and multifaceted way of conducting a revolutionary insurrection reflected in his various roles as Minister for Finance, Director of Intelligence of the IRA and head of the IRB, which represented a formidable alternative power base to that of the political side of the movement.[4]

The Dáil counter-state

It was increasingly evident that throughout the conflict the military side of the movement eclipsed the political side. Eamon de Valera himself was absent from Ireland for most of the war, leaving for the USA in June 1919, not to return until December of 1920. Arthur Griffith remained in charge in Ireland itself but lacked de Valera's unimpeachable militarist credentials and subsequently drew little respect from the Volunteers. The Minister of Defence, Cathal Brugha, attempted to assert nominal political control over the Volunteers, but with little success. While managing to get the Volunteers to swear an oath of allegiance to the Dáil in August 1919, such a declaration had little practical effect on the ground. Indeed the ambiguous relationship between the military and political sides of the movement would not be clarified until the later stages of the war when the Dáil formally accepted responsibility for the activities of the Volunteers and that a state of war existed between the rebel Republic and the British Crown.

The Dáil government, while accepting the reality of military control, concentrated on furthering its propaganda efforts with the creation of a revolutionary counter-state. While much lauded by later historians the Dáil's attempts to build a comprehensive system of local government were stillborn. However, the collapse of state authority in so many areas meant that attempts to set up an alternative system of justice were more successful. This idea drew directly on similar courts established during the Land War of the late 1870s. However, with the collapse of law and order in many parts of the south and west of the island and the growing rise in agrarian outrages and land seizures some form of justice was a vital necessity, if only to maintain support for Sinn Fein in provincial areas and ensuring that the party did not come to be associated with anarchy. As such, local Sinn Fein clubs, backed up by the coercive power of local Volunteers, established a local ad hoc system of justice. While the lack of prison facilities meant that more serious crimes were difficult to punish, often being dealt with by the brutal methods of the local IRA through beatings, forced exile or execution, the courts settled local land disputes and many other petty crimes, which would have been the everyday responsibility of the now departed RIC.

As with so much during the war, these local initiatives were eventually taken up by the Dáil government and transformed into a distinct national policy. The implementation of this policy was certainly helped by Sinn Fein victories in the local elections of January and June 1920 which left the party, although faring less well in large urban areas, in control of almost all rural councils in the south and west. Winning these local elections whilst demonstrating the continued strength of support for Sinn Fein across the country, also presented the movement with a profound problem calling into question the pretensions of the revolutionary Dáil government to offer workable alternative power structures. While all councils lauded their revolutionary credentials by throwing off British state authority and proclaiming their allegiance to the Dáil, they also had to accept the more mundane responsibility for maintaining local services. The withdrawal of British grants for these disloyal authorities meant that they were constantly short of money and only with great effort, and resorting to all kinds of nefarious moneymaking schemes, were they able to provide a rudimentary form of local government. The fundamental contradiction of creating positive local government, while at the same time seeking to spread revolution and disorder, was never really addressed during the conflict and there were numerous examples of local Sinn Fein-run councils taking responsibility for the repair of roads and bridges that its allies in the IRA had destroyed.

While Dáil control over provincial political initiatives was progressing it was obvious that shorn of political control and with central direction from Dublin more imagined than real, local IRA units continued to act largely on their own initiative. While the Volunteer GHQ in Dublin attempted to assert control over the movement on a nationwide basis with the despatch of numerous organisers and officers to provincial areas, they rarely made an impact. Local loyalties and suspicion of central control meant that only where the IRA was weak did GHQ have any notable impact in shaping their activities. When it came to the more active counties GHQ had little success in directing or controlling the often rampant excesses of areas that had already fallen into a state of war.

The relationship between the centre and the periphery remained tenuous and was due in no small part to the nature of the conflict in local areas. With attacks being planned in an ad hoc fashion, informed by superior local knowledge and opportunities, making appeals to GHQ in Dublin for specific authority to carry out an operation was unrealistic and rarely sought. The IRB, which offered one possible alternative power base, was also dictated by local peculiarities and continued to play an ambiguous role in the conflict proving itself just as likely to be a force for restraint as it was for radical action. Communication with GHQ by provincial IRA units tended to be practical demands for arms and ammunition while orders of an operational variety were largely ignored.

Indeed the war, into its final most dramatic phase of full-scale guerrilla warfare, was very much affected by local circumstance and local initiative. With so many IRA Volunteers on the run from the authorities, they would band together for protection or to pool their resources. These men, accused of the most extreme of crimes, and as such the most active and committed fighters, would emerge almost organically as the first Flying Columns, full-time guerrilla fighters operating on the margins of their local communities and striking the enemy at every opportunity in a series of ambushes, raids and assassinations. The ambush was the ideal form of warfare for the small and limited columns to engage in. With crown forces now located in larger reinforced military barracks in major towns, attacks on these fortified positions were well beyond the ability of the ill-equipped IRA. As the British however became more static and defensive in their strategy the Flying Columns shifted their focus to attacks on army supply columns and regular daily and nightly police patrols around the most troubled areas. For the British it proved to be a devastating form of warfare where there was no defined front line and GHQ would later send out orders to local areas to form these columns (or Active Service Units) but the reality was that in the most radical areas they had already been formed and were operating effectively. Such strategic developments showed markedly how Dublin was following rather than leading events on the ground.[5]

The Flying Columns would become home to the most hardened and committed members of the various IRA brigades. While there was much paperwork involved in GHQ keeping track of IRA numbers and activities, in reality this new fluid form of warfare would become the main cutting edge of the movement. Its members were the elite of the Volunteer movement and had access to the weapons, support and resources held within each command area. Other IRA members remained part-time and played the part of support staff, hiding weapons, keeping lookout or offering food or a safe house for the evening.

While the British painted these IRA Volunteers as either brutish ruffians or anti-social outsiders, analysis of the social character of the men who formed these columns has undergone something of a revolution in recent years. The IRA was an overwhelmingly Catholic organisation with only one or two notable and high profile exceptions. While older men tended to join Sinn Fein, the IRA was made up of men notable for their youth, with the rank and file usually in their late teens or early twenties and officers only slightly older on average. They were drawn from a variety of backgrounds with many clerks, shop assistants, publicans and schoolteachers filling the ranks. The poorest members of the community were unlikely to join as were those from the higher professions and affluent farming classes. Although many IRA members in rural areas were drawn from a farming background this was less predominant statistically as may have been expected. Much like the Fenian movement of the late nineteenth century the IRA was very much a small town lower middle-class movement. The localism of the Volunteers was reflected in its organisation with IRA units often mirroring membership of Gaelic sporting or cultural organisations and consisting of a tight knit group of young men who had grown up together in the same provincial community.

Women were also to play a significant, if more diverse role in the revolution. Members of Cumann na mBan played a crucial role in providing logistical and medical support for the IRA columns. The reluctance of the police to carry out searches of women made them invaluable in their ability to pass through checkpoints, moving weapons and ammunition or carrying sensitive orders to other units on a local or even national level. Women also played a key role in intelligence gathering with large numbers of typists, secretaries, maids and postmistresses carrying out spying activities for the IRA, something Michael Collins in particular was adept at taking advantage of. More generally women often provided a key link for imprisoned Volunteers and those on the outside, be it their families or comrades. Aside from this covert role many women were to assume a prominent role in public life. Four of the six female members of the Second Dáil were bereaved family members of men killed in the conflict, becoming for many the closest link to their martyred male relatives. As an organisation Cumann na mBan tended to be strongly linked to the growth of Volunteer organisation in provincial areas. Roughly speaking the stronger the IRA in a particular area, the stronger the women's organisation linked to it. Also similar was their social background with members of Cumann na mBan tending to be made up, much like the IRA, of young, single individuals from a lower middle-class background.

The final phase of the conflict

The fine-tuning of the IRA's military effectiveness in the shape of the Flying Columns heralded a move toward the creation of an elite fighting force and the moving of the war into its third and most bloody final phase from the autumn of 1920 when the war began to spiral into a vicious conflict of ambushes, assassinations and reprisal. The growing sophistication of the IRA was matched by the British Government who, in order to support the demoralised RIC and arrest the breakdown of British authority in many parts of Ireland, set about establishing a new auxiliary police force. Recruiting ex-war veterans from across Britain they formed two distinct units, the Black and Tans named after their mismatched uniforms and the Auxiliaries who were drawn exclusively from ex-British army officers and were set up to directly challenge the Flying Columns of the IRA. The escalation of the conflict that such a move entailed would see the return of state control to many areas of Ireland which had been devoid of organised authority for over a year. This British counter-attack was also to prove severely crippling to the embryonic Dáil counter-state and would finally undermine any attempt to ensure the war remained a limited conflict.

Certainly from the autumn of 1920 the war became a profoundly brutal and dirty affair and it was during this final phase, running up to its end in July 1921, that many of the worst atrocities on both sides would occur. There was a comparatively huge escalation of violence with many parts of Ireland experiencing outright terror as the IRA and security forces both sought to outdo each other with a series of vicious and bloodthirsty acts. The British response to IRA attacks would often focus on the local community who were suspected of offering succour to the rebels although the IRA themselves did little to protect the local community from such raids. The focus also moved to softer targets as both sides became more adept at fighting the new type of guerrilla war.

Minorities were often targeted and the IRA carried out numerous sectarian attacks on local Protestants whom they suspected of being spies and informers. The revelation of sectarian motives behind the activities of the IRA in the south and west of Ireland has proved to be a profoundly controversial topic. Peter Hart's 1998 book, The I.R.A. and its Enemies, uncovered large-scale targeting of Protestants and their property in County Cork between 1920 and 1922. In a provocatively titled chapter 'Taking it out on the Protestants', Hart points out the high proportion of civilian victims of IRA violence who were Protestant (36 per cent despite making up only around 7 per cent of the population) and even more striking that over 80 per cent of IRA arson attacks were launched against property owned by Cork Protestants. He also highlights the notorious attacks in late April 1922, the so-called 'Bandon Valley Massacre', where eighteen Protestants were killed by the IRA in the space of three days. In a broader sense it is argued that the increased targeting of Protestants in Ireland, especially in 1922, led to a large-scale exodus which amounted to (in some interpretations) a form of ethnic cleansing. The dramatic decline of the Protestant population by one-third in only fifteen years (from 250,000 in 1911 to 165,000 in 1926) has been presented as evidence of a sustained sectarian campaign by the IRA. However, Hart's research was confined to Cork and it has been notable that other county studies such as Longford, Limerick and Sligo have not revealed similar evidence. While the north-east of Ireland is largely ignored in such analyses, itself raising fundamental questions about the accepted parameters used by historians for studying violence during the revolution, it appears that sectarianism, while no doubt a motive in some areas cannot be generalised across Ireland. Similarly the notable decline in the Protestant population has been put down to other reasons such as the number of casualties in the Great War, the withdrawal of British crown forces and their families after the signing of the Treaty and a conscious decision by many not to live under what they perceived would be a hostile and Catholic-dominated Irish government. While it is certainly true that in some areas Protestants were targeted disproportionately by the IRA who were inspired by a perception of their disloyalty, the research demonstrates once again the profound local character of the revolution and how important local circumstance and the history of inter-communal relations was in defining the nature of the violence.[6]

The British employed torture and murder to frighten the local population into submission. The Black and Tans and Auxiliaries exacted devastating revenge against the local community in response to IRA attacks. Hundreds of such incidents were recorded in official records and reported loudly by foreign correspondents in Britain, Europe and the United States. The informal reprisals of crown forces were tacitly condoned by the government with very few voices raised in protest, and if so only to complain about a perceived lack of discipline and the crude targeting employed by the auxiliary police. Sir Maurice Hankey, Secretary of the Committee of Imperial Defence, stated: 'The truth is that these reprisals are more or less winked at by the government.'[7] Indeed hundreds of civilians would also be killed during the war with their numbers escalating sharply as the war progressed. Almost three-quarters of the estimated 200 civilians killed by the crown forces were to die in the final six months of the conflict.

'Bloody Sunday'

Much of this came to a head in the month of November. In the early hours of 21 November 1920, under increasing pressure from the British, Michael Collins ordered a large round of assassinations of suspected British intelligence agents in Dublin. Most of the fourteen fatalities were killed in cold blood; nearly all of them, as Anne Dolan has observed, were wearing their pyjamas when they were shot. Others were shot in front of their wives. Two of the victims were savagely beaten and mutilated with sledgehammers while one of the assassins, Mick White, sat down to eat the dead man's breakfast after he had shot him. Bloody Sunday pushed the stakes even higher in Dublin. A reward of £10,000 was offered for Collins and gates were attached to the front of Downing Street for the first time. It was rumoured that from then on Lloyd George always slept with a loaded revolver under his pillow. The British response to the shootings would occur that afternoon at Croke Park, Dublin's largest stadium, where a large crowd had gathered to watch a Gaelic football match between Tipperary and

Dublin. Always the site of radical Nationalist protest, arguments had been made and accepted by Collins to call off the game, only being overruled by the GAA leadership. Certainly the British authorities expected many of the most prominent Republicans to attend the match and made plans to cordon off the area and search fans for weapons, later claiming to find a large number of revolvers. However, before the cordon was completed firing broke out and the crowd stampeded. In the end eleven of the crowd, including Michael Hogan, a Tipperary player, were killed with numerous others being injured in the rush. Although there remained, and still does remain, confusion over which side fired the first shot, even the most vociferous supporters of the British Government's policy in Ireland found it difficult to deny that crown forces had fired wildly into the crowd. Furthermore that evening two prominent leaders of the IRA in Dublin who had been captured earlier in the day, along with Conor Clune, the nephew of the Australian Archbishop of Perth, were shot dead after a sustained period of interrogation and torture. In the all too familiar parlance of the day the authorities claimed they had been shot while trying to escape.

Despite the horror of such reprisals, for Collins Bloody Sunday remained an absolute necessity and one he defended for the rest of his life, stating:

> My one intention was the destruction of the undesirables who continued to make miserable the lives of ordinary decent citizens. I have proof enough to assure myself of the atrocities which this gang of spies and informers have committed. If I had a second motive it was no more than a feeling such as I would have for a dangerous reptile. By their destruction the very air is made sweeter. For myself, my conscience is clear. There is no crime in detecting in wartime the spy and the informer. They have destroyed without trial. I have paid them back in their own coin.[8]

Bloody Sunday was a ruthless act and there seems little doubt that it could have been even more devastating. Originally Collins had over fifty names on his hit list but this was reduced to around thirty. In reality despite all the hyperbole we have about the ruthless efficiency of the killings most of the attacks were failures. As one volunteer, Todd Andrews, admitted 'the fact is that the majority of the IRA raids were abortive. The men sought were not in their digs or in several cases, the men looking for them bungled their jobs'. Many of the original targets were not at home when the IRA called, much to the relief of many of the assassins, as they later admitted. Certainly it was not simply a matter of opportunistic assassination but clear that, for such a radical action as Bloody Sunday to be undertaken, Collins was aware the net was closing very tightly around him. Indeed by the time of the Truce in July 1921 it became clear that Collins would have to organise another similar mass shooting or risk having his organisation compromised.

Bloody Sunday occurred during what was a bloody and emotive year, incorporating the death of Terence MacSwiney, Lord Mayor of Cork City in October after 74 days on hunger strike in Brixton Prison. This was to be followed by the hanging of eighteen-year-old Dublin student Kevin Barry, the first rebel to be executed by the British since the Easter Rising. One week later an IRA Flying Column in West Cork under the command of Tom Barry carried out a devastating ambush at Kilmichael where an eighteen-strong Auxiliary patrol was set about and slaughtered leaving only one survivor. In response the Black and Tans set about burning down large parts of Cork city centre.

In the short-term the British reaction to Bloody Sunday was unprecedented in its harshness. Internment without trial was introduced on 10 September and martial law extended across the south and west of the country. The following day a party of Auxiliaries and Michael Collins now became the subject of a full-scale manhunt. Collins became something of a mythical figure even to his enemies. In January 1921, a newly arrived English soldier named J. P. Swindlehurst noted in his diary (published recently in William Sheehan's fascinating *British Voices from the Irish War of Independence 1918–1921*) that, 'We have two extremely fast cars with Rolls Royce engines, we had a talk to the drivers this morning, and were told they are kept in readiness to catch the elusive Michael Collins when news of his whereabouts comes to hand. He must be famous, £500 is being offered dead or alive for his capture, but all the Black and Tans . . . and CID [Criminal Investigation Department] men from Scotland Yard can't get hold of him.' Six weeks later, he was still complaining that 'night after night we have been ordered out, "Michael Collins had been located, he was imprisoned in such and such a house, the CID had him surrounded," and all sorts of rumours. At the time of writing, he is still at large.' One Dublin university student wrote in her diary in 1921 that there was a rumour that 'Michael Collins was killed in the battle . . . while leading his men on a white charger.'[9]

British policy was no doubt now a policy of terror and reprisal. Such a war soon took on its own momentum and would prove extremely difficult to control. The campaign also targeted the wider Sinn Fein movement with censorship introduced for Sinn Fein newspapers threatening the most successful aspect of the separatist campaign. However, this was to prove ineffectual as the mainstream press continued to print details of attacks and reprisals furnished by their various correspondents on the ground. In a similar way the attempt to bottle up the most rebellious areas of Ireland by introducing martial law in Munster proved ineffective as Volunteers could simply move outside of the proscribed area. Indeed the removal of the most radical IRA units merely helped to spread the war to other previously quiescent areas. However, brutal and unpopular as the harsh British security policy was, it did provide results. For the first time in many months the government reasserted control over large parts of the country, broke up IRA columns and carried out large-scale arrests. It was evident that Lloyd George wanted to crush the rebellion so he could begin any negotiations from a position of strength.

Even so despite the many mythologies which the War of Independence has spawned about the brutality of British policy, when viewed in context the British were nowhere near as harsh to Ireland as would have been expected for any other rebellious colony in the Empire. Even so it was evident that the longer the IRA held out against the onslaught the more uncomfortable liberal opinion in Britain would become. The government certainly felt pressure from all kinds of directions, the left and liberals in general symbolised by the vociferous *Manchester Guardian* whose reporter J. L. Hammond sent home detailed eye-witness reports of events in Ireland. This was matched by pressure from the churches, especially the Church of England, who constantly called for a negotiated settlement and an end to the violence. Foreign governments, including the French and perhaps most importantly the United States, also made clear their concerns. Even the King, George V, was at times heard to voice his concerns.

The path to the Truce

As such it was imperative that the conflict was brought to an end one way or another. For all the horrors of November 1920, the month also saw attempts at peace talks. Through an informal channel, contact was made with Michael Collins and other Sinn Fein leaders. Lloyd George had hoped to be able to speak to Arthur Griffith, who he perceived to hold a more moderate line, but was thwarted when Griffith was arrested in December, much to the annoyance of the British Prime Minister.

While behind closed doors there was talk of some kind of negotiation, especially after the return of de Valera to Ireland in December 1920, such a speedy resolution seemed unrealistic. There were a number of reasons for this. De Valera could see the extent to which the military side was predominant in the movement. It would take time for the political side to gain ground. De Valera's re-arrival just after the arrest of Griffith was to prove significant only in the longer term. Perhaps most significant was the British desire to complete the establishment of Northern Ireland with elections due to be held in May 1921. After the creation of this Ulster parliament with its own bureaucracy and functioning executive, the government could then sit down to negotiate with the Sinn Fein leadership. It was also evident that there remained in Lloyd George a lingering belief that the war could be won and that the IRA campaign was on the brink of collapse.

Certainly the IRA remained largely on the defensive in response to the British counter-attack. However this made little seeming difference in lessening the intensity of the conflict or the operational effectiveness of the IRA. The IRA was certainly under increasing pressure. Their methods of guerrilla warfare had become increasingly refined with larger and better equipped columns operating much like a full-time guerrilla army. It was obvious that the British policy of counter-terror was reaping dividends, perhaps many of them unforeseen with the public growing increasingly wary of the IRA as their presence invited broader reprisals on the community. It was also true that the IRA did virtually nothing to defend local communities against reprisal attacks throughout the course of the conflict.

There can be little doubt that the final months of the war would see an increasing gulf between the IRA and the civilian population, something which would be even more evident when the IRA resumed its campaign during the civil war the following year. The IRA was still a functioning entity however when the conflict came to an end. Indeed the final few months of the conflict saw them launch even more dramatic and large-scale attacks, the most notable of which was the large-scale attack on the Customs House in central Dublin in late May. While disastrous as a military venture the operation grabbed the headlines and helped to paint the IRA campaign in a more favourable light as a conventional military endeavour. Richard Mulcahy would later criticise the IRA campaign, during the bitter Treaty debates, noting sarcastically that the Volunteers could not even get the British out of a medium-sized police barracks. Whilst there was an element of truth in this statement it did not reflect the incredible achievement of the IRA in managing to hold out against a sustained onslaught from the British.

Certainly the sheer intensity of the war from November 1920 led many to consider how long such a conflict could continue. The renewed British offensive was not simply part of a general policy of reprisal but also had a political motive, that of so weakening the Republican movement that the British Government would be able to negotiate from a possible position of strength. It was certainly clear that there was a desperate need for a political compromise. Michael Hopkinson suggests, for example, that Collins was prepared to agree a Truce in December 1920, and that this did not happen for another six months because of the stubbornness and lack of political bravery of Lloyd George, who allowed himself to be convinced by hawks in his Cabinet.[10]

These moves were a reflection of increased pressure on the IRA. Collins suggested in early December 1920 that 'It is too much to expect that IRA force could beat English force for any length of time if the directors of the latter could get a free hand for ruthlessness'. It took a further six months to end the war with both sides concerned about how the calling of a truce would reflect on their negotiating position. The reality however was that the conflict had now reached a military stalemate and any kind of full military victory was impossible for either side. With the agreement of a cessation of hostilities in the shape of an official Truce to begin on 11 July 1921, it was clear that IRA violence had proved successful in forcing the British to open negotiations short of complete victory, a fact they would not hesitate to remind the political side of the movement of in the coming months.

Sample essay and examination questions

Who won the Irish War of Independence?

Why did the IRA prove far more successful than previous Nationalist physical force movements in Ireland?

How accurately does the phrase 'coercion and conciliation' describe British Government policy in Ireland during the War of Independence?

Further reading

J. Augusteijn, *From Public Defiance to Guerrilla Warfare: The Experience of Ordinary Volunteers in the Irish War of Independence, 1916–1921* (Dublin, 1996)

M. Coleman, *County Longford and the Irish Revolution, 1910–1923* (Dublin, 2003)

A. Dolan, 'Killing and Bloody Sunday', *The Historical Journal*, 49, no. 3 (September 2006)

R. Fanning, *The Irish Department of Finance, 1922–58* (Dublin, 1978)

D. Fitzpatrick, *Politics and Irish Life, 1913–21: Provincial Experience of War and Revolution* (Dublin, 1977)

P. Hart, 'The Geography of Revolution in Ireland 1917–1923', *Past & Present*, no. 155 (May 1997)

P. Hart, *The I.R.A. and its Enemies: Violence and Community in Cork, 1916–1923* (Oxford, 1998)

P. Hart, *Mick: The Real Michael Collins* (London, 2005)

M. A. Hopkinson, *The Irish War of Independence* (Dublin, 2004)

A. Mitchell, *Revolutionary Government in Ireland: Dáil Eireann 1919–22* (Dublin, 1995)

C. Townshend, *The British Campaign in Ireland, 1919–1921: The Development of Political and Military Policies* (Oxford, 1975)

C. Townshend, 'The Irish Republican Army and the development of guerrilla warfare, 1916–1921', *English Historical Review*, 91, no. 371 (April 1979).

6

Truce and Treaty

The Anglo-Irish Treaty signed on 6 December 1921 is arguably the most important document in modern Irish history (Document 14). In the short-term it caused a splintering in the previously unified Sinn Fein movement leading eventually to civil war between pro-Treaty moderates and Republican idealists. In the longer term the agreement, referred to simply as 'the Treaty', the subject of numerous books, articles and historical dramatisations, was to have a profound influence on the character of the political culture which emerged to shape independent Ireland. In short its signing was one of the great defining moments of twentieth-century Irish history.

The War of Independence came to a halt, what would become a full stop, with the agreement of a truce on 11 July 1921. This hiatus was largely to allow negotiations to take place between Sinn Fein and the British Government. Despite a number of incidents of low-level skirmishing and continual grumbling from some provincial IRA units who wished to continue the war, an uneasy peace was sustained. All sides in the conflict, especially the IRA, were exhausted and the sheer bloody intensity of the first six months of 1921 did not bode well for the future direction of the conflict if it continued into the summer months. For many it appeared that by July 1921 there was a stark choice between reaching a final settlement of the conflict and falling further into the abyss. It was evident that the military wing of the Republican movement, who had up to now dominated the direction of the independence struggle, was allowing the political side a chance to bring the conflict to a successful conclusion by negotiation. Throughout the long months ahead the IRA would maintain a watching brief, their sensitivities needing at times to be both appeased and flattered.

Initially a series of four meetings were held between de Valera and Lloyd George in London. Although they involved tough negotiations the British Prime Minister grew increasingly frustrated with the Irish leader, famously comparing negotiating with the pedantic de Valera as akin to trying to pick up mercury with a fork. As such Lloyd George made a clear and unambiguous offer of Dominion status for the twenty-six counties of Southern Ireland as defined by the Government of Ireland Act. The offer of Dominion status was a huge advance on the previous Irish Nationalist demand for devolution in the shape of home rule. It meant in effect full independence. Since their emergence from the mid-nineteenth century the other major self-governing colonies of the Empire such as Canada, New Zealand, Australia and South Africa had already done a great deal to extend their powers of self-government. The Colonial Conference of 1907 had explicitly replaced the term 'Colony' with 'Dominion' and these symbolic advances were given concrete form when all of the Dominions had signed the Treaty of Versailles separately becoming individual members of the newly established League of Nations. As such for Nationalist Ireland becoming a Dominion meant joining a group of proactive states who through negotiation were moving toward fuller and fuller independence. Thus it could be argued, membership of this Dominion club was an easy way of eventually achieving the Sinn Fein demand of full separation without the need for further conflict.

De Valera met this candid offer with a non-committal and ambiguous response. It was clear to him that there was no pressure on the Irish side to hurry into formal negotiations. The Sinn Fein movement needed time to take stock. The IRA was exhausted and needed time to rearm and recuperate in case of a resumption of hostilities and many commanders were similarly concerned about the prospect of fighting in the summer where the light evenings would, they felt, hinder the effectiveness of their particular form of covert guerrilla warfare. The hiatus also allowed for the movement to consolidate its control over the country at all levels. The Dáil courts for example were re-established and strengthened as was Sinn Fein control of local government whose effectiveness had been severely disrupted during the war. Propaganda efforts were stepped up with a particular focus on the heroic achievement of the IRA in fighting the British to a standstill. The force became more visible, openly parading in local areas for the first time, and as such recruitment to the IRA accelerated enormously with thousands of young men flocking to join. Although largely treated with disdain by the few thousand hardened veterans of the War of Independence, who sarcastically dubbed these new recruits 'Trucileers', their numbers continued to rise with close to 180,000 men joining the Volunteers by the end of the year. There was nothing in the Truce agreement itself to stop this kind of activity and Sinn Fein and the IRA were happy to bide their time while they consolidated their hold on the country. This control, however, although good for propaganda, was to prove illusory and deeply counterproductive. It gave the false impression to many that the war had been already won and the British presence ended. Thus when the compromises of the Treaty were revealed it appeared that this palpable sense of self-government many had experienced during the Truce was being inexplicably taken away.

The Treaty negotiations

The relaxed manner in which the Sinn Fein leadership approached the search for a permanent settlement meant that it was not until October 1921 that formal negotiations got under way. There were many other reasons for delay including Lloyd George's abortive idea of holding the talks out in a secluded spot near Inverness in Scotland. However, the idea fell through and the negotiations were switched to London, beginning on 11 October with the state aim of deciding 'how the association of Ireland with the community of nations known as the British Empire can best be reconciled with Irish national aspirations'. They would last a little short of two months.

Rather than attend himself, de Valera took the momentous decision to send a group of plenipotentiaries in his stead. This controversial move would prove to be of huge significance considering his later hostility to the agreement. He would argue that his best contribution was to remain in Ireland to shore up support amongst the Volunteers especially as he was the one politician whom they respected due to his role in the Easter Rising. However, for many his failure to attend was due to a wish not to be associated with what he knew would be an inevitable compromise of the demand for a full Republic. In a later letter to an American supporter de Valera stated that his 'intention was to balance the delegation to a point where it was almost paralysed'.[1]

Both the British and Irish delegations however were led by senior figures from each side. The British delegation was led by Lloyd George, Winston Churchill and Austen Chamberlain while on the Irish side Arthur Griffith and Michael Collins, chosen largely to reassure hard-line Republicans back home, were the key delegates. Although given the status of plenipotentiaries de Valera provided them with vague instructions to submit any final draft agreement back to Dublin for ratification by the full Cabinet.

The fact that Sinn Fein had chosen to attend the negotiations inevitably implied that they would have to compromise on their Republican separatist demand. During a long series of bitter debates the two sides laid out their positions which revolved less around the practical powers of the new state but rather the vexed issue of its relationship to the British Empire. The British maintained that they wanted overt royal authority with the creation of a Governor-General and an oath of allegiance taken to the monarch. Contrarily the Irish side pushed for de Valera's rather quirky idea of 'external association' whereby Ireland would be associated with the Empire on matters of common concern and the King would be relegated to the position of head of that association rather than the state itself. In reality this was merely semantics although, as the reaction to the treaty would show, constitutional symbols were of profound importance to Republican die-hards.

The Treaty, signed in the early hours of 6 December 1921, after a frustrated Lloyd George theatrically threatened the resumption of 'immediate and terrible war' if things were not brought to a conclusion, offered Ireland Dominion status with full fiscal autonomy and the right to create a military defence force. The state was to be styled the 'Irish Free State' and maintained a remarkable degree of independence with the British Government failing to insist on the reservation of rights over the internal workings of the new state. However, there were some peculiar restrictions attached. These included the retention by the British of a number of naval installations (the so-called 'Treaty Ports') and Irish liability for its part of the British national debt. In a sop to Nationalist concerns over the oath, the wording was changed from 'allegiance' to 'fidelity' with the former being kept for the as yet unwritten Free State constitution.

Most notably the issue of the North was largely sidestepped. Northern Ireland, while included in the overall agreement, was given the option to opt out of the agreement if they made such a request to the King within a month of the ratification of the new Free State. However, the decision of the Irish delegation to accept the creation of a boundary commission to determine the future border between the two new Irelands was an implicit acceptance of partition. The idea of altering the boundary was left as ill-defined as possible, the wording of the infamous Article XII stating that the frontier would be decided 'in accordance with the wishes of the inhabitants, so far as may be compatible with economic and geographic conditions.' This vague statement was the closest the Treaty got to dealing with the partition issue. With no timetable set and no formal mechanism established to determine what exactly the inhabitants' wishes were, the ambiguities of the idea were glaring. Indeed when the Boundary Commission was finally convened in 1924, the uncertainty surrounding the clause, not to mention the gulf in the perception of its remit between Nationalists and Unionists, caused the whole idea to be scrapped and the border to remain exactly the same as that outlined in the original Government of Ireland Act.

Reactions to the Treaty

If an initial reaction to news of the signing of the Treaty can be discerned it was one of widespread relief. There can be little doubt that the vast majority of people at all levels of Irish society desired peace above all else. The key establishment elites were strongly in favour of the Treaty including the Catholic Church, the press and the farming and business elites. So, notably, was the IRB whose Supreme Council supported the Treaty by an overwhelming majority of eleven to four at a meeting on 11 December 1921. One of those voting against was Liam Lynch, later Chief of Staff of the Republicans in the civil war, who claimed that when it came to the IRB the rank and file were largely anti-Treaty while the higher ranks followed Collins and Mulcahy. Indeed Collins' role in the IRB had proved crucial and it was Collins himself who would now control so much of the patronage of the new state. One Cork IRB man later claimed to Ernie O'Malley that 'The IRB were placing men in jobs . . . just before the Treaty was signed.'[2] To add to the general atmosphere of positivity the British also released the approximately 4,000 prisoners interned during the War of Independence in order to reinforce the good will behind the Treaty.

However, right from the start there was also opposition. The split began ironically at the top, right at the heart of the revolutionary government in the Cabinet. De Valera had wanted the document referred back to the Cabinet before being signed, but this agreement was not honoured by the delegates in London who believed themselves to have full plenipotentiary powers. De Valera claimed to be furious when he heard the contents of the Treaty although there can be little doubt that he was well aware of the details beforehand, having been kept informed of developments by various members on the Irish delegation. However, his anger, real or imagined, led him to threaten to sack those Cabinet ministers who had signed the document, though he was persuaded against this by W. T. Cosgrave, later Chairman of the Provisional Government. Cathal Brugha, the uncompromising Dáil Minister of Defence, made a threat to have all of the delegates arrested as soon as they arrived back in Dublin.

A stormy meeting of the seven-member inner Cabinet followed where the more hard-line members, Austen Stack and Brugha, argued that the Treaty was asking all Teachtaí Dála (TDs) to renege on their oath of allegiance to the Republic. Both sided with de Valera in rejecting the Treaty although they were outvoted four to three by the other members (Robert Barton, one of the Treaty signatories, later rescinding his support). To add more perplexity a vote in a fuller meeting of the whole Cabinet went against the Treaty again by the narrow majority of one, being rejected eight to seven. Following this ambiguous response from the Dáil government leadership, attention turned to the Dáil itself which would prove to be the key forum for an infamous series of Treaty debates, which spanned a two week period covering the turn of the year. The debates (Document 16), which were based at University College Dublin rather than the usual meeting place at the Mansion House, were passionate and bitter affairs right from the start.

The case of the pro-Treaty side was less an appeal to the unblemished virtues of the Treaty but rather a plea for pragmatism, arguing that it was the best deal that could have been reached and, in Collins' famous phrase offered, 'if not the ultimate freedom that all nations desire . . . but the freedom to achieve it'. Collins, Griffith and Kevin O'Higgins would all be the key spokesmen for the Treaty side arguing that an unwinnable war and more bloodshed was the only likely outcome of rejecting the Treaty.

The anti-Treaty side on the other hand appealed to idealism and the sanctity of the Republic. They argued that the Treaty would not in any way end conflict but was merely yet another false dawn on the road to inevitable separation, the only true way to bring peace to Ireland. Their appeal was passionate and ideological, painting the Treaty as a betrayal of the dead martyrs of 1916. They reserved particular ire for the notion of taking an oath of allegiance to the British monarch, a feature of the Treaty which particularly enraged Robert Erskine Childers, the editor of the *Irish Bulletin* who had acted as a secretary to the London delegation. Overwhelmingly the oath would prove to be the single most offensive clause in the Treaty for the Republican side. The anti-Treaty appeal to emotion was demonstrated markedly by the strong presence of female TDs in their ranks. These widows, wives and sisters of Republican martyrs, such as Mary MacSwiney, were treated by many as substitutes for their dead male relatives and were thus destined to cast their vote for a more radical political path. So strong was opposition to the Treaty amongst female members of the Dáil that the pro-Treaty side soon sarcastically dubbed the opposition the 'Women and Childers Party'.

The bitterness of the Dáil debates led de Valera to propose a compromise agreement in which he revived, in typically opaque language, the idea of Ireland having an 'external association' with the British Empire placing it somewhere between a Dominion and a fully independent Republic. The proposals, dubbed 'Document No. 2' (Document 15), rather than helping to heal the rift proved to be deeply counterproductive and damaging for de Valera personally. Whilst it is true that some anti-Treaty politicians smiled on the idea many, especially IRA commanders, were outraged at this watering down of the Republican demand. Most importantly Document No. 2 led to a growing mistrust of de Valera amongst the Volunteers who would take steps to marginalise his influence on the military side of the movement both before and during the civil war. The document itself however was little more than a paper exercise. Even if it had proved acceptable to hard-line Republicans, few appear to have realised that it would not be so to the British, who after all were the other party to the agreement and not the Republicans.

De Valera's alternative was itself a rather meek attempt to shift the Treaty in a slightly more radical direction and it is notable that most of the Treaty clauses remained the same. One area which was not changed were those issues affecting the north, with the clauses on partition and the creation of a later boundary commission remaining the same. This mirrored what was largely a failure to address the northern issue in the debates themselves, with only Sean McEntee and Eoin O'Duffy, both of them notably from Ulster counties, raising the issue. The lack of reference to the north was peculiar particularly considering its key role in precipitating the revolution and the fact that it was an increasingly violent area of the country amid the quiet Truce period elsewhere. It appears obvious that southern Nationalist leaders made little priority of the north and placed a great deal of undeserved faith that the Boundary Commission would lead to the transfer of large amounts of territory from north to south. Certainly there is no substance whatsoever in the long-standing popular myth that the Treaty split and subsequent civil war were caused by partition. Such perceptions largely grew because they reflected well on the integrity of southern Nationalists who, it could be argued, were willing to go to war in defence of Irish unity and the northern Catholic minority, rather than the real, and far more indulgent, cause, namely the oath and the sanctity of constitutional symbols.

The debates were suspended for a short Christmas break before any final decision was reached on the Treaty. This break was to prove to be vital in shaping the later responses of TDs when called on to vote. Most returned to their constituencies where they engaged, often, due to imprisonment or war service, for the first time, with grass-roots opinion in their counties. Most encountered pressures for peace from local business, press and farming interests. Certainly on returning the debates became more bitter and personal with insults and dramatic gestures, such as de Valera's offer to resign, dominating the more substantive issues of the Treaty clauses. In the end the Treaty would be passed by an extremely narrow majority, being passed by sixty-four votes to fifty-seven, demonstrating the profound divisions which had emerged at the very top of the Sinn Fein movement. De Valera, after losing to Griffith in his attempted re-election to the position of President of the Dáil, walked out of the Dáil followed by all of the anti-Treaty deputies, never to return.

The triumph of the pro-Treaty side of Sinn Fein left the newly emerging state in a profoundly confused constitutional mess. Griffith was now President of the Dáil, a body which would continue in existence alongside the new Provisional Government, which itself had been established by the forgotten parliament of 'Southern Ireland' set up under the Government of Ireland Act in 1921, a parliament which met only once for a mere thirty minutes, where after passing an order to establish the Provisional Government, it promptly dissolved itself. All these bodies were now dominated by the pro-Treaty side. Both the Dáil and the Provisional Government continued to exist and thus there were two cabinets and two sets of ministers who, to add further confusion, were as often as not the same people. In reality however it was the Provisional Government which would make all of the running, paving the way for the creation of the Irish Free State. The Dáil was kept in existence largely as a symbol of unity for both the public and the Republican opposition, but as the structures of the new state began to form, its power would dwindle away to nothing.

The military split

While the confused constitutional position of the Dublin government, and the semantic twists and turns of its various assemblies, was to underpin the later legitimacy of the new state, in reality such issues were becoming largely irrelevant. With the civil government divided it was the military side of the movement that would become the focus for opposition to the Treaty. Political debate and attempts at compromise would certainly continue but it was the IRA that would increasingly make all of the running.

The majority of experienced IRA Volunteers were against the Treaty. Indeed aside from the GHQ staff in Dublin and a few isolated brigades, the provincial IRA stood full-square in opposition to the agreement. Most key IRA leaders such as Liam Lynch, Sean Moylan, Tom Barry and Seamus Robinson all went anti-Treaty. Roughly speaking it was the most active areas during the War of Independence which became the most virulently Republican during the civil war. There was little doubt also that distance from GHQ was key and built on the growing resentments which had occurred between provincial IRA units and the Dublin leadership during the later years of the War of Independence. Added to this also were curious cases of counties where there had been little violence or IRA activity during the War of Independence but now became hard-line Republican areas. These included counties such as Wexford and Sligo which would see much fighting during the civil war. It is hard to explain the radicalism of these newly active counties but it may be a case of overcompensation for their previous poor performance against the British. Alternatively it may simply have been that they were slow starters and that by the time they were finally trained and prepared to fight the Truce had intervened. There was certainly much resentment in more inactive counties at the constant criticisms they had received from GHQ in Dublin during the War of Independence. Ernie O'Malley claimed that many local officers in such areas were quick to join the Provisional Government Army thus allowing for those who had been frustrated by their lack of action over the previous three years to take charge. Whatever the reasons it soon became very clear that it was the anti-Treaty IRA who would be the face of radical Republicanism as opposed to anti-Treaty politicians. It certainly appeared as in 1916 that the military was acting as a vanguard, viewing itself once again as the guardian of the morals of what they perceived as the authentic Irish nation.

The IRA certainly made all the running in establishing alternative power bases to those of the Treatyites. An Army Convention was called in March, the first since 1918, to decide on a new IRA policy. Although banned by pro-Treaty Chief of Staff Richard Mulcahy, who was well aware how dominant the Republicans would be at any such gathering, the Convention went ahead regardless. Reaffirming their commitment to the Republic as established in 1916 the delegates elected their own Executive, appointing Liam Lynch as the new Chief of Staff.

Politically things also began to draw apart. While the image of unity was maintained with Sinn Fein and the retention of a Dáil government, in reality there were now two new political parties and two new armies, a move which was given concrete expression when de Valera established a new political party in the shape of Cumann na Poblachta ('Party of the Republic') on 15 March 1922. Meanwhile Michael Collins was increasingly attempting to draw together the two sides with a variety of ever more desperate measures. His main policy was one of delaying a definitive split by constant postponement, holding up crucial votes and arguing that no significant changes should occur until the new Free State constitution was published.

However, on the ground the military situation was polarising alarmingly. The British garrison began to leave in large numbers from the spring of 1922 after gathering together in larger urban barracks in major cities and towns. The British Government was certainly keen to get out of Ireland as soon as possible. The first unit, 1st Battalion, Duke of Wellington's Regiment, left Dublin for Holyhead late in the evening of 20 January 1922, with one news report observing 'the soldiers cheering and waving their caps as the vessel drew out. Except for the quay labourers in the vicinity her departure was practically unnoticed and there were no answering cheers'.[3] The *Evening Herald* reported the next day, 'To-day a row of cold and empty "cookers" [armoured cars] standing in line at the Alexandra Basin premises, some handed-over hutments, small flags trampled into the mud and some floating flotsam and jetsam are the sole reminders of the departed British troops.'[4]

By the end of February the fourteen counties of Sligo, Mayo, Galway, Kerry, Tipperary, Laois, Offaly, Kilkenny, Carlow, Wexford, Westmeath, Longford, Cavan and Roscommon had been evacuated. However, unaware of the complexities of the IRA split the British handed over barracks and equipment to the local IRA units regardless of their attitude to the Treaty. Emerging from this power vacuum was a new struggle on the ground between the few isolated pro-Treaty IRA units in the provinces and the Republicans who now controlled most of the country. A struggle emerged for key towns and key barracks, the most notable of which occurred at the strategic city of Limerick where a stand-off between pro-Treaty IRA units led by Clare commander Michael Brennan faced off against Republican forces under the command of Ernie O'Malley. In the end an open confrontation was averted although this was only due to the intervention of Mulcahy and Lynch at the last moment.

There was certainly growing tension and chaos on the ground. The number of Republican bank raids increased as the IRA sought money to fund the Volunteers. Some killings occurred also; although it was largely low level acts of intimidation and beatings which added to the atmosphere of anarchy and chaos. Particular targets were prominent pro-Treaty supporters with Griffith himself being forced to call off a speech in Sligo after shots were fired in the crowd. Those political speeches which did go ahead often merely added to the confrontational rhetoric, most notoriously that of Eamon de Valera who in a speech in Thurles in late March (Document 18) said that the IRA 'would have to wade through the blood of the soldiers of the Irish Government, and perhaps through that of some members of the Irish Government to get their freedom'. Although often misunderstood as an incitement to violence rather than the warning against civil war that it actually was, it certainly was not a helpful turn of phrase to use at the time.

Confrontation seemed inevitable to many but the war itself would not break out for a number of months. This had much to do with hopes on the side of Collins that playing for time would allow the heat to be taken out of the situation. For Republicans the hope was that unity could be achieved and their former comrades would join them once again in war against the British. Time was not on the Republicans' side, however. The old Dáil government and Sinn Fein itself were little more than rhetorical symbols. The Provisional Government now held the real power in the state with new ministries being set up and the old Dáil courts and counter-state being phased out. The new National Army was also beginning to form around those few veterans who had sided with the Treaty side. Certainly as these moves became ever more clear to Republicans it engendered an increasingly radial response. In April Executive IRA Officer, Rory O'Connor, took over the Four Courts and several other buildings in central Dublin. Moving into the courts was itself a very provocative move and a profound challenge to the infant Provisional Government. O'Connor himself made his hard-line stance clear when in answer to a question as to whether he was talking of setting up a military dictatorship he responded 'you can take it that way if you like'.

While the military side of the split was radicalising, the political side of the movement still attempted to hold things together. With elections due in May, Collins and de Valera, after long and arduous negotiations, agreed an electoral pact where both pro- and anti-Treaty candidates would stand under the Sinn Fein banner and return sixty-four and fifty-seven candidates respectively to represent the original Dáil vote. The various offices of the government were to be parcelled out in a similar fashion with the President being a pro-Treaty TD while the Minister of Defence would be chosen from anti-Treaty ranks in order to represent the view of the army. Other Cabinet posts were to be divided up in a 5:4 split. The Treaty itself was to be ignored in the campaign.

The pact decision was a sign of profound political corruption, desperation and a failure to accept the reality of the situation and act accordingly. Certainly Collins' colleagues on the pro-Treaty side were outraged as were the British when they got wind of the pact. Collins himself still hung on, however, arguing that the pact was the only way to hold any kind of working election as any attempt to make the election about the Treaty would have been made unworkable by the IRA. Collins also argued that there were other non-Sinn Fein candidates to choose for those stuck with an anti-Treaty candidate in their constituency and so they could express their view on the Treaty democratically if they so wished.

In the end Collins certainly showed himself to be a very devious and clever operator. During a speech on 16 June, the morning of the elections, he informed the crowd to vote for whomever they saw fit, inciting the public to choose their preference based on their attitude to the Treaty. When the election results were announced it represented a crushing defeat for the Republican side with pro-Treaty candidates, of both the Sinn Fein and Labour variety, winning a large majority. Anti-Treaty candidates won only thirty-five seats compared to eighty-six for pro-Treaty candidates. However, in the end, despite Collins' seeming clear victory in the pact election, his Janus-faced policy of trying to stay true to the Treaty while at the same time remaining faithful to Republican aims would unravel and all his schemes and plots would collapse into civil war less than two weeks later.

Sample essay and examination questions

Assess the arguments of both sides for and against the Treaty.
How justified were Republican objections to the Oath of Allegiance?
'In the fullness of time, history will come to see the greatness of Collins and it will be recorded at my expense.' To what extent has this statement, made by de Valera in 1966, been substantiated by recent historiography on Michael Collins and Eamon de Valera?

Further reading

J. Curran, *The Birth of the Irish Free State* (Alabama, 1980)
G. Doherty and D. Keogh (ed.), *Michael Collins and the Making of the Irish State* (Cork, 2010)
D. Fair, 'The Anglo-Irish Treaty of 1921: Unionist aspects of the Peace', *Journal of British Studies*, 12 (1972–3)
B. Kissane, *The Politics of the Irish Civil War* (Oxford, 2005)
J. Knirck, *Imagining Ireland's Independence: The Debates over the Anglo-Irish Treaty* (Lanham, MD, 2013)
K. Middlemass (ed.), *T. Jones, Whitehall Diary*, Volume 3 (Oxford, 1969)
F. Pakenham, *Peace by Ordeal* (London, 1992)
J. Regan, *The Irish Counter-Revolution, 1921–1936* (Dublin, 1999)
T. Towey, 'The Reaction of the British Government to the 1922 Collins-De Valera Pact', *Irish Historical Studies*, xxii, no. 85 (March 1980)

Useful web links

A full copy of the Treaty debates is available online at http://celt.ucc.ie/published/E900003-001/index.html [accessed 2 June 2014].

A fascinating virtual exhibition on the Treaty is also available at http://treaty.nationalarchives.ie/ [accessed 2 June 2014].

7

The Establishment of Northern Ireland, 1920–5

The partition of Ireland has played a curious role in histories of the Irish revolutionary period. In many ways the events in the north-east do not fit into the more straightforward narrative of Nationalist revolution which has dominated perspectives of the period. Ulster's experience was certainly unique. The north-east saw partition with the establishment of a new state in the shape of Northern Ireland, an arguably far more fundamental change than any other part of revolutionary Ireland. Indeed even if one uses a crude measurement such as the extent of violence, then the north-east is by far the most violent part of Ireland, with Belfast experiencing a higher per capita loss of life than even the most violent counties in Munster. In the two-year period running from June 1920 to June 1922 over 600 people were killed within the borders of what would become the new state of Northern Ireland, the vast majority of them in bouts of intense sectarian rioting in the city of Belfast. It appears that the events of the revolutionary period in the north-east of Ireland are by any measure a serious, if not defining, aspect of the conflict.

Partition, the division of Ireland into two new self-governing administrations, was arguably the most important concrete outcome of the Irish revolution. Both new states came to embody a particular vision of Irishness; Gaelic Catholic Nationalism in the south and Protestant Ulster Unionism in the north. The two new Irelands also retained significant ethno-religious minorities within their borders, especially Northern Ireland where a full third of the population was Catholic which equated in most cases to a Nationalist political allegiance. This would lead to the violence of the 'Troubles' which plagued the province for over thirty years, only ending in an uneasy peace with the Good Friday Agreement in 1998.

The issue of Ulster of course also lay arguably as the root cause of the revolution in the first place. The strength and militancy of Ulster Unionist resistance to the Third Home Rule Bill was key in destabilising Irish politics and undermining support for moderate nationalism, whose perceived complicity in the exclusion of Ulster from the Home Rule scheme was a source of constant condemnation from advanced Nationalists and one of the most caustic criticisms used by Sinn Fein in its victorious electoral campaign of December 1918.

However, the problem of Ulster, which had done so much to confound the architects of the Home Rule Bill prior to the First World War, had not gone away. Indeed the agreement reached in 1914, by promising the addition of some kind of amending legislation for Ulster, was merely a postponement of the vexing issue of how to accommodate Unionist demands within a broader Irish settlement. That the solution would involve a permanent partition of the country was as unrealistic in 1914 as it was a reality in 1921.

During the war itself various solutions were put forward. While this was a convoluted and at times confusing process, the general trend was toward special treatment of Ulster involving either all or part of the province being excluded from the application of the Home Rule Act. However, with the radicalisation of Irish nationalism and the slide into confrontation and conflict, the need to find a concrete policy became paramount. Damaging as the Ulster Crisis had been to British politics before the war, the expediencies of the conflict would do much to heal these wounds. The Liberal Lloyd George now headed a Conservative-dominated coalition, a state of affairs that proved so harmonious that it was anticipated the arrangement would continue to function in peacetime. As such by 1918 there emerged a general consensus in British politics about the Irish question that, whilst granting that self-government was inevitable, any settlement would have to meet two strict criteria as spelled out in the Conservative party manifesto for the December 1918 general election: 'there are two paths which are closed – the one leading to a complete severance of Ireland from the British Empire, and the other the forcible submission of the six counties of Ulster to a Home Rule parliament against their will.' Realising that the Third Home Rule Bill was effectively a dead piece of legislation in the new political context, Lloyd George decided to introduce a new political compromise which was placed firmly within these parameters. It took the form of a fourth home rule bill, the Government of Ireland Act, also know pejoratively as the 'partition act' (Document 10). It was this piece of legislation, enacted in December 1920 just as the War of Independence entered its most extreme stage, and so often overshadowed by the later Anglo-Irish treaty, which would bring about the most fundamental change in modern Irish history.

While Edward Carson made threatening noises to once again revive the UVF 'if any attempt were made to interfere with the rights and liberties of Ulster', in reality the case for permanent exclusion for a large part of the province was to be the cornerstone of the new settlement. The act itself proposed the creation of two separate home rule parliaments in Dublin and Belfast. The two new states, 'Northern Ireland' and 'Southern Ireland', would consist of six and twenty-six counties respectively. Northern Ireland was made up of the four majority Protestant counties of Armagh, Down, Antrim and Londonderry and also, most controversially, the two counties of Fermanagh and Tyrone where Catholics formed a slim majority. The decision on the extent of the northern state was an attempt to provide the Unionist government with a strong local majority whilst at the same time including as many Ulster Protestants as possible. The Protestant populations of the other three Ulster counties of Donegal, Cavan and Monaghan were sacrificed despite their vociferous protests. Their inclusion in an expanded nine county Ulster state would have left the Unionists with only a slight majority over Nationalists and would have, it was felt, made the state unworkable as a viable political entity. Similarly the exclusion of Fermanagh and Tyrone would have made Northern Ireland look too small on a map and also given the southern state control of areas right in the heart of the new Ulster state including the west bank of Lough Neagh. Major cities, such as Derry and Newry, which lay on the periphery of the new border were included despite their local Catholic majorities. Derry, the site of the famous siege of 1689, was retained due to its fundamental place in the historical mythologies of Protestant Unionism while Newry was included due to its vital economic position. Forty-two Irish MPs would continue to sit at Westminster and the British Government would retain control over war and peace, foreign affairs, customs and excise, law and order, the armed forces and land and agricultural policy. A Council of Ireland was also created, comprising twenty members from each of the two parliaments, being trumpeted as some kind of embryonic all-Ireland government. How this cross-border component would actually operate was left as vague as possible and was little more than a gesture to the idea of Irish unity.

The superficial impression was that Irish Unionists had achieved a great victory. Craig was represented as the great practical hero of the hour. As one British journalist reported:

> Ulster is safe in James Craig's hands, said an old covenanter, when I asked him what the six counties thought of their new prime minister; we trust him absolutely, and an Ulsterman cannot say more ... His is the outstanding personality in the new Government ... he is a tower of strength for Ulstermen and he faces with serene confidence a task which might well stagger any statesman.[1]

The *Daily Chronicle* said of Craig:

> He is a man of character rather than subtlety. He is ready with a plan and goes straight to his object, disregarding cross currents and side issues. A man of great common sense, he has much of the nature of General Botha. It may be added that he has as difficult a part to play as General Botha but his friends believe he will succeed.[2]

However, for Irish Unionists outside of the excluded area the Government of Ireland Act represented a profound defeat. Hugh Montgomery, a Unionist leader from Fivemiletown, County Tyrone called the settlement 'humiliating' for Unionists and that the alternatives were between this 'miserable' settlement' and 'chaos'. Many Protestant Unionists along the new border were bitter about their abandonment by their Ulster allies, miles from safety in the new Northern state. While a number of East Ulster leaders described the new 'Northern Ireland' as 'dry land', the implication was that those Unionists who found themselves on the wrong side of the border were now lost in a sea of Catholic nationalism.[3]

The Sinn Fein response was to ignore the act, using the scheduled elections in May 1921 for the new parliament of 'Southern Ireland' merely to elect a second Dáil before continuing their own struggle, with all 124 Sinn Fein candidates and four independent Unionist representatives for Trinity College being elected unopposed. The British had fully anticipated this rejection, Lord Birkenhead stating plainly of the bill: 'I am absolutely satisfied that the Sinn Feiners will refuse it. Otherwise in the present state of Ireland I could not even be a party to making such an offer.' However, the reaction of the Unionists was different and they embraced the idea wholeheartedly.

With the election in the twenty-six counties (19 May 1921) being a formality with no contests or need for political campaigning, Sinn Fein was able to concentrate all of its resources and propaganda on the election in the North. This, the so-called 'partition election,' held on 24 May 1921, was arguably the most important election in modern Irish history. The poll was the first to be held under the new system of Proportional Representation with fifty-two seats in total up for grabs within the six counties. Nationalist unity had already been assured when on 17 March, after a series of tortuous negotiations, a pact agreement was signed between Sinn Fein and the Nationalists who stood together on an anti-partitionist ticket.[4]

Prior to the election Sinn Fein launched a huge propaganda campaign in Ulster. However, its tone was far from conciliatory. Louis J. Walsh, the prominent northern Sinn Feiner, argued: 'Ulster has really never had the truth preached to her, and having regard to the obstacle she is in our way I do think that you should concentrate on the problem of her enlightenment.'[5] Advertisements were placed in almost fifty northern newspapers spelling out a whole series of arguments against partition. Sinn Fein even went so far as to print a newspaper, *The Unionist,* 50,000 copies of which were sent out to prominent Protestants in East Ulster. A letter to the editor of the Unionist *Northern Whig* claimed that 'practically all the Unionist voters in all parts of County Antrim have had this paper sent them'.[6]

The campaign, while vast in scale, was also marked by its crudity and lack of reference to Unionist sensibilities. At one meeting in Armagh a Sinn Fein speaker argued 'the man who claimed to have common-sense and voted for Partition, should go at once to the nearest lunatic asylum, and find out what was wrong with him'.[7] Eamon Donnelly, the Armagh Republican and

Sinn Fein's Chief Organiser, admitted in a letter on the day of the poll: 'The only effect that all our literature and leaflets etc. will have upon them is to bring them out to vote against us in great numbers.'[8] Overall Sinn Fein propaganda was patronising to Unionists, focusing on their perceived ignorance about the situation in Ulster and scaring them with dire predictions about the economic effects of partition, citing tactlessly (and inaccurately) the Belfast Boycott as a sign of the economic strength of southern nationalism. Efforts were also made to recruit agricultural workers in Ulster whom it was argued would be at the mercy of East Ulster's urban industrial elites.[9]

Despite all this, Nationalist hopes for the election were high. Eamon de Valera felt that they would win at least one-third of the fifty-two northern seats but possibly half.[10] Indeed most commentators expected the Nationalists to secure a minimum of seventeen seats. When the result was announced on 27 May 1921 it was a huge shock. While Nationalists won over one-third of the vote they received only 23 per cent of the seats with only twelve elected representatives (six from Sinn Fein and six from the UIL). Every single one of the forty Unionist candidates who stood were elected. While no doubt it can be argued that Sinn Fein was poorly organised in the north and that some intimidation did take place, this was not at a level to profoundly alter the result which by any account represented a dreadful failure for the Sinn Fein project. One month after the election in June 1921 King George V opened the Northern Irish parliament in Belfast, using the opportunity to make a conciliatory speech which was widely seen as opening the way for negotiations with Sinn Fein, the Truce following only a matter of weeks later (Documents 12 and 13).

The character of violence in Ulster

Violence itself had been slow to arrive in the North. During the first eighteen months of the War of Independence, Ulster was one of the quietest parts of Ireland. However, a series of local government election victories in the elections of January and June 1920 saw Nationalists take control of a number of significant local authorities including Derry City which had its first ever Catholic Mayor. Indeed it was in Derry that violence first erupted in June to be followed one month later by Belfast, where the vast majority of violence would occur over the next two years. In the context of the Twelfth of July holiday, many Unionists reflected on the growing anarchy in the south which was increasingly finding its way into border areas of Ulster. After a fiery speech by Edward Carson in which he called on Ulster Protestants to 'take matters into their own hands', others made vociferous attacks on perceived Loyalist apathy in the local press, with one correspondent to the *Belfast Newsletter* writing: 'the Protestants of Ulster are asleep while the Sinn Feiners, who are pouring into our province, are wide awake; they are busy organising, while we prate on the deeds of our forefathers and do nothing ourselves'. When Protestant workers returned after the holiday this growing sense of Loyalist frustration and paranoia was taken out on thousands of their Catholic co-workers who were violently expelled from the shipyards and engineering works of East Belfast. These attacks set the pattern for the following two years with the city engulfed in periodic bouts of brutal sectarian violence (Document 19) leading to the deaths of over 550 people and millions of pounds worth of property damage.

The IRA in the north would have little to do with this violent outbreak. The organisation was a small and irrelevant part of the political scene. Not only did they face an actively hostile majority population, but even amongst northern Nationalists republicanism was never the dominant political force. Despite its collapse elsewhere the old Home Rule party hung on in the north, retaining the allegiance of the vast majority of northern Catholics, shown during the by-election defeats of Sinn Fein in 1918 in South Armagh and East Tyrone by moderate Nationalists. Even more notably this division was intensely bitter. There are numerous cases of the IRA and the Catholic nationalist fraternal organisation, the Ancient Order of Hibernians, coming to blows, with the IRA carrying out a number of shootings, beatings and arson attacks against their co-religionists. In fact throughout much of the violence, the Hibernians, not the IRA, were the organisation whose members manned the barricades in defence of Catholic areas in Belfast. They themselves were also extremely aggressive at times, assaulting IRA members or raiding the houses of Republicans in search of weapons.[11]

Indeed when large-scale sectarian violence began in Belfast with the shipyard expulsions of July 1920, the IRA was largely an irrelevance, not wishing, in the words of Roger McCorley, one of their commanders, 'to get involved in the usual stone-throwing competition'. Those IRA attacks that did occur were inspired and carried out by southern IRA members. The two most notable were the assassinations of Colonel Gerard Smyth in Cork on 17 July 1920 and RIC District Commander Oswald Swanzy on 22 August, both of which led to appalling levels of reprisal violence in Belfast and other northern towns. In particular, the shooting of Oswald Swanzy in Lisburn led to the expulsion of almost the entire Catholic population of the town (Document 11). One of the assassins, sent north by Michael Collins to carry out the killing, recalled seeing Lisburn in flames in the distance as he headed south to safety on a train.

It was this dynamic of small-scale IRA actions along the border leading to reprisal rioting and expulsions in Belfast which was the chief characteristic of violence in Ulster. The casualties stemming from such incidents were unprecedented. A rough estimate suggests that around 550 people were killed in Northern Ireland during the almost exactly two years running from July 1920. The first half year of the conflict saw around seventy deaths, rising to 100 in 1921 and then escalating massively in the first six months of 1922 which saw almost 300 murders, running at an average of thirty per month and peaking at almost eighty in May 1922 at the height of the IRA's northern offensive. Remarkably all but 100 of these deaths occurred in the city of Belfast, this single city alone accounting for almost half as many deaths as occurred in the twenty-six counties of the south and west during the whole of the War of Independence.

Dáil policy and Ulster

It had become clear that the IRA in the north alone had little ability to carry out substantial attacks themselves without the support of their southern allies. Indeed it was the southern Republican leadership which instigated almost all of the major offensives which were to occur in the north. Many northern Nationalists and even Republicans were wary of the dangers of such a strategy. Time and again the shooting of a policeman or the burning of a barracks during a border incursion would lead to sectarian atrocities in Belfast. Bishop MacRory, the Catholic Bishop of Down and Conor which covered Belfast, would characterise the violence as the 'Catholics of Belfast being punished for the sins of their brethren elsewhere', while Cahir Healy the northern Nationalist politician actually contacted the IRA leadership in Dublin to plead with them to halt attacks due to its counterproductive nature. It was a request the southern leadership failed to agree to.

The revolutionary Dáil Cabinet was largely passive when it came to the northern issue. While they issued various token protests about the treatment of northern Catholics they were reluctant to take any proactive steps against the Belfast government. Their approach to the ominous threat of partition was one of denial, sticking to an all-Ireland Republican irredentism with a misplaced belief that the British presence, rather than Irish Unionist resistance, lay at the root of all the problems. In such views partition was an example of British perfidy and yet another colonialist scheme from Britain. The Nationalist newspaper *Nationality* for example summed up this approach as early as 1918:

> There is no such political entity as 'Ulster' . . . it is not Sir Edward Carson, but the Government of England which incited and secretly incites a minority in the north-east of Ireland to oppose the Republic. The so-called 'Ulster' question had neither its root nor its origin in Ulster. Its root and origin are English, and with the disappearance of English Government it would also automatically disappear.[12]

Throughout the period Nationalists would refer to Northern Ireland derisively as 'Carsonia' or 'Ulsteria', matching the later pious nomenclature of the 'North of Ireland' or the 'Six Counties'. This long-standing view was expressed as early as 1904 when Arthur Griffith wrote that 'the frontier of Ireland has been fixed by nature'.[13]

Southern Nationalist denial meant that even referring to the northern state by its name was an act of unnatural blasphemy. Father Michael O'Flanagan, in a speech in Derry City in May 1921, stated that:

> The boundaries of Ireland were marked by the finger of Almighty God when He surrounded it with the circling sea. No country in the world had so clearly marked boundaries as Ireland had, and there could never be any dispute about them.[14]

The Government of Ireland Act, much like the Irish Convention of 1917–18, was in this view simply another unworkable British scheme which would ultimately collapse as the revolution continued. However, the violence in the north and pressure once again from grass-roots Sinn Fein activists, this time shopkeepers in Galway city, forced the Dáil Cabinet to instigate an economic boycott of goods going to and from the north-east. This so-called 'Belfast Boycott' was designed to hit northern traders in the pocket, playing largely on southern stereotypes about the grasping materialism of the average Ulster Protestant businessmen. The IRA were ordered to intercept and destroy any products which originated in the north-east and southern traders were banned from doing business with their northern counterparts. Such a policy was almost impossible to maintain and in reality became an excuse for sporadic acts of violence and sectarian intimidation on both sides of the border. Most significantly however, it was at base a partitionist policy, actually helping to partition the Irish economy and reinforce northern Unionist perceptions about the aggressive objectives of radical Irish nationalism.

The economic war instigated by Dáil politicians along with the profoundly self-defeating decision of the military side of the movement to carry out attacks in the north, were also counterproductive in another sense. Both of these policies did much to reinforce the paranoia of the Unionist population and the new government of Northern Ireland, increasing the perception that the new state was under siege. In response to the perceived threat of the IRA, the UVF had revived, with local patrols in isolated border areas resuming during the summer of 1920. By October the Northern Ireland government was calling for the creation of its own auxiliary police force. The RIC were increasingly viewed by the Belfast government as at best passive and at worst colluding with the IRA at the local level. Certainly the composition of the force had changed somewhat during the early part of the War of Independence. With Ulster the quietest province in the country, many older Catholic officers had been transferred to the north from more troublesome areas in Munster with officers from Ulster making the journey in the other direction. While these changes were modest, Richard Dawson Bates, the Northern Ireland Minister of Home Affairs, whose paranoia knew no bounds (even voicing his concerns about the loyalty of the British Under-Secretary James MacMahon because of his Catholicism), saw the RIC in the north as an increasingly Catholic and disloyal force. In the face of Unionist calls for a locally recruited loyal police force, in July 1920 Churchill asked the Cabinet, 'What would happen if the Protestants in the six counties were given weapons and . . . charged with maintaining law and order and policing the country?' The answer to this question would be the Ulster Special Constabulary (USC). The new force, established in October 1920 would grow to have a membership of 35,000 by June 1922. Its members were organised in three classes. The 'A' class were full-time uniformed police auxiliaries, many of whom would go on to form the nucleus of the new Royal Ulster Constabulary (RUC) established in June 1922. While the 'C' class were the largest group they were only to be called out in the direst emergencies such as invasion which never materialised, and the 'B' group would become the most notorious arm of the new force. Employed on a part-time basis and allowed to keep their weapons at home, these 'B' Specials were soon to be implicated in a whole range of unsavoury incidents.

The decision by the British to support the establishment of the new force was heavily criticised at the time. On 2 September Sir John Anderson, the Under-Secretary at Dublin Castle, wrote to Bonar Law:

> You cannot, in the middle of a faction fight, recognize one of the contending parties and expect it to deal with disorder in the spirit of impartiality and fairness essential in those who have to carry out the order of the Government.

While officially northern Catholics were allowed to join the force, few did or were actively encouraged to do so. Right from the beginning northern Nationalists saw the Specials as being 'nothing more and nothing less that the dregs of the Orange lodges, armed and equipped to overawe Nationalists and Catholics, and with . . . an inclination to invent "crimes" against Nationalists and Catholics.' Certainly the 'B' Specials would prove deeply unpopular with northern Catholics for the rest of their long existence, coming to an end fifty years later in March 1970, symbolic for many of the partial and discriminatory nature of the northern state. The existence of the USC would highlight the main feature of the Northern government: a paranoid obsession with security and the, largely non-existent, threat from the IRA. In early April 1922 the Belfast government introduced draconian legislation in the form of the Civil Authorities (Special Powers) Act (Document 20) which allowed for a whole range of coercive measures including the death penalty, flogging and internment without trial. Although intended as a short-term emergency measure, the act would eventually become permanent, not being repealed until 1973.

Ulster and the Anglo-Irish Treaty

While the character and duration of violence in the north appeared to have little relation to that occurring in the south, the week spanning the instigation of the Truce for example seeing sixteen deaths in Belfast alone, there was little doubt that British negotiations with Sinn Fein would have direct implications for the north. While the six counties of Northern Ireland were nominally included in the Anglo-Irish Treaty, in reality the inclusion of a clause allowing the north-east to opt out of Dublin jurisdiction, something they were to do at the first opportunity in December 1922, was merely window-dressing to disguise the established fact of partition. Despite the rhetoric there was little likelihood that any agreement between Sinn Fein and the British Government would seriously affect the existence or status of Northern Ireland. Like the Government of Ireland Act, the Treaty's claim to provide an all-Ireland settlement was a rhetorical illusion. It was a separate settlement for the south and west with only token idealistic allusions to an all-Ireland resolution. Richard Mulcahy himself would later reflect that the setting up of the Northern government was a British prerequisite 'before they would grapple in any way realistically with a settlement of the south.' The fact that both governments involved in the talks ruled out the use of coercion against the North even before the talks had started meant that Unionists would themselves have to agree to their own state's dissolution. Michael Collins, reflecting on the Treaty negotiations in May 1922 recalled it had been decided 'there would not be coercion of the North East . . . the plenipotentiaries had guided their actions by that policy.'

However, discussions over the status of the six counties in the Treaty could not be avoided. Aside from the unrealistic statements about Irish unity contained in the rest of the agreement, a more substantial clause involving the creation of a boundary commission was added promising to look anew at the whole basis of partition. The notorious Article XII, described shortly after the signing of the Treaty as 'full of grave and dangerous ambiguity',[15] stated that at an unspecified time a commission would sit, made up of northern and southern members, and readjust the border between north and south 'in accordance with the wishes of the inhabitants'. However, the addition of the caveat 'so far as social and economic conditions will allow' created a profound degree of confusion and misinterpretation. This deliberate ambiguity allowed Lloyd George to give the impression to the Sinn Fein delegation that a good deal of territory would be transferred to the south including Fermanagh, Tyrone, South Down, South Armagh and the border cities of Derry and Newry. However, it also allowed him to reassure James Craig that the commission was only going to rationalise the cumbersome border and that perhaps majority Protestant areas, currently in the south, such as North Monaghan and East Donegal, would be incorporated into Northern Ireland.

During the early stages of the negotiations the Sinn Fein delegation had concentrated largely on the perceived injustices of partition, de Valera telling the delegates that if a break were to be made then they should make it on the Ulster issue rather than the more rarefied topics of constitutional symbols. Due to their confused analysis of the partition issue it is easy to dismiss Sinn Fein as naive or unprepared when it came to the practical preparations for the Treaty debates. However, this is far from the case with a number of sub-committees established prior to the Treaty negotiations to articulate the Nationalist arguments against partition. It was obvious though that no matter how prepared they were, the Sinn Fein delegation were still profoundly limited by their refusal to acknowledge the reality of the new government in the north-east. Lloyd George in a letter to Craig highlighted this peculiar denial in Nationalist circles, stating that de Valera 'must realise that Ulster is a fact which he must recognise, not a figment bolstered up by the British Government as a counter to Sinn Fein.' Prior to this the South African leader General Smuts had acted as an intermediary with de Valera and reinforced this curious dismissal of the authenticity of the partition settlement. He advised the Sinn Fein president:

> My conviction is that for the present no solution based in Ulster coming into the Irish state will succeed. Ulster will not agree, she cannot be forced, and any solution on these lines is at present foredoomed to failure . . . My strong advice to you is to leave Ulster alone for the present . . . to concentrate on a free constitution for the remaining twenty-six counties, and work a successful running of the Irish state and so by the pull of economic and other peaceful forces, eventually to bring Ulster into that state.

The southern delegation however failed to listen to such warnings. Instead they retreated into a safe fundamentalism which saw partition as a perfidious British scheme rather than a reflection of realities on the ground. George Gavan Duffy recorded during the negotiations: 'If England would stand aside there would be no difficulty.' An exasperated Lloyd George wrote:

> They with the instinct of trained politicians saw that Ulster was the stumbling block. They got the whole force of the opposition concentrated on Ulster. Ulster was arming and would fight. We were powerless. It is no use ignoring facts however unpleasant they may be. The politician who thinks he can deal out abstract justice without reference to forces around cannot govern. The first axiom is whatever happened we could not coerce Ulster. There was the same strain in the argument of De Valera as I have heard this morning, that Ulster would come in if we let her alone . . . It is a mistake to assume that the population of Ulster for the time being is opposed to partition. It is not. I am glad that De Valera has come to the conclusion that force is not a weapon you can use. It would break in our hands. We should have a whirlpool . . . We do not care in the slightest degree where Irishmen put Tyrone and Fermanagh, but it is no use making peace with you if we are going to have civil war with Ulster.[16]

As such the Boundary Commission was presented as a way of bypassing the 'stumbling block' of Ulster. Less a solution, than a deferment of the partition problem, the Boundary Commission idea was presented to Collins and Griffith at a meeting on 8 November 1921. While the Sinn Fein reaction to the idea was qualified they gave just enough to accept the principle and allow negotiations to move forward. The idea itself of an impartial commission deciding on the frontier between the two partition states was not new and reflected back to earlier ideas presented during the Ulster Crisis and ironically by James Craig himself in 1919. Collins had also discussed various options including plebiscites and county opt-outs earlier in the negotiations. It was obvious that the challenges of partition were as unfathomable in 1921 as they had been in 1914. Griffith himself seized on the solution as a way of ensuring that 'we would save Tyrone and Fermanagh, part of Derry, Armagh and Down' although there was little in the way of concrete declarations from the participants that such large-scale transfers were to be involved. Lloyd George himself was happy to allow Irish minds to take as much as they wanted from the vague scheme as long as the partition issue no longer stopped the negotiations from proceeding.

While Griffith was able to persuade himself of the value of the Boundary Commission, Collins seemed to have little faith in the scheme. Certainly if he is judged by his actions rather than his words, Collins had little belief that anything except coercion would shift the border. As such over the next six months he would instigate a sustained military and propaganda war against the new Northern government. Collins, almost alone amongst the leadership of Sinn Fein, had come to accept the reality of partition and strove to do something to undermine it. By comparison the general unreality of Nationalist thinking on the north meant that, much as during the Treaty negotiations in general, the northern issue could be put aside for later. The lack of reference to the Ulster clauses during the passionate Treaty debates which followed in the Dáil and the unaltered presence of the Boundary clauses in de Valera's Document No. 2 reflected the almost magical thinking which Nationalist dogma had instilled in the Sinn Fein leadership over the previous years when it came to the issue of partition. De Valera, despite all that had transpired, was still able to state dogmatically that: 'The difficulty is not the Ulster question. As far as we are concerned this is a fight between Ireland and England. I want to eliminate the Ulster question out of it.' This failure to accept the reality of partition could not disguise the fact that the Treaty had accepted the division of the island. Despite the promise of boundary adjustments, it remained the case that no matter how generous any future award might have been, some kind of Northern Ireland would remain. The Treaty and Document No. 2 were thus by definition partitionist documents. The failure to accept this and not to back-pedal on past rhetorical dogmas meant the worst of all possible worlds. What followed in 1922 was disaster.

The Treaty's northern clauses were yet again an ad hoc response to circumstance. Once again the government had altered its policy to meet the ongoing situation despite the rhetorical claims of the 1920 Government of Ireland Act to offer a final solution to the problem. When the attempt to link up that Act with the Treaty was made things would go horribly wrong. Certainly the Treaty and especially its clause on the boundary caused profound alarm in northern Unionist circles. Craig warned Austen Chamberlain in stark terms soon after the Treaty was signed:

> Far from feeling that I have exaggerated the situation I believe that civil war is not necessarily the only end to which we have to look forward under the Treaty. So intense is local feeling at the moment that my colleagues and I may be swept off our feet, and contemporaneously with the functioning of the Treaty, Loyalists may declare independence on their own behalf, seize the Customs and other Government Departments and set up an authority on their own. Many already believe that violence is the only language understood by Mr Lloyd George and his Ministers.[17]

Craig was alarmed at the failure of a Conservative-dominated government to defend the interests of the new Northern Ireland government. It was very apparent that the radical support for Ulster Unionism which had characterised the Ulster Crisis had now dissipated. While prominent Conservatives had supported Craig's resistance to any all-Ireland settlement in the early months of the Treaty negotiations, they would not support his opposition to the Boundary Commission clauses. The Conservative party chairman, Sir George Younger, noted in late 1921 that:

> [A]ny intractable attitude on the part of Ulster would be bitterly resented. There is a natural fear of the appalling results which may follow a breakdown and while there will be no coercion of Ulster if she disagrees, there is a strong feeling that she ought in the interests of the Empire and of Great Britain to make every reasonable concession to secure a settlement.

J. P. Croal, the editor of the *Scotsman* newspaper, informed Bonar Law in November that he detected 'very little public support anywhere for supporting Ulster up to the hilt, especially after Sinn Fein had abandoned the republic.' Lord Derby writing to Lloyd George noted: 'Ulster may ask for some concessions which are clearly preposterous and that then it will be said that Ulster is evidently so unreasonable that no attention be paid to her.' It was evident that unlike in 1914 British opinion now knew what lengths it was prepared to go to in support of the Ulster cause.

The change in Conservative support for Ulster had much to do with Lloyd George's skilful handling of the Ulster issue in the wider context of the Treaty settlement. He had ensured that senior Conservatives would be party to the settlement by making them key members of the Treaty negotiating team. Not only did this move ensure that leading Conservatives were tied to the agreement, it also made sure that the coalition government he headed would not break over the vexed issue of Ireland. Indeed it is astonishing, considering events during the Ulster Crisis, that so few Conservatives were prepared to ally with Craig during the crisis. Only mavericks such as Sir Henry Wilson, later to become military adviser to the Northern government, re-invoked the old Tory radicalism of the pre-war years.

The promise not to use coercion against Ulster would ensure Conservative support but also the government's hands in any future dealings with the partition issue. The Conservative party were ironically the most supportive of the Treaty. Austen Chamberlain and Winston Churchill became its chief defenders against Craig's threats. It represented perhaps Lloyd George's greatest political achievement. While the Irish situation had proved to be the most divisive issue for the coalition government, he had effectively defused it as an issue in British politics. Thomas Jones, Deputy Secretary to the British Cabinet, noted in his diary: 'This was the one topic on which the Liberals could criticise the coalition policy – our Irish policy, and here we've got rid of it.' Indeed even when the coalition government fell in the autumn of 1922, the new Conservative administration continued its support of the agreement.

While the Treaty was a major achievement in that it ended the poisonous influence of the Irish question on British politics, it would prove disastrous for Ireland itself. The response of Craig's Cabinet in the face of this wrangling was to resist all compromise. While Lloyd George pressed for some kind of all-Ireland settlement, Craig threatened independence or Dominion status for Northern Ireland. Even though successful in averting an all-Ireland settlement, the transformation of a unitary settlement into the idea of a boundary commission would prove just as disagreeable. Unionist claims revolved around the fact they had not been party to the Treaty agreement and had no intention of participating in any of its clauses in so much as they affected the six counties. Craig claimed that they had never wanted a parliament in the first place, accepted it reluctantly for only six counties, and now were being asked to have even that settlement amended by an agreement they had taken no part in.

The underlying priority behind the Treaty was the aim of normalising relations between the two new Irish states. However the reality was exactly the opposite. The first six months of 1922 would see rising tensions between the two new governments. While radicals such as Collins and his IRB allies would launch a sustained military, propaganda and economic war against the new Northern government, the Boundary Commission hung over the situation as a longer-term threat to the existence of the Northern government. The effect of this clause on stability in border regions was to lead to devastating levels of violence during the first half of 1922, encouraging on the one hand Nationalist hopes of reclaiming property and reclaiming land, whilst on the other hand adding to the vulnerability and paranoia of the Protestant community. To add to the tension the Boundary Commission did not make it clear when it would sit, how it would decide which areas to transfer, and what criteria were to be employed in its decision-making process.

Craig summed up these fears in a letter to Churchill in May 1922:

> The Boundary Commission has been at the root of all evil. If you picture Loyalists on the borderland being asked by us to hang on with their teeth for the safety of the Province, you can also picture their unspoken cry to us, 'if we sacrifice our lives and our property for the sake of the Province, are you going to assent to a Commission which may subsequently by a stroke of the pen, take away the very area you now ask us to defend?'

Lloyd George warned that no Treaty would be worth anything if its only effect was 'transferring the agony from the South to the North'.[18] However, this is precisely what the Treaty would do.

January–June 1922

Unionist fears over the implications of the Treaty and growing mistrust of the British Government would lead to a whole new focus on military solutions to the partition question in the first six months of 1922. The disbandment of the RIC throughout the spring of 1922 reinforced these fears. The ad hoc special constabulary of 1920 would now be massively reinforced and armed to defend the northern state against a perceived imminent onslaught from southern Nationalists. By May 1922 there would be over 30,000 men under arms in Northern Ireland. The rest of the male Unionist population was also effectively mobilised as reservists in case of dire need. Stephen Talents, the British civil servant sent over to investigate the Northern government, noted in his report that these 'C' Specials were made up of 'a high proportion of the remaining adult male population.' Major-General Arthur Solly-Flood, appointed as military adviser to the Northern government in the spring of 1922, would call for the arming of an intermediate force of 15,000 more 'CI' Specials and wide-ranging military plans to defend border areas. The total cost of the Specials alone in the post-Treaty period would amount to the enormous sum of £2,561,865 but for radicals such as Wickham and Fred Crawford, both of whom called for a general mobilisation, such preparations were barely adequate.

All of the most extreme paranoias of the Unionist psychology would be reinforced by events in Ireland after the signing of the Treaty: a pernicious minority population within its own borders, supported by aggressive elements in the south and an untrustworthy British Government ready to sell them out at the earliest possibility. Balfour reported to the British Cabinet in June 1922: 'In the view of the Northern government the present disturbances were being deliberately aimed at destroying Ulster – they were part of a great conspiracy for exacerbating the feeling between the Roman Catholics and Protestants.' Stephen Tallents gave an even more searching analysis of Unionist paranoia when he noted:

> The Protestant community of the North feel that it is an outpost of civilisation set precariously on the frontiers of Bolshevism. It believes that the British Government has betrayed it and at best that its cause is misunderstood in England.

Unionist paranoia would be reinforced by an increase in IRA attacks across the border. The rise in the level of violence which would occur in the first six months of 1922 was not dependent on how much of a real threat such sporadic attacks were to the security of Northern Ireland. They fed into already pre-existing perceptions. Thus in early February a series of kidnapping raids by the IRA in retaliation for the arrest of a number of prominent Northern IRA figures, dubbed the 'Monaghan Footballers', near Derry City led to huge tensions along the border. Guerrilla attacks and sniping along the border would remain for the next three months and kidnapping became a prominent tactic. In Belfast responses to this imagined threat of imminent invasion led to large-scale reprisals and rioting in which the IRA and the Specials were both implicated. This was civil war in Ireland in all but name.

Certainly the Truce had allowed for the revival and reinforcement of the IRA in Ulster which had come to rely increasingly on southern support for its effectiveness. In September 1921 the Lord Lieutenant of Ireland, Lord Fitzalan, wrote to Lloyd George: 'The chief danger at present in my opinion is in Ulster, where the S[inn] F[einer]'s have started training camps, and there is, therefore, constant imminent risk of disturbances with Craig's Special Constables.'

The chief legacy of the Treaty for northern Catholics however was that southern Nationalist leaders were the acknowledged representatives of the northern minority. Throughout the long debates no one sought input from Catholic minority leaders when it came to the issue of the North making the huge assumption that the interests of southern and northern Nationalists were identical. This fact meant that they had little recourse but to look to southern leaders to advocate on their behalf. As Tallents noted:

> In the spring of 1921 the Nationalists and Sinn Fein representatives made a pact not to recognise the Northern government nor to sit in the Northern Parliament. One result of this attitude has been that Belfast Catholics with grievances have had recourse to Mr Collins instead of approaching the Northern Government directly.

The Northern Catholic minority were forced to hitch their mast to southern nationalism. Any changes in the southern political situation were bound to impact on northern minority aspirations and an unsteady ship it would prove to be.

However, it became apparent that northern minority opinion was far too complex to be dictated by a one-size-fits-all Nationalist perspective. Joe Devlin retained a strong power base in Belfast and East Ulster and Sinn Fein had never managed to become the predominant political force amongst northern Catholics. Collins himself, whilst receiving some support as their spokesman, received his patronage from Bishop McCrory and the increased role of the IRA in defining Nationalist policy. Southern initiatives such as the Belfast Boycott, the abstention policy and the decision to pay northern schoolteachers received only qualified support. Abstention particularly meant there was no forum for northerners to express their opinions and they were reduced to an advisory role or direct appeal to Collins and other Provisional Government colleagues. The unsteady nature of the post-Treaty southern state would do much to dictate the direction of northern policies amongst southern Nationalists. The lack of stability in the southern state undermined Nationalist criticisms of similar problems in the North. Arthur Griffith admitted in April 1922 that their critiques of Craig not being able to control his government would illicit the simple response from the northern leader that 'we have not been able to control ours'.

There is little doubt however that southern Nationalists felt that a combination of the Boundary Commission and a policy of direct confrontation would so reduce the territory of the Belfast government that it would no longer prove to be a viable state and soon collapse. The Northern government certainly did face a coherent military and political threat from the South during the first six months of 1922. With the signing of the Treaty in December 1921 and the subsequent formation of a Provisional Government in Dublin under Michael Collins, the Irish leader quickly moved to instigate an aggressive anti-partition policy in the South. Nationalist-controlled local authorities were urged to opt out of the northern state, their employees, particularly schoolteachers were paid by the South, and the bitterly divided IRA south of the border was united behind an aggressive policy aimed at launching an all-out offensive in the North. A sustained propaganda campaign was also launched in the South aimed at both pointing out the repressive policies of the Unionist government against the Nationalist majority and also publicising the Nationalist case for a radical adjustment to the boundary with the creation of the North-Eastern Boundary Bureau. The IRA in the North was reorganised and reinforced massively with thousands of weapons and men being sent north to take part in attacks along the border. A number of northern IRA leaders were also given commissions in the new Provisional Government Army and Eoin O'Duffy, Collins' key deputy, given the role of co-ordinating IRA activity in Ulster. An all-out offensive was planned for mid-May which, although collapsing due to poor co-ordination, caused widespread panic amongst the Unionist authorities. The involvement of the Provisional Government however was to be kept a secret and Collins kept up the diplomatic pressure by meeting James Craig on two occasions, January and March 1922, to discuss settling of the boundary question and make representations on behalf of the northern minority. Although the resultant Craig–Collins pacts (Document 17) failed miserably, the most important implication of the negotiations was that the South, and Collins in particular, was now acknowledged as the representative of the northern Catholic minority. For good or ill, the fate of the Nationalist minority was thus inextricably linked to the future policy of the southern administration and its leadership.

The increased level of IRA violence in the North led to unprecedented reprisal violence in Belfast with over 250 people losing their lives in the city during the five months running from February to June and millions of pounds worth of damage caused. Although profoundly counterproductive, almost in spite of itself this policy came close to success with the very existence of the Northern Irish government under threat. The Unionist government was growing increasingly mistrustful of the British Government, fearing that the constant disorder would eventually lead the London government to tire of the situation and move to appease southern Nationalists. It was certainly clear that the British Government were becoming increasingly exasperated by the failure of the Northern government to maintain control of its allotted area and the role of many of its security forces in a number of high profile atrocities. These included the so-called 'MacMahon murders' in March where masked policemen murdered six male members of the Catholic MacMahon household in north Belfast in cold blood. The British Government were also tired of the crippling costs of maintaining such a large, and one-sided, security apparatus with Lloyd George reminding Churchill: 'our Ulster case is not a good one'. British troops had already been forced to intervene in the west when the IRA seized an area around the Belleek-Pettigo triangle and a continuation of the violence may have led inevitably to their wider intervention to keep the peace. In June 1922 Churchill despatched a senior British civil servant, Stephen Tallents, to investigate the workings of the Northern government. Certainly by the end of June things were not looking good for the future sustainability of the partition settlement.

The Unionist backlash, May–August 1922

However, it was at this crucial point that two developments took the pressure off the Belfast government. The first was its own decision to employ the full rigour of the Special Powers Act after the shooting of a Unionist MP, William Twadell, in late May. Mass round-ups were carried out and over 700 IRA Volunteers and leading Nationalist politicians were interned, many of them on an old cargo ship, the *Argenta*, moored in Belfast Lough. More significant perhaps was the opening of the civil war in the South on 28 June

1922. Immediately southern support for northern Nationalists collapsed with the supply of money and arms drying up.

Furthermore in August 1922, Michael Collins, the one southern politician who had made a priority of northern affairs, was killed in an ambush in West Cork. The emerging Irish Free State leadership under William Cosgrave chose not to make an issue of the North and instigated 'a policy of peaceful obstruction towards the Northern government', turning its back on any kind of offensive policy with regard to the North. IRA units were withdrawn from the North and offensive action suspended (Document 21). The thousands of Belfast refugees who had fled to Dublin in the spring of 1922 were sent back to the North and the Provisional Government moved to recognise partition and normalise relations with the Northern government, closing down its various advisory bodies and establishing customs posts along the border in 1923. As such Tallents, while making a number of critical reports about aspects of the Unionist government, especially the Ministry of Home Affairs under Dawson Bates, was able to report that the situation was now coming under control. By the skin of its teeth, Northern Ireland had survived.

The Boundary Commission

The outbreak of civil war in Dublin was also to have a profoundly detrimental effect on the potential of convening the much anticipated Boundary Commission. It was to prove unfeasible for the new Free State government to make an issue of the boundary when it was struggling to assert its control over the area it already had. As such it was only when the civil war was over that the southern government got round to putting a commission in place and by that time the context has almost completely changed.

History has not been kind to the Boundary Commission. While there remains a general view that the border is in the wrong place, few have presented an alternative which would satisfy both communities in Ulster. The border certainly appears unwieldy and impractical as it did to contemporaries. Lady Lillian Spender noted on a tour of the border that her 'route corkscrewed about in the most bewildering manner' through numerous small roads in a futile effort to avoid crossing over the border.[19]

Hindsight has also inevitably given the impression that the border had a permanence that did not exist at the time of its creation. Many parties on both sides painted the border as provisional. Lloyd George defined the area to be excluded as simply 'using six counties as a basis' while Carson himself dismissed the idea of using county lines to set the frontier of the new state. Even in May 1917 when the partition idea was still in its infancy, some Ulster Unionist leaders looked towards some kind of amended border in some unforeseeable future. Charles D'Arcy, Church of Ireland Bishop of

Down and later a member of the Irish Free State Senate, argued that: 'It will be very wise policy to demand the exclusion of all Ulster. Bad bits could be cut out at a later stage.'[20]

The 'bad bits' of course were the major problem. Chief amongst these were Fermanagh and Tyrone. In 1924, Asquith, long out of office, spoke in the House of Commons on the question of the Boundary Commission, stating that as in 1914 it faced 'precisely the same problem . . . centred, as it centres now, mainly on the position of the two counties of Fermanagh and Tyrone'; what one official had called the 'Alsace-Lorraine of Ireland'.[21] Churchill himself recalled:

> I remember on the eve of the Great War we were gathered together at a Cabinet meeting in Downing Street, and for a long time, an hour or an hour and a half, after the failure of the Buckingham Palace Conference, we discussed the boundaries of Fermanagh and Tyrone. Both of the great political parties were at each other's throats. The air was full of talk of civil war. Every effort was made to settle the matter and bring them together. The differences had been narrowed down, not merely to the counties of Fermanagh and Tyrone, but to parishes and groups of parishes inside the areas of Fermanagh and Tyrone, and yet, even when the differences had been so narrowed down, the problem appeared to be as insuperable as ever, and neither side would agree to reach any conclusion.[22]

The Boundary Commission was the distillation of the partition question. There had been so much denial over the reality of partition amongst Irish Nationalists that it is hard to escape the conclusion that most parties wanted someone else to make the inevitable decision that moving the border in any kind of equitable way was almost impossible. Austen Chamberlain noted in 1922 that 'partition was a compromise, and like all compromises indefensible and illogical'.[23] Cosgrave later admitted that the Boundary Commission was an attempt 'to secure a Divine Solution by human agency'.[24] Lord Curzon in the Lords in 1924 found the vagueness of the idea so bad that he expressed his sympathy for the 'the unhappy man who is going to be Chairman'[25].

The 'unhappy man' was the South African judge Richard Feetham, who was chosen to chair the enterprise. In a very profound sense the whole partition question fell on the shoulders of this one man. The idea of reconciling Nationalist demands for the award of two and a half counties to the South contrasted sharply with that of Craig. Speaking in December 1922 in the Northern Ireland House of Commons, he claimed dominion over:

> the whole of Fermanagh and Tyrone, and if I pay I am not going to give away one inch of the soil of Fermanagh and Tyrone, does it not immediately mean that the destinies of these two counties rest in the hand of one man? Was there ever such a preposterous suggestion? If I cannot give way on the question of Tyrone and Fermanagh, and the other man

[i.e. Cosgrave] will not by any sort or manner of means reduce his demand for the two counties, is there not a complete deadlock without a chance of success, and is not any Chairman, whoever he may be, in the position of having to decide the fate of these two places, and of Derry City?[26]

Feetham was a respected judge but lacked any experience of arbitrating border disputes and had never set foot in Ireland before. For some this appeared to be an advantage and reinforced his impartiality but the convoluted nature and bitter history of Ulster's religious demographics confounded even those with a long experience of Irish politics. The vagueness of Article XII of the Treaty was made even more problematic by the material the commission had to deal with. The census figures they worked with were thirteen years out of date and there was little knowledge of how the experience of war and revolution had altered the situation.

Even an up-to-date census though would have caused problems. The main problem was which unit of population to use in order to 'ascertain the wishes of the inhabitants', something which remained unspecified in the original article. In their lengthy discussions the commissioners agonised over which would provide a coherent and consistent measure.[27] The example of the 'Communes' used at Versailles was used throughout the discussions as the potential unit for transfer. However, Article 88 of the Versailles Treaty was far more precise than that of the Anglo-Irish Treaty and the various Irish units did not match the 'commune'. As such it was left to the commissioners themselves to make the decision.

The smallest administrative areas were the Poor Law Unions. Each county was divided into three to six of them, clustered around market towns. They were also the easiest areas to transfer, as they could continue to function if they were 'transferred with all their machinery.' However, Feetham pointed out that administrative practicalities were not his concern, only geographic and economic conditions, voicing his concern that the administrative units 'may be bad economically and geographically'. Smaller units such as the polling districts of the District Electoral Divisions were also considered but they were small and had no administrative function. By contrast parliamentary constituencies and counties were rejected as being too large an area. In the south changes to the Poor Law union system meant their complete overhaul so there was no comparative unit of measurement on the other side of the border. The situation was bewildering.

When the commission did finally sit in late 1924, after all manner of procrastination and delay, including bouts of illness for both Irish premiers, with a South African chairman and a Northern government refusing to choose a representative, what followed was little short of farce.

After gathering up evidence by touring round the border and holding a series of public meetings, the commission recommended that only minor adjustments were made to the boundary in which some of South Armagh went into the South, but also parts of East Donegal were awarded to the

North. While never made public, a map was leaked to the right-wing *Morning Post*, probably by J. R. Fisher, the representative appointed on behalf of the Northern government. In response all hell broke loose in the South. The southern representative, Eoin MacNeill, resigned from the commission as a result and a hasty compromise was agreed in London whereby the border was to remain as it was with no changes whatsoever, in response to a few changes with regard to southern Irish responsibility for paying off the war debt to the British Government (Document 22). The report itself was to be suppressed and not published, only being opened to the public in the 1960s.

It is difficult not to see the Boundary Commission as a betrayal of the Northern Irish Catholic minority by its southern allies. Northern Nationalists had been given to believe that large amounts of territory would be involved and they would soon be reintegrated into the South. In the end the failure of the Boundary Commission removed any chance of them escaping from Unionist control. As Cahir Healy, a leading northern Nationalist politician of the time, poignantly noted of the northern minority in the aftermath of the Boundary commission, 'we have been abandoned to Craig's mercy'.

Ulster's experience of the Irish revolution is important for a number of reasons. Firstly it shaped the rather draconian defensiveness of the Unionist government which emerges in its aftermath, and a state which many would argue never got over the torrid experience of its birth, remaining in almost a permanent state of emergency. Secondly, it led to a huge amount of disunity amongst the northern Catholic minority not only between Nationalists and Republicans but also between border and Belfast Nationalists, something which would cripple minority politics for decades to come. Thirdly, the experience of the Northern IRA, being at points courted and then abandoned, meant that the IRA in Ulster was virtually destroyed in this period, failing to recover in any meaningful way until the 1960s. Finally the revolution in Ulster created profound divisions between northern and southern Nationalists which were slow to heal.

The Boundary Commission was hailed as a great victory for Craig but it was in many ways his worst defeat. The loss to the South of some of the most virulently Nationalist areas would have rid Northern Ireland of areas which would become hotbeds of Republicanism in later years. Unlike with the South, the North was left with a large and unmanageable minority. The failure of the Boundary Commission thus made the minority issue largely a northern phenomenon. Indeed, seeing partition as a victory for Ulster Unionists in this sense is flawed. It is interesting to speculate on what a generous award from the Boundary Commission from the southern point of view would have done to the dynamics and political culture of the southern state. In December 1921, shortly after the signing of the Treaty, Lloyd George summed up the ominous implications of the partition settlement:

> There is no doubt – certainly since the Act of 1920 – that the majority of
> the people of two counties prefer being with their Southern neighbours to

being in the Northern Parliament. Take it either by constituency or by Poor Law unions, or, if you like, by counting heads, and you will find that the majority in these two counties prefer to be with their Southern neighbours. What does that mean? If Ulster is to remain a separate community, you can only by means of coercion keep them there, and although I am against the coercion of Ulster, I do not believe in Ulster coercing other units. Apart from that, would it be an advantage to Ulster? There is no doubt it would give her trouble. The trouble which we have had in the South the North would have on a smaller scale, but the strain, in proportion, on her resources would be just as great as the strain upon ours. It would be a trouble at her own door, a trouble which would complicate the whole of her machinery, and take away her mind from building. She wants to construct; she wants to build up a good Government, a model Government, and she cannot do so as long as she has got a trouble like this on her own threshold, nay, inside her door.[28]

The whole legacy of the revolution meant that southern Nationalists gave much greater priority to their own independence than they did on Irish unity. Thus in a very profound sense the responsibility for partition resides not only with the British Government and Ulster Unionists but with the policies of the revolutionary Irish Nationalist generation itself.

Sample essay and examination questions

How have historians understood the place of partition in the wider 'Irish revolution' of 1916–23?
Why did the IRA in Ulster prove unable to successfully impede the establishment of Northern Ireland between 1920 and 1922?
Account for the failure of the Craig-Collins pacts of January and March 1922.
To what extent was Northern Ireland 'a state under siege' between 1920 and 1922?
Was the Boundary Commission anything more than an exercise in futility?

Further reading

M. Farrell, *Arming the Protestants: The Formation of the Ulster Special Constabulary and the Royal Ulster Constabulary 1920–1927* (London, 1983)
B. Follis, *A State Under Siege. The Establishment of Northern Ireland 1920–1926* (Oxford, 1995)
G. Hand (ed.), *Report of the Irish Boundary Commission* (Shannon, 1969).
M. Harris, *The Catholic Church and the Foundation of the Northern Irish State* (Belfast, 1993)

A. C. Hepburn, *A Past Apart: Studies in the History of Catholic Belfast, 1850–1950* (Belfast, 1996)

M. A. Hopkinson, *Green Against Green: The Irish Civil War* (Dublin, 1988), pp.77–88

M. A. Hopkinson, 'The Craig-Collins Pacts of 1922: two attempted reforms of the Northern Irish government', *Irish Historical Studies* (November 1990)

R. Lynch, *The Northern IRA and the Early Years of Partition, 1920–22* (Dublin, 2006)

K. Matthews, *Fatal Influence: The Impact of Ireland on British Politics* (Dublin, 2004)

Useful web links

The full report of the Boundary Commission is available for download from the National Archives (London) at http://discovery.nationalarchives.gov.uk/SearchUI/Details?uri=C386829 [accessed 2 June 2014].

8

The Irish Civil War, 1922–3

By the spring of 1922 the Anglo-Irish Treaty had proved itself to be almost the ideal document to spread division within the Sinn Fein movement. It is certainly arguable that any other settlement which had swung to more moderate or more extreme forms of defining the new state would have resulted in its rejection or embrace by an overwhelming majority of the population. In the end the Treaty was just objectionable enough to give the idealists within the Republican movement enough support from more mainstream sections of the Sinn Fein movement, typified by de Valera's defection and his trumpeting of his own semantic separatism in the form of Document No. 2, as an acceptable political alternative.

The military situation

If the Treaty issue was to be settled by war, then at first glance the anti-Treaty IRA held all of the advantages. This was certainly the case in the period immediately preceding the start of the war. The Republican IRA were in control of most of the country and outnumbered those in the IRA who had gone pro-Treaty by 2:1. They also contained the vast majority of veterans from the War of Independence who made up the most radical and ideologically committed parts of the Republican movement. Notably the most active IRA counties in Munster had overwhelmingly chosen to reject the Treaty. Even previously inactive IRA areas such as Sligo and Connemara joined the anti-Treaty side. The make-up of the anti-Treaty IRA was heterogeneous but largely provincial and all shared to some extent a hostility to control from GHQ in Dublin with had proved a point of tension during the War of Independence. Certainly the various splits which had developed after the March 1922 Convention between the Executive in Dublin and Liam Lynch's Munster command were healed by the time war began.

The 'Trucilleers', despite their large numbers, would be largely irrelevant to the conflict. As during the War of Independence, IRA numbers on paper were misleading and the organisation tended to rely on a relatively small number of committed guerrillas. In the case of the anti-Treaty IRA this would amount to around 15,000 Volunteers. Indeed the Republicans' main problem would be supplying even this small number of Volunteers with weapons. By the start of the war the IRA had less than 7,000 rifles, many of its men relying on antiquated shotguns or revolvers, and lacked artillery or heavy weapons of any kind. Aside from a few armoured cars acquired from British forces when they hurriedly left Ireland in the spring of 1922, the Republicans were an ill-equipped and poorly supplied force, constantly short of ammunition and reliant as previously on captured weaponry from the enemy. As such the IRA was to be limited in terms of its military strategy and found the possibility of large-scale offensive action difficult to sustain, instead reverting to a defensive strategy which, while giving them little chance of all-out victory, helped to prolong the war.

While the anti-Treaty IRA faced some major problems, the Provisional Government barely had an army worth the name once the conflict began. Aside from one or two notable command areas in the provinces such as Joe Sweeney's in Donegal and Sean MacEoin's in Longford, the Provisional Government Army would begin as a largely Dublin-based enterprise. The one reliable unit came directly from Collins' old Squad men and the Dublin Active Service Unit, which had formed early in January 1922 largely to oversee the handing over of Dublin Castle to the new regime. Aside from these Volunteers the army would be largely made up of officers from the old GHQ so was top-heavy from the start. It was obvious that time was vital for the building up of an efficient military force for the new state, although it would not be until August 1922, two months after the war began, that the Provisional Government was able to muster as many troops as the anti-Treaty side. Certainly from this point the army grew quickly, reaching 38,000 by the end of 1922 and ending the war with almost 60,000 officers and men. However, this rapid increase was only sustainable if the quality of the recruits would match the veterans of the anti-Treaty side. This was largely achieved by the enlistment of large numbers of men who had served in the British Army during the First World War. Indeed by the end of the conflict over half of the Free State Army, as the force became at the turn of the year, was made up of ex-British Army veterans. The army would also have a strong advantage in terms of weaponry and was liberally supplied with equipment including artillery, armoured cars and even aircraft by the British.

The war itself began largely through the failure of various attempts to patch together some kind of workable compromise and the collapse of those unifying crusades, most notably the offensive in the North, which were already underway. It was clear also that patience was running out on many fronts. The British were especially exasperated by the continued presence of the anti-Treaty IRA garrison in Dublin who it was believed were sponsoring and supplying weaponry for the ongoing attacks aimed at destabilising Northern Ireland. The British found the excuses of Collins and his allies increasingly difficult to believe, especially when they offered the new Provisional Government ample means in terms of military equipment to dislodge the insurgents. It was also clear that Collins was becoming an increasingly isolated figure within the Provisional Government with many leading figures, most notably Arthur Griffith, finding the IRA's partial occupation of the capital an increasing impediment to the establishment of the new state. Indeed the IRA were far from a passive force in Dublin, having occupied numerous prominent buildings in the city as well as commandeering material to house refugees from Belfast. Such initiatives included the raiding of shops and the intimidation of large numbers of private citizens, while in the country at large there was a similar increase in anarchy and disorder. This was not helped by the rapid demobilisation of the RIC which, although formally ceasing to exist on 31 August 1922, was steadily wound up throughout March, this process all but completed by mid-May.

On 25 June, having finally reached the end of its tether, the British Cabinet took the decision to launch an attack on the Four Courts garrison the following day. Although the attack itself was postponed largely due to fears of repeating the mistakes of 1916, there is little doubt that a major British offensive was only a matter of time. This decision had been hastened by the shooting of Sir Henry Wilson, the outspoken recently appointed military adviser to the Northern government, in London by two members of the IRB. It is still unclear who, if anyone, gave the order to the assassins, many historians seeing Collins' conspiratorial hand in the background, but nonetheless its impact was to be the final straw for the British. For the Provisional Government the situation was becoming impossible. With an overwhelming popular mandate and ample supplies of weaponry, Republican provocations, such as the high profile kidnapping of the new National Army's Deputy Chief of Staff J. J. ('Ginger') O'Connell on 26 June, could no longer be tolerated, although it was British impatience which was to prove decisive.

While British political pressure had been key, it was also British arms that would deal the first blow of the civil war. In the early hours of 28 June 1922 Provisional Government forces began an artillery bombardment of the Four Courts. Although there had been increasing disorder since the military split in March the shelling of the Four Courts was of a different magnitude. The attack itself demonstrated the inexperience of the new Provisional Government Army with one shell landing accidently on the nearby British barracks. Despite such blunders and the provocative actions of Republicans, the British refused to be drawn into the war and would stay disciplined and aloof throughout the conflict. During the early civil war the strength of the garrison in Dublin would remain at 5,500 with a watching brief to assert the Imperial authority should the need arise until the Irish Free State had come into being. Indeed it was largely with relief that the British sat back and watched the previous united Irish Nationalist movement collapse into open civil war.

The early civil war

The shelling of the Four Courts began a week-long battle for control of Dublin. The various Republican occupied buildings in the centre of the city were steadily reduced and abandoned by their occupants to be followed by uncoordinated skirmishes and street battles. The Four Courts garrison themselves lasted barely two days, although not before the building and its precious historical records were destroyed. Efforts to relieve Dublin by anti-Treaty forces outside the city failed miserably when the most serious attempt was halted at Blessington leaving the garrison in the city isolated. Certainly within barely a week Republican resistance in the capital had collapsed leaving the Provisional Government in complete control. The casualties were relatively light with fewer than seventy dead and thirty wounded on both sides. Among those who had died however were prominent individuals, most notably the old Minister of Defence, Cathal Brugha, who chose martyrdom rather than surrender. Again though civilian casualties, much like in 1916, were by far the worst with over 200 people losing their lives in the crossfire. Over 500 Republican prisoners were taken by the Provisional Government including again many prominent leaders of what had been the most aggressive element of the anti-Treaty forces.

The capture of Dublin would prove to be the key moment in the war. The Provisional Government would follow this early success with a seemingly uninterrupted run of major victories as it moved to consolidate control over the country. Holding Dublin would also be crucial as it was the key administrative hub, the main port for the import of weapons and a major training centre for the new army. What was perhaps most surprising was how easily Republican arms had been overcome in the city and how ill prepared they were when the final attack came. In terms of strategy it was clear that the same mistakes of the Easter Rising had been repeated with the concentration on the occupation of prominent buildings and an overall defensive posture. Certainly ideologically the spectre of 1916 hovered over the Dublin fighting. The IRA had taken the Easter rebels as their inspiration with the fighting being notable for the number of individual acts of bravery and martyrdom. However, while such noble self-sacrifice would be a key feature of the Republican war effort it would do little to alter the outcome. There was also a strange sense of unreality in Republican circles about the war, many finding it hard to shed the perception of the British as the main enemy and a belief that their old comrades would soon come to their senses and move to reunify the movement once again. It was very clear that had the Republicans acted with decisiveness in the spring of 1922 they could have fairly easily overcome the new pro-Treaty regime but this failure to accept the reality of civil war would linger well into the early months of the conflict.

By contrast the Provisional Government showed little of such sentimentality. Now that the war had begun the pro-Treaty side would pursue it ruthlessly with Michael Collins, despite his desperate attempts to avert the conflict, at the forefront of the campaign. Having left his role as Chairman of the Provisional Government he became the great rallying point for the pro-Treaty side. All power stemmed from him and during these last few months of his life, Collins wielded the greatest power any Irishmen had over the country in its history. The Republicans would have no such similar figure with central strategic direction proving as problematic for the IRA as it had been during the War of Independence. While Chief of Staff Liam Lynch was the nominal military commander of all Republican forces, in reality the IRA were a disparate group under the control of local commanders who demonstrated little co-ordination in terms of developing an overall strategy or defined war aims.

The Provisional Government offensive

With the seizure of Dublin, the Provisional Government Army began a broad advance into the heart of provincial Ireland. The offensive was rapid and for the most part unopposed. The advance on land would be complemented by a series of innovative sea landings designed to strike right at the heart of the so-called 'Munster Republic', an imagined half-mocking notion of a provincial heartland controlled by the anti-Treaty side. While in hindsight such a move would have been advisable, and in many ways essential to fight a civil war, the Republicans would never manage to control any distinct geographic region. So successful was the National Army's advance that, with the fall of Fermoy on 11 August, every major town in Ireland was now under the control of the new government.

There can be little doubt that the Provisional Government advance was greeted with general support by the Irish public as they moved in to relieve various provincial towns. Even so the Provisional Government dominated the news agenda and the flow of information about the progress of the war. It was publicity and the news agenda where many of the fiercest battles were fought. Press censorship was introduced early on and Republicans were to be categorised and stripped of their chief ideological nomenclature by their christening as 'Irregulars' (a title still erroneously used by many historians when discussing the war). Other public bodies offered high profile and significant support, most notably the Catholic Church whose October Pastoral was a damning attack on the Republican war effort. Even so Republicans managed to keep up their own stream of propaganda under the guiding hand of Erskine Childers, a constant thorn in the side of the Dublin government.

Despite the innovation of the sea landings and the speed of the Provisional Government advance, the truth was that in most cases Republican resistance had been minimal. The chief tactic employed by the IRA was to burn barracks and other buildings before withdrawing and leaving the towns open to the advancing forces. There were few pitched battles of any note.

Even when something akin to a pitched battle did occur such as at Kilmallock, south of Limerick city, where Liam Deasy's force of 2,000 guerrilla fighters faced a smaller National Army contingent, the Republicans chose withdrawal rather than confrontation after engaging in a token fire fight with oncoming enemy forces. The only notable conventional military enterprise undertaken by the Republicans occurred in Dundalk where the South Armagh IRA leader Frank Aiken, who had remained neutral in the conflict until his arrest and imprisonment in the town by pro-Treaty forces, led a daring raid, capturing the town and releasing his comrades. However, once again Aiken, like other IRA commanders, failed to show any desire to hold on to the city and withdrew his forces soon after. The ease with which the Provisional Government Army advanced across Ireland has led to strong criticism of Republican military strategy during the war. It was certainly the case that after the Provisional Government's occupation of urban areas the IRA seemed more comfortable in reverting to the creation of the old Flying Columns which had served them so well during the War of Independence. While Liam Lynch would prove to be a hard-line and uncompromising leader of the Republican forces he showed little dynamism militarily and opted for a strategy of defence and survival, hoping it seemed to win some kind of war of attrition, exactly the kind of strategy the IRA were least suited to engage in.

By August 1922 the war appeared to be all but over. What is perhaps most surprising was that the Republican IRA both chose, and were able, to continue the war. It was certainly true that guerrilla warfare proved to be a far more logical strategy for Republicans to adopt. Its fighters already had long experience of this type of warfare, its effectiveness and limitations, and they also understood how such a strategy could garner public support if they could place the Provisional Government Army in a similar position to that of the British during the War of Independence. Any relation the war had to a conventional conflict for territory shaped by pitched battles and fixed lines was completely abandoned by August 1922. The reversion to guerrilla warfare reaped immediate dividends for the IRA and would prolong the conflict for a further eight months.

Republican commitment to the war was due in large to the dominant role that hard-line militarists had assumed within the movement. Their idealism and profound mistrust of politics undermined any hopes for a negotiated settlement. The lack of any kind of broader social or political strategy from Lynch was a constant frustration to other leading Republicans. Peadar O'Donnell, who consistently voiced his frustration at the failure of Irish Republicanism to exploit its links with a radical socialist ideology, noted of his fellow anti-Treatyites:

They were the stuff that martyrs are made of, but not revolutionaries, and martyrdom should be avoided. We had a pretty barren mind socially; many on the Republican side were against change . . . The city-minded

Sinn Feiner was darkly suspicious of the wild men on the land ... Pure ideals were used as a mask and a blinkers to direct the movement away from revolution.[1]

Similarly Liam Mellows was critical of this one-dimensional and narrow militarism of the struggle, calling for 'a rallying centre, and the movement a focussing point'. Certainly the inertia which underlay the development of the IRA's military strategy during the war did not lead to a concomitant rise in Republican political efforts. The always uneasy relationship between the political and military parts of the anti-Treaty side reached a new low during the civil war. Even such a high profile figure as de Valera cut an increasingly isolated figure and was largely irrelevant in shaping the direction of the conflict. His symbolic enlistment as a lowly Volunteer in his old unit drew a line under his own acceptance of his powerlessness within the wider movement.

Many Republicans however did maintain a dwindling faith that some form of compromise could be found. Despite the rhetoric it was clear that one of the reasons for the rapid collapse of the Republican war effort was a lingering faith that army unity could be restored, certainly far more than those on the pro-Treaty side. Numerous ad hoc peace initiatives were instigated throughout the war especially from the Republican side. In December 1922 the 'Neutral IRA' was formed. Led by Florrie O'Donoghue and Sean Hegarty, the organisation was made up of pre-Truce veterans and was Republican in its political and constitutional outlook. However, its efforts came to little when faced with the inflexibility of the Provisional Government leadership. Overall moves towards peace remained confused and ill co-ordinated and tended to be the work of individuals such as Frank Aiken whose personal visit to Limerick early on the eve of war ended in abject failure.

This attempt to create some form of political facet to the Republican campaign continued with the feeble attempts to form some kind of alternative Republican government. Formed after a meeting of the IRA Executive in October 1922, the government had de Valera, reinstated as 'President of the Irish Republic', at its head. De Valera himself saw the new body as an 'emergency government' and organised a new 'Council of State' made up of a dozen TDs from the Second Dáil. This Republican Cabinet was an odd collection of anti-Treatyites and included leading lights such as Austin Stack, Sean Moylan, and Mary MacSwiney. However, as a functioning body the Republican government was largely imaginary and attempts to engage in any form of civil administration unconvincing. Most of its members were absent, either in gaol or, as with Moylan, abroad in the USA. It was also a government with nothing to exercise its authority over and no real power to exercise even if it did have. Largely it was a symbolic move designed to reinforce Republican legitimacy by shoring up the dwindling political relevance of the Second Dáil, a body which was never formally wound up and from which all later Republicans would draw their perceived political authority, handing that power on to the IRA's Army Council in the 1930s. Mary MacSwiney, languishing in gaol on hunger strike at the time noted: 'The Republican government has been kept alive and that is the most important thing.'[2]

The guerrilla phase of the conflict

Indeed the key spur for the formation of the Republican government was not so much a wish to explore political solutions but a response to the sitting of the Third Dáil. After being postponed five times the Provisional Government allowed the Dáil elected in June to finally have its first sitting on 5 September 1922, its main role being the ratification of the new Free State constitution. The new body was very different from the one which had preceded it. All of the Republicans were now gone including previously prominent individuals such as Harry Boland and Cathal Brugha who had both been killed early in the war along with so many others; Arthur Griffith himself was the next major figure to die, although of natural causes, in August. In a second major blow to the Provisional Government he was to be followed two weeks later by Michael Collins who was shot dead in an IRA ambush in West Cork. Collins, whose lack of familiarity with combat may have contributed ironically to his death, had been the major power figure in the new state. His massive state funeral in late August, attended by an estimated 500,000 people, gave the new state is first prominent martyr to mourn.

Collins' death was to prove to be a hugely significant turning point in the war. From now on the war would become increasingly bitter. With the loss of both Griffith and Collins, the new leadership of the Provisional Government, represented by figures such as Richard Mulcahy, William Cosgrave, Ernest Blythe and Kevin O'Higgins, would be far more hard-line. As the war dragged on through the winter into 1923 it would become an increasingly bitter conflict marked by atrocities on both sides, unthinkable when the conflict began.

Republican strategy descended into widespread and heavily localised guerrilla warfare aimed at crippling the infrastructure of the new state. While direct stand-up fights had proved impossible for the IRA, increasingly they looked to strike at the soft underbelly of the newly established Irish Free State. Railways were targeted in particular which managed to disrupt Free State troop movements around the country and were costly and time consuming to repair. Creameries, local administrative buildings and a wide range of economic targets were also attacked by the IRA. Almost inevitably such focus on the infrastructure of the new state often led to attacks on its supporters. While not directly targeting TDs, the IRA did widen its list of enemies to include a wide range of actual or perceived Free State supporters, including Protestants, especially with the targeting of 'Big Houses', the large country mansions of the old Anglo-Irish elite, almost 200 of which were destroyed by the Republicans during the war. A number of senators were also attacked and Kevin O'Higgins' father was shot dead.

The bitter end

The Provisional Government's response to this descent into terror and reprisal was uncompromising. With the absence of all anti-Treaty TDs, only the Labour party offered any organised opposition within the Dáil to the creation of new emergency public order legislation. Indeed the Third Dáil, far from being a forum for moderation, allowed for the airing of growing criticism of the military and the need for a stronger policy to bring the war to an early end. As such a Public Safety Bill was passed on 27 September involving the introduction of military courts and a policy of execution. However, the bill was not actually used until two months later. On 17 November five Republicans, who had been captured in Dublin carrying weapons, were executed after facing a military tribunal. Most shocking however was the execution of Erskine Childers a week later. Childers' execution by firing squad on 24 November, after being caught carrying a revolver, ironically given to him by Michael Collins, was a profound shock to Irish society. Many viewed his execution as politically motivated. Childers himself was in no way a military leader but, with his stinging criticisms of the new government with his control of the Republican Publicity Department, had arguably had the greatest impact in undermining confidence in the new state.

The Republican response was to meet terror with the threat of even greater terror. On 30 November Liam Lynch issued an order to IRA units to kill prominent Provisional Government supporters. However, the fear of reprisals from the government meant that in reality Republicans proved reluctant to carry out this policy of assassination. Indeed only one shooting was carried out when pro-Treaty TD Sean Hales (whose brother was a prominent Cork IRA leader) was gunned down in Dublin on 7 December. Another TD, Padraic O'Maille was also wounded in the attack. To this single attack the Provisional Government responded savagely. On the day after the shooting four Republicans, Rory O'Connor, Joe McKelvey, Dick Barrett and Liam Mellowes, who had been in prison since the attack on the Four Courts, were summarily executed. There was no pretence at any kind of trial. The choice of these four men was profoundly symbolic as each one hailed from a different Irish province and all of them were notable members of the IRB. The fact that O'Connor had been Kevin O'Higgins' best man at his wedding added to the severity of the decision. O'Higgins himself would later pay with his life after being gunned down by the IRA in Dublin in 1927.

The savagery of the new Provisional Government execution policy caused much alarm in pro-Treaty circles especially considering the almost unanimous dignity with which the victims met their deaths. The Labour party and the Church were shocked by the killings and became increasingly uneasy at the direction the conflict was taking. Even so the executions would continue throughout the war with seventy-seven being carried out in total. Certainly if one looks to explain why Republican military opposition was overcome relatively easily during the civil war when compared to the War of Independence, the unsavoury methods of the Free State government have to be taken into account. Many IRA veterans testified later that the executions had a bad effect on morale and did much to lessen military activity. Indeed despite popular portrayals of the period it is unlikely that the British would have countenanced such a harsh policy against the IRA as that of the Free State.

Less public, but perhaps more insidious, was a whole range of informal atrocities. The closing months of the war would be punctuated by a series of organised massacres of Republicans by units of the National Army. The perpetrators came mostly from the old Squad of Michael Collins and police officers from the notorious Criminal Investigation Department (CID). It certainly appeared that in these final few months the Free State became institutionally terroristic. Of particular note were the shootings of captured Republicans in County Kerry, where the guerrilla campaign had been most successful. In March 1923 after an IRA bomb killed five Free State troops at the village of Knocknagoshel, a number of massacres were carried out, most notoriously at Ballyseedy where nine Republican prisoners were tied together and sent along a road to 'clear' landmines laid by their comrades. Eight of the prisoners were killed with one surviving to later tell his story.

In the face of this uncompromising onslaught Republican resistance, never very coherent in the closing months of the war, began to crumble. The military side had already fallen into disarray and existed largely on paper as a national military organisation, being made up largely of increasingly isolated guerrilla columns. On the ground the grandiose ranks and titles of regional commanders meant little. Ernie O'Malley, who was appointed as commander of a vast and unwieldy area covering the whole of Ulster and the West, wrote to Lynch on numerous occasions asking for some kind of clarification, and at one point directly for an 'outline of your military and national policy, as we are in the dark here?' As the months dragged on through the harsh winter increasing numbers of Republicans were also interned by the new government, totalling some 13,000 by the end of the war.

A significant blow to Republican military commitment came with the death of Liam Lynch in early April. Lynch, who like Collins was killed in a freak ambush, had represented a strange mixture of resolute resolve and military inertia. However, as much as Collins' death had hardened pro-Treaty resolve, Lynch's death would weaken Republican resistance. His replacement Frank Aiken, a close ally of de Valera, had never been strongly committed to the war effort, and indeed had remained neutral during the early months of the conflict, only siding with the Republicans after Free State provocation.

When the end came it was messy, confused and inconclusive. On 24 May Aiken ordered IRA Volunteers to 'dump' their arms. The order was an attempt to maintain Republican dignity with the illusion that the struggle was merely postponed rather than abandoned. No official surrender was ever signed. The war just stopped. Without an agreed peace deal thousands of Republicans, including de Valera, were rounded up and interned. The collapse of Republican morale was complete, and when in October almost 8,000 IRA prisoners launched a co-ordinated hunger strike in protest at their continued imprisonment, it quickly collapsed.

The desperate situation faced by the Volunteers meant that protest from hardliners was muted. Those who were critical of the decision to end the war, such as Mary MacSwiney, were given a blunt explanation of the realities.

> You speak as if we were dictating terms and talk . . . of a military situation. There is no military situation. The situation now is that we have to shepherd the remnant of our forces out of this fight so as not to destroy whatever hope remains in the future by allowing the fight to peter out ignominiously.[3]

The legacy of the civil war

By May 1923 the pro-Treaty government had won a complete victory and had total control of the new state. However, the traumatic birth of the state was to have hugely negative legacies. Although the civil war was in many ways a limited conflict it was to have a profound and enduring impact on the Ireland which emerged in its aftermath.

Perhaps the most notable fact about the civil war was that the north-east played so little part in the conflict with the civil war allowing for, if anything, the further strengthening of partition. The civil war did much to confirm Unionist prejudices about the violent and perfidious nature of Irish nationalism. Having survived near collapse in May–June 1922, the war offered the Northern Irish government the chance to consolidate its position and reinforce its control of the province. The few remaining active IRA Volunteers made their way south to participate in the conflict and the enormous pressure which had been placed on the Unionist government during the first six months of 1922 was eased. In August 1922 Winston Churchill was able to report:

> In the area of the Northern Government the position had sensibly improved: murders and incendiarism had almost entirely ceased, and a state of quiescence established. This might be due to the fact that the gunmen were engaged in the South . . . With their return there might be a

recrudescence of outrage, but at the moment life in Belfast had almost become normal.[4]

The civil war remained solidly a southern phenomenon. Aside from a few incursions in areas such as South Armagh and West Tyrone where the civil war spilled over the frontier, there was virtually no fighting within Northern Ireland. The IRA in the North, shorn of its crucial southern support and suffering expulsion or imprisonment under the Special Powers Act, was almost totally destroyed as a functioning organisation. It would not revive in any meaningful way until the late 1960s and the onset of the 'Troubles'. By the time the partition issue was raised again in 1924 with the ill fated Boundary Commission the context had almost entirely changed. In the event, it was only well after their defeat in the civil war that anti-Treaty Irish Republicans seriously considered whether to take armed action against British rule in Northern Ireland, the first serious suggestion to do this coming only in the late 1930s.

Partition and civil war left the Dublin government with a moth-eaten state to run. Even without the war the new state faced an incredibly difficult economic situation. Indeed one of the reasons the Free State Army was able to grow so quickly had much to do with the large number of unemployed Irishmen desperate to find work of any kind. The war crippled the new state financially costing over £17 million to fight with almost twice as much caused in damage, a direct result of the IRA's campaign against economic targets later in the war.

The most lasting legacy of the civil war however was political. The use of coercive emergency powers by the Free State government certainly shortened the duration of the war but compromised the Free State government's popularity in the longer term. The Free State executions and atrocities were never forgotten with even the mention of 'the 77' poisoning debate. There was no political consensus to rebuild the new state in the aftermath of the war and it left a dysfunctional political culture in the south from which it has barely recovered from decades afterward. The Treaty and Civil War would define Irish politics with the two major political parties, Fine Gael and Fianna Fail, emerging to represent the pro- and anti-Treaty sides respectively. It was not until the 1970s that Ireland's prominent politicians ceased to be veterans of the civil war with the dominance of the civil war division stifling other more expansive political ideologies, particularly on the left where the Labour party came a poor third in all elections until as recently as 2010. Even more, due to the messy end of the war and the lack of any form of negotiated peace, the IRA and its Republican irredentism endured in various forms, becoming the predominant ideology of Nationalist extremists in Northern Ireland during the 'Troubles'.

Although short-lived the civil war was a brutal affair. There are no reliable figures concerning the number of deaths in the civil war although current estimates are that it was somewhere around 4,000–6,000 consisting of 800 pro-Treaty deaths and 1,200 Republicans with the rest, as in all the conflicts of the revolutionary period, made up of civilians. However, it was less a case of how many were killed than who they were. For such a small country as Ireland the loss of almost an entire leadership class, in the shape of Collins, Brugha, Lynch, Griffith, Mellowes, Childers, etc., was a heavy blow to bear.

So damaging had the civil war been it is worth asking what the conflict had been about. With the Treaty lying at the heart of the conflict most analysis focuses on its perfidious influence. As such there is, as with all civil wars, but especially in Ireland, a sense of futility and wastefulness about the civil war, which was seen largely as a pointless conflict between Tweedledum and Tweedledee. Some historians further argue that there were no profound ideological differences between the two sides who can best be described as pro-Treaty pragmatists and anti-Treaty idealists. The Irish Civil War in such analysis was an unnecessary war.

However, other historians have argued that the war had less to do with the semantics of the Treaty but can be better understood as a confrontation between democracy and dictatorship. In such arguments the civil war was a victory for the democratic political tradition within Irish nationalism, which Sinn Fein had inherited from the old Home Rule party, over the militarism of the IRA and their nineteenth-century forebears in the IRB. Sinn Fein itself had merely been a flag of convenience, an artificial alliance of two intrinsically oppositional worldviews. The Provisional Government was by this argument carrying out its duty to enforce the democratically expressed will of the people it represented. In 1932 this commitment to democracy was demonstrated markedly when the old pro-Treaty side handed over power to the first elected majority government formed by its old rivals on the anti-Treaty side, now reconstituted as Fianna Fail. Despite the countless other examples of post-colonial struggles falling under the sway of a military dictatorship, this was not the case with Ireland where the principles of popular sovereignty won out and Ireland became a functioning liberal democracy.

However, it is unfair to paint Republican opposition as merely anti-democratic or based on irrational romanticism as so many historians have done. Indeed if the Irish revolution was driven by anything it was idealism rather than more pragmatic goals such as land reform or religious freedom. It was a revolution about Nationalist symbols. The importance of those symbols, whose perceived sacrifice so many Republicans saw in the Anglo-Irish Treaty, would be demonstrated markedly by the fact that for the next quarter of a century Irish political culture would be defined by attempts to regain those symbols and the sovereignties they represented. Indeed that is what the revolution in a very profound sense had been about.

Sample essay and examination questions

Why was Republican military opposition overcome so easily?
Assess the impact of the civil war on Irish political culture.

Who were the winners and losers in the civil war?
To what extent did the severity of Free State government security policy win the war at the expense of long-term popularity?

Further reading

A. Dolan, *Commemorating the Irish Civil War* (Cambridge, 2006)

R. Dwyer, *Michael Collins and the Civil War* (Cork, 2012)

T. Garvin, *1922: The Birth of Irish Democracy* (Dublin, 1996)

M. Hayes, 'Dáil Eireann and the Irish Civil War', *Studies: An Irish Quarterly Review*, 58, no. 229 (Spring 1969)

M. A. Hopkinson, *Green Against Green* (Dublin, 1988)

M. Ryan, *Liam Lynch: The Real Chief* (Cork, 2012)

C. Younger, *Ireland's Civil War* (London, 1982)

Conclusion

The most lasting legacy of the Irish Revolution would be the two states which emerged in its aftermath. Despite their mutual antipathy it is remarkable how similar the experience of these two new Irelands had been. Both had shared a similarly traumatic birth resisting fiercely attempts by political or religious minorities to undermine the authority of the new states. Both of the two dominant ideologies in Ireland in the form of constitutional nationalism and Ulster Unionism would triumph largely by marginalising the influence of radical Republicans, northern Catholics, southern Unionists and labour activists, who had all played a prominent role in the revolution.

Both states were certainly defined by their experience in the revolutionary period. However, while in the south the bitterness of the civil war suffused all parts of the political culture, there also emerged a democratic consensus and a functioning parliamentary political system. This was shown markedly with the transformation of the anti-Treaty side of the Sinn Fein movement into Fianna Fail, a populist Nationalist party founded in 1926 under Eamon de Valera. Fianna Fail, whilst Republican in doctrine, remained wedded to constitutionalism and broke away from the physical force side of the movement leaving a militarist IRA to endure. Despite some notable periods of activity: the assassination of Kevin O'Higgins in 1927; street fighting with the 'fascist' Blueshirts in the 1930s; and various abortive campaigns against the British, most notably in 1939 and 1956–62, the organisation never had enough power to seriously challenge the new democratic status in the twenty-six counties with the Dublin governments of all shades prepared to use coercive legislation against them. This victory of democracy was demonstrated markedly in 1927 when Fianna Fail members entered the Dáil, dismissing their signing of the oath as 'merely a form of words', to be followed by the formation of their first government under de Valera in 1932. While many were concerned that the pro-Treaty party, Cumann na nGaedheal, would not relinquish power, in the end they moved dutifully into political opposition.

Politically, southern politics was dominated by two key dynamics: reconstruction and constitutional change. Economically, the south was a virtually bankrupt state after the civil war whose total cost including military expenditure and material destruction was well over £50 million. The pro-Treaty government of Cumann na nGaedheal pursued a conservative economic policy and managed to build up support amongst Irish elites including notably ex-Unionists and larger farming interests in the Irish provinces. Viewed as parsimonious by many, the government closely followed British Treasury practices in order to balance their strained budgets, making numerous unpopular cuts to public expenditure. In 1924, the Minister for Industry and Commerce, Patrick McGilligan, crudely spelled out the implications of this policy when he said that 'people may have to die in this country and die of starvation'. The fact that the revolution did little to overthrow the conservative structures of Irish economic life meant that the Free State was able to achieve stability fairly rapidly in the wake of the civil war. Indeed Cumann na nGaedheal presented themselves as the party of law and order and economic stability with little intention of continuing the revolutionary struggle by other means. The Anglo-Irish Treaty thus became less a regrettable but pragmatic compromise, as defined by Michael Collins, but rather a key foundation document on which the new state was built.

Fianna Fail made a number of key constitutional changes, including the introduction of a virtual Republican constitution in 1937. The power of this new constitutional arrangement was shown markedly when Ireland chose neutrality during the Second World War, with the creation of a full Republic following soon after in 1949, demonstrating ironically how adept de Valera had proved in carrying out Michael Collins' strategy of using 'freedom to achieve freedom'. The obsession with stability and more rarefied constitutional change which so defined the two major political parties in the south meant that there was little room for any radical attempts to end partition. Although rhetorically the issue of the north was given a high profile, little in the way of constructive political initiatives followed. The southern state certainly did little to reassure Irish Protestants and independence was marked by a consensus over the issues of Catholicising and Gaelicising the new state. In 1925 divorce was outlawed and by 1930 a clerical-dominated censorship board had been established. A good working knowledge of the Irish language was made compulsory for the school leaving certificate and for employment in the state's civil service. The steady decline of the southern Protestant population, although having multifarious causes, was no doubt a sign of their growing isolation from the mainstream ideology of the new state.

In the north by contrast a rapprochement with previous political opponents in the northern Catholic minority was never achieved. Compared to the south the sheer size of the minority religious population in the north and its deeply held commitment to see the end of partition, meant that repression and exclusion was the option chosen by the Belfast government. The safeguards of Proportional Representation for elections enshrined in the Government of Ireland Act were removed by the Belfast government in 1922 for local elections and in 1929 for the Northern Ireland parliament. This led to the return of a comfortable Unionist majority in the Northern Irish parliament, sustained over many decades by the gerrymandering of political boundaries in a number of prominent councils in the west of the province, most notably Derry City itself. This was added to by discrimination in employment terms of both the private and public sector and in the allocation of housing leading to widespread unemployment and deprivation in many Catholic communities.

Despite opposition to home rule being its defining ideological principle, the Unionist government quickly moved to embrace the idea after the establishment of the Northern state with the Government of Ireland Act. Control of its own devolved legislature and executive gave Unionists a safeguard against what it increasingly came to believe was a fickle and potentially treacherous British Government. In particular the perceived hostility of the Catholic minority meant that local control of security and law and order legislation was crucial for Unionist security. The Northern state also maintained its coercive legislation with the eventual permanent adoption of the Special Powers Act and the part-time 'B' Specials whose numbers would remain at almost 12,000 long after the IRA threat had receded, almost three times the size of the official police force in the shape of the RUC. While Catholic membership was officially encouraged, the security forces remained overwhelmingly Protestant in terms of their membership, increasingly so as the post-revolutionary period drew on and older Catholic RIC men who had made the switch to the new force retired.

In many senses the Northern Irish government, unlike the south, never managed to get over the traumatic nature of its birth, remaining in a virtual state of emergency for the fifty years of its existence. Under such circumstances politics ossified as did northern nationalism as a proactive political force. Despite efforts by Belfast Nationalists to encourage minority participation in the Belfast parliament, the more numerous and radical Catholics in the west of the six counties, where lingering hopes of a favourable boundary settlement were slow to fade, continued to insist on a policy of abstention. Indeed it was not until the 1960s that northern Catholics managed to create a broad-based political movement with calls for an end to civil rights abuses leading to further conflict in the shape of the 'Troubles'. As such in many senses the Irish Revolution instigated by Sinn Fein after the Easter Rising remains for many unfinished. Ironically, while partition itself was to play a minor role in the deliberations of Irish Nationalists, its continuation despite decades of violence and political agitation is still the greatest legacy of the revolution on the island. It would only be if the aspiration shared by many of ending partition and reuniting the country peacefully through mutual understanding was achieved, that Ireland could finally be said to have escaped its past and brought a final end to the Irish Revolution.

DOCUMENTS

DOCUMENT 1: Ulster's Solemn League and Covenant (for men)

BEING CONVINCED in our consciences that Home Rule would be disastrous to the material well-being of Ulster as well as of the whole of Ireland, subversive of our civil and religious freedom, destructive of our citizenship, and perilous to the unity of the Empire, we, whose names are underwritten, men of Ulster, loyal subjects of His Gracious Majesty King George V., humbly relying on the God whom our fathers in days of stress and trial confidently trusted, do hereby pledge ourselves in solemn Covenant, throughout this our time of threatened calamity, to stand by one another in defending, for ourselves and our children, our cherished position of equal citizenship in the United Kingdom, and in using all means which may be found necessary to defeat the present conspiracy to set up a Home Rule Parliament in Ireland.

And in the event of such a Parliament being forced upon us, we further solemnly and mutually pledge ourselves to refuse to recognize its authority. In sure confidence that God will defend the right, we hereto subscribe our names.

Source: Buckland, P. *Irish Unionism: The Anglo-Irish and the New Ireland, 1885–1923: A Documentary History* (HM Stationery Office, 1973), p. 224.

DOCUMENT 2: The Ulster Declaration (for women)

We, whose names are underwritten, women of Ulster, and loyal subjects of our gracious King, being firmly persuaded that Home Rule would be disastrous to our Country, desire to associate ourselves with the men of Ulster in their uncompromising opposition to the Home Rule Bill now before Parliament, whereby it is proposed to drive Ulster out of her cherished place in the Constitution of the United Kingdom, and to place her under the domination and control of a Parliament in Ireland.

Praying that from this calamity God will save Ireland, we hereto subscribe our names.

Source: Buckland, P. *Irish Unionism, 1885–1923: A Documentary History* (HM Stationery Office, 1973), p. 225.

DOCUMENT 3: John Redmond's speech at Woodenbridge, 20 September 1914

Wicklow Volunteers in spite of the peaceful happiness and beauty of the scene in which we stand, remember this country at this moment is in a state of war, and your duty is two-fold. Your duty is, at all costs to defend the shores of Ireland from foreign invasion. It is a duty, more than that of taking care that Irish valour proves itself on the field of war, as it has always proved itself in the past. The interests of Ireland as a whole are at stake in this war. This war is undertaken in defence of the highest principles of religion, morality and right, and it would be a disgrace for ever to our country, a reproach to her manhood, and a denial of the lessons of her history, if young Irishmen confined their efforts to remaining at home to defend the shores of Ireland from an unlikely invasion and shrinking from the duty of proving upon the field of battle that gallantry and courage which have distinguished your race all through its history. I say to you, therefore, your duty is two-fold. I am glad to see such magnificent material for soldiers around me, and I say to you, go on drilling and make yourselves efficient, and then account yourselves as men, not only in Ireland itself, but wherever the firing line extends in defence of right, of freedom and religion in this war.

Source: *Irish Independent*, 21 September 1914.

DOCUMENT 4: Patrick Pearse's graveside oration at the funeral of Jeremiah O'Donovan Rossa, Glasnevin Cemetery, Dublin, 1 August 1915

It has seemed right, before we turn away from this place in which we have laid the mortal remains of O'Donovan Rossa, that one among us should, in the name of all, speak the praise of that valiant man, and endeavour to formulate the thought and the hope that are in us as we stand around his grave. And if there is anything that makes it fitting that I, rather than some other, rather than one of the grey-haired men who were young with him and shared in his labour and in his suffering, should speak here, it is perhaps that I may be taken as speaking on behalf of a new generation that has been re-baptised in the Fenian faith, and that has accepted the responsibility of carrying out the Fenian programme. I propose to you then that, here by the grave of this unrepentant Fenian, we renew our baptismal vows; that, here by the grave of this unconquered and unconquerable man, we ask of God, each one for himself, such unshakable purpose, such high and gallant courage, such unbreakable strength of soul as belonged to O'Donovan Rossa.

Deliberately here we avow ourselves, as he avowed himself in the dock, Irishmen of one allegiance only. We of the Irish Volunteers, and you others who are associated with us in to-day's task and duty, are bound together and must stand together henceforth in brotherly union for the achievement of the freedom of Ireland. And we know only one definition of freedom: it is Tone's definition, it is Mitchel's definition, it is Rossa's definition. Let no man blaspheme the cause that the dead generations of Ireland served by giving it any other name and definition than their name and their definition.

We stand at Rossa's grave not in sadness but rather in exaltation of spirit that it has been given to us to come thus into so close a communion with that brave and splendid Gael. Splendid and holy causes are served by men who are themselves splendid and holy. O'Donovan Rossa was splendid in the proud manhood of him, splendid in the heroic grace of him, splendid in the Gaelic strength and clarity and truth of him. And all that splendour and pride and strength was compatible with a humility and a simplicity of devotion to Ireland, to all that was olden and beautiful and Gaelic in Ireland, the holiness and simplicity of patriotism of a Michael O'Clery or of an Eoghan O'Growney. The clear true eyes of this man almost alone in his day visioned Ireland as we of to-day would surely have her: not free merely, but Gaelic as well; not Gaelic merely, but free as well.

In a closer spiritual communion with him now than ever before or perhaps ever again, in a spiritual communion with those of his day, living and dead, who suffered with him in English prisons, in communion of spirit too with our own dear comrades who suffer in English prisons to-day, and speaking on their behalf as well as our own, we pledge to Ireland our love, and we pledge to English rule in Ireland our hate. This is a place of peace, sacred to the dead, where men should speak with all charity and with all restraint; but I hold it a Christian thing, as O'Donovan Rossa held it, to hate evil, to hate untruth, to hate oppression, and, hating them, to strive to overthrow them. Our foes are strong and wise and wary; but, strong and wise and wary as they are, they cannot undo the miracles of God who ripens in the hearts of young men the seeds sown by the young men of a former generation. And the seeds sown by the young men of '65 and '67 are coming to their miraculous ripening to-day. Rulers and Defenders of Realms had need to be wary if they would guard against such processes. Life springs from death; and from the graves of patriot men and women spring living nations. The Defenders of this Realm have worked well in secret and in the open. They think that they have pacified Ireland. They think that they have purchased half of us and intimidated the other half. They think that they have foreseen everything, think that they have provided against everything; but the fools, the fools, the fools! — they have left us our Fenian dead, and while Ireland holds these graves, Ireland unfree shall never be at peace.

Source: *Collected Works of Padraic H. Pearse: Political Writings and Speeches* (Dublin, 1922), p. 125.

DOCUMENT 5: The Easter Proclamation of the Irish Republic

IRISHMEN AND IRISHWOMEN: In the name of God and of the dead generations from which she receives her old tradition of nationhood, Ireland, through us, summons her children to her flag and strikes for her freedom.

Having organised and trained her manhood through her secret revolutionary organisation, the Irish Republican Brotherhood, and through her open military organisations, the Irish Volunteers and the Irish Citizen Army, having patiently perfected her discipline, having resolutely waited for the right moment to reveal itself, she now seizes that moment, and, supported by her exiled children in America and by gallant allies in Europe, but relying in the first on her own strength, she strikes in full confidence of victory.

We declare the right of the people of Ireland to the ownership of Ireland, and to the unfettered control of Irish destinies, to be sovereign and indefeasible. The long usurpation of that right by a foreign people and government has not extinguished the right, nor can it ever be extinguished except by the destruction of the Irish people. In every generation the Irish people have asserted their right to national freedom and sovereignty: six times during the past three hundred years they have asserted it in arms. Standing on that fundamental right and again asserting it in arms in the face of the world, we hereby proclaim the Irish Republic as a Sovereign Independent State, and we pledge our lives and the lives of our comrades-in-arms to the cause of its freedom, of its welfare, and its exaltation among the nations.

The Irish Republic is entitled to, and hereby claims, the allegiance of every Irishman and Irishwoman. The Republic guarantees religious and civil liberty, equal rights and equal opportunities to all its citizens, and declares its resolve to pursue the happiness and prosperity of the whole nation and of all its parts, cherishing all the children of the nation equally, and oblivious of the differences carefully fostered by an alien government, which have divided a minority from the majority in the past.

Until our arms have brought the opportune moment for the establishment of a permanent National Government, representative of the whole people of Ireland and elected by the suffrages of all her men and women, the Provisional Government, hereby constituted, will administer the civil and military affairs of the Republic in trust for the people.

We place the cause of the Irish Republic under the protection of the Most High God, Whose blessing we invoke upon our arms, and we pray that no one who serves that cause will dishonour it by cowardice, inhumanity, or rapine. In this supreme hour the Irish nation must, by its valour and discipline and by the readiness of its children to sacrifice themselves for the common good, prove itself worthy of the august destiny to which it is called.

signed on behalf of the Provisional Government

Thomas J. Clarke,
Sean MacDiarmada, Thomas MacDonagh
P. H. Pearse, Eamon Ceannt
James Connolly, Joseph Plunkett
Source: Dunne, S. (ed.) *The Irish Anthology*
(Dublin, 1997), pp. 264–5.

DOCUMENT 6: Sinn Fein general election manifesto, December 1918 (Extracts)

GENERAL ELECTION — MANIFESTO TO THE IRISH PEOPLE

THE coming General Election is fraught with vital possibilities for the future of our nation. Ireland is faced with the question whether this generation wills it that she is to march out into the full sunlight of freedom, or is to remain in the shadow of a base imperialism that has brought and ever will bring in its train naught but evil for our race.

Sinn Féin gives Ireland the opportunity of vindicating her honour and pursuing with renewed confidence the path of national salvation by rallying to the flag of the Irish Republic.

Sinn Féin aims at securing the establishment of that Republic.

1. By withdrawing the Irish Representation from the British Parliament and by denying the right and opposing the will of the British Government or any other foreign Government to legislate for Ireland.

2. By making use of any and every means available to render impotent the power of England to hold Ireland in subjection by military force or otherwise.

3. By the establishment of a constituent assembly comprising persons chosen by Irish constituencies as the supreme national authority to speak and act in the name of the Irish people, and to develop Ireland's social, political and industrial life, for the welfare of the whole people of Ireland.

4. By appealing to the Peace Conference for the establishment of Ireland as an Independent Nation . . .

Sinn Féin stands less for a political party than for the Nation; it represents the old tradition of nationhood handed on from dead generations; it stands by the Proclamation of the Provisional Government of Easter, 1916, reasserting the inalienable right of the Irish Nation to sovereign independence, reaffirming the determination of the Irish people to achieve it, and guaranteeing within the independent Nation equal rights and equal opportunities to all its citizens.

The policy of our opponents stands condemned on any test, whether of principle or expediency. The right of a nation to sovereign independence rests upon immutable natural law and cannot be made the subject of a compromise . . .

Those who have endeavoured to harness the people of Ireland to England's war-chariot, ignoring the fact that only a freely-elected Government in a free Ireland has power to decide for Ireland the question of peace and war, have forfeited the right to speak for the Irish people . . .

The present Irish members of the English Parliament constitute an obstacle to be removed from the path that leads to the Peace Conference . . .

Sinn Féin goes to the polls handicapped by all the arts and contrivances that a powerful and unscrupulous enemy can use against us. Conscious of the power of Sinn Féin to secure the freedom of Ireland the British Government would destroy it. Sinn Féin, however, goes to the polls confident that the people of this ancient nation will be true to the old cause and will vote for the men who stand by the principles of Tone, Emmet, Mitchel, Pearse and Connolly, the men who disdain to whine to the enemy for favours, the men who hold that Ireland must be as free as England or Holland, Switzerland or France, and whose demand is that the only status befitting this ancient realm is the status of a free nation.

ISSUED BY THE STANDING COMMITTEE OF SINN FÉIN
    Source: National Library of Ireland, MS. 25,588 (no. 54).

DOCUMENT 7: Declaration of Independence

Whereas the Irish people is by right a free people:

And Whereas for seven hundred years the Irish people has never ceased to repudiate and has repeatedly protested in arms against foreign usurpation:

And Whereas English rule in this country is, and always has been, based upon force and fraud and maintained by military occupation against the declared will of the people:

And Whereas the Irish Republic was proclaimed in Dublin on Easter Monday, 1916, by the Irish Republican Army acting on behalf of the Irish people:

And Whereas the Irish people is resolved to secure and maintain its complete independence in order to promote the common weal, to re-establish justice, to provide for future defence, to insure peace at home and goodwill with all nations and to constitute a national polity based upon the people's will with equal right and equal opportunity for every citizen:

And Whereas at the threshold of a new era in history the Irish electorate has in the General Election of December, 1918, seized the first occasion to declare by an overwhelming majority its firm allegiance to the Irish Republic:

Now, therefore, we, the elected Representatives of the ancient Irish people in National Parliament assembled, do, in the name of the Irish nation, ratify the establishment of the Irish Republic and pledge ourselves and our people to make this declaration effective by every means at our command:

We ordain that the elected Representatives of the Irish people alone have power to make laws binding on the people of Ireland, and that the Irish Parliament is the only Parliament to which that people will give its allegiance:

We solemnly declare foreign government in Ireland to be an invasion of our national right which we will never tolerate, and we demand the evacuation of our country by the English Garrison.

We claim for our national independence the recognition and support of every free nation in the world, and we proclaim that independence to be a condition precedent to international peace hereafter:

In the name of the Irish people we humbly commit our destiny to Almighty God who gave our fathers the courage and determination to persevere through long centuries of a ruthless tyranny, and strong in the justice of the cause which they have handed down to us, we ask His divine blessing on this the last stage of the struggle we have pledged ourselves to carry through to Freedom.

Source: Minutes of the proceedings of the first parliament of the republic of Ireland, 1919–1921, official record (Dublin Stationery Office, 1994), pp. 14–16.

DOCUMENT 8: Dáil Eireann address to the free nations of the world, 21 January 1919

To the Nations of the World—Greeting

The Nation of Ireland having proclaimed her national independence, calls, through her elected representatives in Parliament assembled in the Irish Capital on January 21, 1919, upon every free nation to support the Irish Republic by recognising Ireland's national status and her right to its vindication at the Peace Congress.

Naturally, the race, the language, the customs and traditions of Ireland are radically distinct from the English. Ireland is one of the most ancient nations in Europe, and she has preserved her national integrity, vigorous and intact, through seven centuries of foreign oppression; she has never relinquished her national rights, and throughout the long era of English usurpation she has in every generation defiantly proclaimed her inalienable right of nationhood down to her last glorious resort to arms in 1916.

Internationally, Ireland is the gateway to the Atlantic; Ireland is the last outpost of Europe towards the West; Ireland is the point upon which great trade routes between East and West converge; her independence is demanded by the Freedom of the Seas; her great harbours must be open to all nations, instead of being the monopoly of England. To-day these harbours are empty and idle solely because English policy is determined to retain Ireland as a barren bulwark for English aggrandisement, and the unique geographical position of this island, far from being a benefit and safeguard to Europe and America, is subjected to the purposes of England's policy of world domination.

Ireland to-day reasserts her historic nationhood the more confidently before the new world emerging from the war, because she believes in freedom and justice as the fundamental principles of international law; because she believes in a frank co-operation between the peoples for equal rights against the vested privileges of ancient tyrannies; because the permanent peace of Europe can never be secured by perpetuating military dominion for the profit of empire but only by establishing the control of government in every land upon the basis of the free will of a free people, and the existing state of war, between Ireland and England, can never be ended until Ireland is definitely evacuated by the armed forces of England.

For these among other reasons, Ireland—resolutely and irrevocably determined at the dawn of the promised era of self-determination and liberty that she will suffer foreign dominion no longer—calls upon every free nation to uphold her national claim to complete independence as an Irish Republic against the arrogant pretensions of England founded in fraud and sustained only by an overwhelming military occupation, and demands to be confronted publicly with England at the Congress of the Nations, that the civilised world having judged between English wrong and Irish right may guarantee to Ireland its permanent support for the maintenance of her national independence.

Source: Minutes of the proceedings of the first parliament
of the republic of Ireland, 1919–1921, official record
(Dublin Stationery Office, 1994), p. 20.

DOCUMENT 9: Democratic Programme of Dáil Eireann

We declare in the words of the Irish Republican Proclamation the right of the people of Ireland to the ownership of Ireland, and to the unfettered control of Irish destinies to be indefeasible, and in the language of our first President, Pádraíg Mac Phiarais, we declare that the Nation's sovereignty extends not only to all men and women of the Nation, but to all its material possessions, the Nation's soil and all its resources, all the wealth and all the wealth-producing processes within the Nation, and with him we reaffirm that all right to private property must be subordinated to the public right and welfare.

We declare that we desire our country to be ruled in accordance with the principles of Liberty, Equality, and Justice for all, which alone can secure permanence of Government in the willing adhesion of the people.

We affirm the duty of every man and woman to give allegiance and service to the Commonwealth, and declare it is the duty of the Nation to assure that every citizen shall have opportunity to spend his or her strength and faculties in the service of the people. In return for willing service, we, in the name of the Republic, declare the right of every citizen to an adequate share of the produce of the Nation's labour.

It shall be the first duty of the Government of the Republic to make provision for the physical, mental and spiritual well-being of the children, to secure that no child shall suffer hunger or cold from lack of food, clothing, or shelter, but that all shall be provided with the means and facilities requisite for their proper education and training as Citizens of a Free and Gaelic Ireland.

The Irish Republic fully realises the necessity of abolishing the present odious, degrading and foreign Poor Law System, substituting therefor a sympathetic native scheme for the care of the Nation's aged and infirm, who shall not be regarded as a burden, but rather entitled to the Nation's gratitude and consideration. Likewise it shall be the duty of the Republic to take such measures as will safeguard the health of the people and ensure the physical as well as the moral well-being of the Nation.

It shall be our duty to promote the development of the Nation's resources, to increase the productivity of its soil, to exploit its mineral deposits, peat bogs, and fisheries, its waterways and harbours, in the interests and for the benefit of the Irish people.

It shall be the duty of the Republic to adopt all measures necessary for the recreation and invigoration of our Industries, and to ensure their being developed on the most beneficial and progressive co-operative and industrial lines. With the adoption of an extensive Irish Consular Service, trade with foreign Nations shall be revived on terms of mutual advantage and goodwill, and while undertaking the organisation of the Nation's trade, import and export, it shall be the duty of the Republic to prevent the shipment from Ireland of food and other necessaries until the wants of the Irish people are fully satisfied and the future provided for.

It shall also devolve upon the National Government to seek co-operation of the Governments of other countries in determining a standard of Social and Industrial Legislation with a view to a general and lasting improvement in the conditions under which the working classes live and labour.

Source: Minutes of the proceedings of the first parliament
of the republic of Ireland, 1919–1921, official record
(Dublin Stationery Office, 1994), pp. 22–3.

DOCUMENT 10: The Government of Ireland Act (Extracts)

(1) On and after the appointed day there shall be established for Southern Ireland a Parliament to be called the Parliament of Southern Ireland consisting of His Majesty, the Senate of Southern Ireland, and the House of Commons of Southern Ireland, and there shall be established for Northern Ireland a Parliament to be

called the Parliament of Northern Ireland consisting of His Majesty, the Senate of Northern Ireland, and the House of Commons of Northern Ireland.

(2) For the purposes of this Act, Northern Ireland shall consist of the parliamentary counties of Antrim, Armagh, Down, Fermanagh, Londonderry and Tyrone, and the parliamentary boroughs of Belfast and Londonderry, and Southern Ireland shall consist of so much of Ireland as is not comprised within the said parliamentary counties and boroughs.

2. Constitution of Council of Ireland. –

(1) With a view to the eventual establishment of a Parliament for the whole of Ireland, and to bringing about harmonious action between the parliaments and governments of Southern Ireland and Northern Ireland, and to the promotion of mutual intercourse and uniformity in relation to matters affecting the whole of Ireland, and to providing for the administration of services which the two parliaments mutually agree should be administered uniformly throughout the whole of Ireland, or which by virtue of this Act are to be so administered, there shall be constituted, as soon as may be after the appointed day, a Council to be called the Council of Ireland.

(2) Subject as hereinafter provided, the Council of Ireland shall consist of a person nominated by the Lord Lieutenant acting in accordance with instructions from His Majesty who shall be President and forty other persons, of whom seven shall be members of the Senate of Southern Ireland, thirteen shall be members of the House of Commons of Southern Ireland, seven shall be members of the Senate of Northern Ireland, and thirteen shall be members of the House of Commons of Northern Ireland.

The members of the Council of Ireland shall be elected in each case by the members of that House of the Parliament of Southern Ireland or Northern Ireland of which they are members . . .

3. Power to establish a Parliament for the whole of Ireland. –

(1) The Parliaments of Southern Ireland and Northern Ireland may, by identical Acts agreed to by an absolute majority of members of the House of Commons of each Parliament at the third reading (hereinafter referred to as constituent Acts), establish, in lieu of the Council of Ireland, a Parliament for the whole of Ireland consisting of His Majesty and two Houses . . .

(2) On the date of Irish union the Council of Ireland shall cease to exist and there shall be transferred to the Parliament and

Government of Ireland all powers then exercisable by the Council of Ireland, and (except so far as the constituent Acts otherwise provide) the matters which under this Act cease to be reserved matters at the date of Irish union, and any other powers for the joint exercise of which by the Parliaments or Governments of Southern and Northern Ireland provision has been made under this Act . . .

4. Legislative powers of Irish Parliaments. –

1 Subject to the provisions of this Act, the Parliament of Southern Ireland and the Parliament of Northern Ireland shall respectively have power to make laws for the peace, order, and good government of Southern Ireland and Northern Ireland with the following limitations, namely, that they shall not have power to make laws except in respect of matters exclusively relating to the portion of Ireland within their jurisdiction, or some part thereof, and (without prejudice to that general limitation) that they shall not have power to make laws in respect of the following matters in particular, namely: –

(1) The Crown . . . or the Lord Lieutenant, except as respects the exercise of his executive power in relation to Irish services as defined for the purposes of this Act . . .

(2) The making of peace or war, or matters arising from a state of war . . .

(3) The navy, the army, the air force, the territorial force . . .

(4) Treaties, or any relations with foreign states, or relations with other parts of His Majesty's dominions . . .

(5) Dignities or titles of honour;

(6) Treason, treason felony, alienage, naturalization, or aliens as such, or domicile . . .

(7) Trade with any place out of the part of Ireland within their jurisdiction, except so far as trade may be affected by the exercise of the powers of taxation given to the said parliaments, or by regulations . . .

(8) Submarine cables;

(9) Wireless telegraphy;

(10) Aerial navigation;

(11) Lighthouses, buoys, or beacons . . .

(12) Coinage; legal tender; negotiable instruments . . .

(13) Trade marks, designs, merchandise marks, copyright, or patent rights; or

(14) Any matter which by this Act is declared to be a reserved matter, so long as it remains reserved. Any law made in contravention of the limitations imposed by this section shall, so far as it contravenes those limitations, be void . . .

8. Executive Power. –

(1) The executive power in Southern Ireland and in Northern Ireland shall continue vested in His Majesty the King, and nothing in this Act shall affect the exercise of that power. . .

> Source: http://www.legislation.gov.uk/ukpga/1920/67/pdfs/
> ukpga_19200067_en.pdf [accessed 2 June 2014].

DOCUMENT 11: Fred Crawford's description of his visit to Lisburn after the violence expulsion of Catholics from the town following the assassination of Oswald Swanzy on 22 August 1920

It reminded me of a French town after it had been bombarded by the Germans as I saw in France 1916. We visited the ruins of the Priest's house on Chapel Hill. It was burnt or gutted and the furniture all destroyed. When coming down the avenue I found a small pair of manicure scissors that had been through the fire. I kept them as a souvenir of the event. We called at Mr Stephenson's and had tea there. Mrs Thompson his sister was also with him. They told me of some very hard cases of where Unionists had lost practically all they had by the fire of the house of a Catholic spreading to theirs, and also of some very decent respectable families of the brutal cold blooded murder of Inspector Swanzie [sic] one does not wonder at the mob loosing [sic] its head with fury . . . it has been stated that there are only four of five RC [Roman Catholic] families left in Lisburn. Others say this is wrong that there are far more. Be that as it may there certainly are practically no shops or places of business left to the RC's.

> Source: Buckland, P. *Irish Unionism: The Anglo-Irish and the
> New Ireland 1885–1923: A Documentary History*
> (HM Stationery Office, 1973), p. 445.

DOCUMENT 12: Speech of King George V on the occasion of the opening of the Northern Ireland parliament, June 1921

Members of the Senate and of the House of Commons

For all who love Ireland, as I do with all my heart, this is a profoundly moving occasion in Irish history. My memories of the Irish people date back to the time when I spent many happy days in Ireland as a midshipman. My affection for the Irish people has been deepened by the successive visits since that time, and I have watched with constant sympathy the course of their affairs.

I could not have allowed myself to give Ireland by deputy alone. My earnest prayers and good wishes in the new era which opens with this ceremony, and I have therefore come in person, as the Head of the Empire, to inaugurate this Parliament on Irish soil.

I inaugurate it with deep-felt hope, and I feel assured that you will do your utmost to make it an instrument of happiness and good government for all parts of the community which you represent.

This is a great and critical occasion in the history of the Six Counties, but not for the Six Counties alone, for everything which interests them touches Ireland, and everything which touches Ireland finds an echo in the remotest parts of the Empire.

Few things are more earnestly desired throughout the English speaking world than a satisfactory solution of the age long Irish problems, which for generations embarrassed our forefathers, as they now weigh heavily upon us.

Most certainly there is no wish nearer My own heart than that every man of Irish birth, whatever be his creed and wherever be his home, should work in loyal co-operation with the free communities on which the British Empire is based.

I am confident that the important matters entrusted to the control and guidance of the Northern Parliament will be managed with wisdom and with moderation, with fairness and due regard to every faith and interest, and with no abatement of that patriotic devotion to the Empire which you proved so gallantly in the Great War.

Full partnership in the United Kingdom and religious freedom Ireland has long enjoyed. She now has conferred upon her the duty of dealing with all the essential tasks of domestic legislation and government; and I feel no misgiving as to the spirit in which you who stand here to-day will carry out the all important functions entrusted to your care.

My hope is broader still. The eyes of the whole Empire are on Ireland to-day, that Empire in which so many nations and races have come together in spite of ancient feuds, and in which new nations have come to birth within the lifetime of the youngest in this Hall.

I am emboldened by that thought to look beyond the sorrow and the anxiety which have clouded of late My vision of Irish affairs. I speak from a full heart when I pray that My coming to Ireland to-day may prove to be the first step towards an end of strife amongst her people, whatever their race or creed. In that hope, I appeal to all Irishmen to pause, to stretch out the hand of forbearance and conciliation, to forgive and to forget, and to join in making for the land which they love a new era of peace, contentment, and goodwill.

It is My earnest desire that in Southern Ireland, too, there may ere long take place a parallel to what is now passing in this Hall; that there a similar occasion may present itself and a similar ceremony be performed.

For this the Parliament of the United Kingdom has in the fullest measure provided the powers; for this the Parliament of Ulster is pointing the way. The future lies in the hands of My Irish people themselves.

May this historic gathering be the prelude of a day in which the Irish people, North and South, under one Parliament or two, as those Parliaments may themselves decide, shall work together in common love for Ireland upon the sure foundations of mutual justice and respect.

Source: Northern Ireland Parliamentary Debates,
House of Commons, vol. 1, 19–22, 22 June.

DOCUMENT 13: Lady Craig recalling the visit of the King to Belfast in June 1921

The great day. The King and Queen have the most wonderful reception, the decorations everywhere are extremely well done and even the little side streets that they will never be within miles of are draped with bunting and flags, and the pavement and lampposts painted red white and blue, really most touching, as a sign of their loyalty. Imagine Radicals in England thinking they would ever succeed in driving people like that out of the British Empire, or wanting to!

Source: Diary of Lady Craig, 22 June 1921, PRONI (D 1415/B/38).

DOCUMENT 14: The Anglo-Irish Treaty (Extracts)

Extracts from the final text of the Articles of Agreement for a Treaty between Great Britain and Ireland as signed in London, 6 December 1921.

ARTICLE 1. Ireland shall have the same constitutional status in the Community of Nations known as the British Empire as the Dominion of Canada, the Commonwealth of Australia, the Dominion of New Zealand, and the Union of South Africa with a Parliament having powers to make laws for the peace order and good government of Ireland and an Executive responsible to that Parliament, and shall be styled and known as the Irish Free State.

ARTICLE 2. Subject to the provisions hereinafter set out the position of the Irish Free State in relation to the Imperial Parliament and Government and otherwise shall be that of the Dominion of Canada, and the law, practice and constitutional usage governing the relationship of the Crown or the representative of the Crown and of the Imperial Parliament to the Dominion of Canada shall govern their relationship to the Irish Free State.

ARTICLE 3. The representative of the Crown in Ireland shall be appointed in like manner as the Governor-General of Canada and in accordance with the practice observed in the making of such appointments.

ARTICLE 4. The oath to be taken by Members of the Parliament of the Irish Free State shall be in the following form:–

I . . . do solemnly swear true faith and allegiance to the Constitution of the Irish Free State as by law established and that I will be faithful to H.M. King George V., his heirs and successors by law, in virtue of the common citizenship of Ireland with Great Britain and her adherence to and membership of the group of nations forming the British Commonwealth of Nations . . .

ARTICLE 5. The Irish Free State shall assume liability for the service of the Public Debt of the United Kingdom as existing as the date hereof and towards the payment of War Pensions as existing at that date in such proportion as may be fair and equitable, having regard to any just claim on the part of Ireland by way of set-off or counter claim, the amount of such sums being determined in default of agreement by the arbitration of one or more independent persons being citizens of the British Empire . . .

ARTICLE 12. If before the expiration of the said month, an address is presented to His Majesty by both Houses of the Parliament of Northern Ireland to that effect, the powers of the Parliament and the Government of the Irish Free State shall no longer extend to Northern Ireland, and the provisions of the Government of Ireland Act, 1920, (including those relating to the Council of Ireland) shall so far as they relate to Northern Ireland, continue to be of full force and effect, and this instrument shall have effect subject to the necessary modifications. Provided that if such an address is so presented a Commission consisting of three persons, one to be appointed by the Government of the Irish Free State, one to be appointed by the Government of Northern Ireland, and one who shall be Chairman to be appointed by the British Government shall determine in accordance with the wishes of the inhabitants, so far as may be compatible with economic and geographic conditions the boundaries between Northern Ireland and the rest of Ireland, and for the purposes of the Government of Ireland Act, 1920, and of this instrument, the boundary of Northern Ireland shall be such as may be determined by such Commission.

(Signed)

On behalf of the British Delegation   On behalf of the Irish Delegation

D. LLOYD GEORGE   ARTHUR GRIFFITH
AUSTEN CHAMBERLAIN   MICHAEL COLLINS
LORD BIRKENHEAD   ROBERT BARTON
WINSTON S. CHURCHILL   EAMON DUGGAN
L. WORTHINGTON-EVANS   GEORGE GAVAN DUFFY
HAMAR GREENWOOD
GORDON HEWART

Source: National Archives of Ireland, Department of the Taoiseach, 2002/5/1.

DOCUMENT 15: Eamon de Valera's Document No. 2

That inasmuch as the "Articles of Agreement for a treaty between Great Britain and Ireland," signed in London on December 6th, 1921, do not reconcile Irish National aspirations and the Association of Ireland with the Community of Nations known as the British Commonwealth, and cannot be the basis of an enduring peace between the Irish and the British peoples, Dáil Eireann, in the name of the Sovereign Irish Nation, makes to the Government of Great Britain, to the Government of the other States of the British Commonwealth, and to the peoples of Great Britain and of these several States, the following Proposal for a Treaty of Amity and Association which, Dáil Eireann is convinced, could be entered into by the Irish people with the sincerity of goodwill:

PROPOSED TREATY OF ASSOCIATION BETWEEN IRELAND AND THE BRITISH COMMONWEALTH

In order to bring to an end the long and ruinous conflict between Great Britain and Ireland by a sure and lasting peace honourable to both nations, it is agreed

STATUS OF IRELAND

(1) That the legislative, executive, and judicial authority of Ireland shall be derived solely from the people of Ireland.

TERMS OF ASSOCIATION

(2) That, for purposes of common concern, Ireland shall be associated with the States of the British Commonwealth, viz.: the Kingdom of Great Britain, the Dominion of Canada, the Commonwealth of Australia, the Dominion of New Zealand, and the Union of South Africa.

(3) That when acting as an associate the rights, status, and privileges of Ireland shall be in no respect less than those enjoyed by any of the component States of the British Commonwealth.

(4) That the matters of "common concern" shall include Defence, Peace and War, Political Treaties, and all matters now treated as of common concern among the States of the British Commonwealth, and that in these matters there shall be between Ireland and the States of the British Commonwealth "such concerted action founded on consultation as the several Governments may determine."

(5) That in virtue of this association of Ireland with the States of the British Commonwealth citizens of Ireland in any of these States shall not be subject to any disabilities which a citizen of one of the component States of the British Commonwealth would not be subject to, and reciprocally for citizens of these States in Ireland.

(6) That for purposes of the Association, Ireland shall recognize His Britannic Majesty as head of the Association.

DEFENCE . . .

(7) That, so far as her resources permit, Ireland shall provide for her own defence by sea, land, and air, and shall repel by force any attempt by a foreign Power to violate the integrity of her soil and territorial waters, or to use them for any purpose hostile to Great Britain and the other associated States . . .

ADDENDUM

North-East Ulster

That, whilst refusing to admit the right of any part of Ireland to be excluded from the supreme authority of the Parliament of Ireland, or that the relations between the Parliament of Ireland and any subordinate Legislature in Ireland can be a matter for treaty with a government outside Ireland, nevertheless, in sincere regard for internal peace, and in order to make manifest our desire not to bring force or coercion to bear upon any substantial part of the province of Ulster, whose inhabitants may now be unwilling to accept the national authority, we are prepared to grant to that portion of Ulster which is defined as Northern Ireland in the British Government of Ireland Act of 1920, privileges and safeguards not less substantial than those provided for in the Articles of Agreement for a Treaty between Great Britain and Ireland signed in London on December 6th, 1921.

Source: National Archives of Ireland, Department
of the Taoiseach (TSCH/3/S9302 A).

DOCUMENT 16: Excerpts from the Treaty Debates, 19 December 1921

ARTHUR GRIFFITH: Nearly three months ago Dáil Eireann appointed plenipotentiaries to go to London to treat with the British Government and to make a bargain with them. We have made a bargain. We have brought it back. We were to go there to reconcile our aspirations with the association of the community of nations known as the British Empire. That task which was given to us was as hard as was ever placed on the shoulders of men. We faced that task; we knew that whatever happened we would have our critics, and we made up our minds to do whatever was right and disregard whatever criticism might occur. We could have shirked the responsibility. We did not seek to act as the plenipotentiaries; other men were asked and other men refused. We went. The responsibility is on our shoulders; we took the responsibility in London and we take the responsibility in Dublin. I signed that Treaty not as the ideal thing, but fully believing, as I believe now, it is a treaty honourable to Ireland, and safeguards the vital interests of Ireland.

And now by that Treaty I am going to stand, and every man with a scrap of honour who signed it is going to stand. It is for the Irish people—who are our masters (hear, hear), not our servants as some think—it is for the Irish people to say whether it is good enough. I hold that it is, and I hold that the Irish people—that 95 per cent of them believe it to be good enough. We are here, not as the dictators of the Irish people, but as the representatives of the Irish people, and if we misrepresent the Irish people, then the moral authority of Dáil Eireann, the strength behind it, and the fact that Dáil Eireann spoke the voice of the Irish people, is gone, and gone for ever . . .

It has been stated also here that the man who made this position, the man who won the war—Michael Collins— compromised Ireland's rights. In the letters that preceded the negotiations not once was a demand made for recognition of the Irish Republic. If it had been made we knew it would have been refused. We went there to see how to reconcile the two positions, and I hold we have done it . . .

It is the first Treaty between the representatives of the Irish Government and the representatives of the English Government since 1172 signed on equal footing. It is the first Treaty that admits the equality of Ireland. It is a Treaty of equality, and because of that I am standing by it. We have come back from London with that Treaty—Saorstat na hEireann recognised—the Free State of Ireland. We have brought back the flag; we have brought back the evacuation of Ireland after 700 years by British troops and the formation of an Irish army (applause). We have brought back to Ireland her full rights and powers of fiscal control. We have brought back to Ireland equality with England, equality with all nations which form that Commonwealth, and an equal voice in the direction of foreign affairs in peace and war . . . At all events, the Irish people are a people of great common sense. They know that a Treaty that gives them their flag and their Free State and their Army (cheers) is not a sham Treaty, and the sophists and the men of words will not mislead them, I tell you . . .

SEAN MACKEON [Longford I.R.A. Commander]: A Chinn Chomhairle I rise to second the motion, as proposed by the Deputy for West Cavan (Arthur Griffith) and Chairman of the Irish Delegation in London. In doing so, I take this course because I know I am doing it in the interests of my country, which I love. To me symbols, recognitions, shadows, have very little meaning. What I want, what the people of Ireland want, is not shadows but substances, and I hold that this Treaty between the two nations gives us not shadows but real substances, and for that reason I am ready to support it. Furthermore, this Treaty gives Ireland the chance for the first time in 700 years to develop her own life in her own way, to develop Ireland for all, every man and woman, without distinction of creed or class or politics. To me this Treaty gives me what I and my comrades fought for; it gives us for the first time in 700 years the evacuation of Britain's armed forces out of Ireland . . .

EAMON DE VALERA: I think it would scarcely be in accordance with Standing Orders of the Dáil if I were to move directly the rejection of this Treaty. I daresay, however, it will be sufficient that I should appeal to this House not to approve of the Treaty. We were elected by the Irish people, and did the Irish people think we were liars when we said that we meant to uphold the Republic, which was ratified by the vote of the people three years ago, and was further ratified—expressly ratified—by the vote of the people at the elections last May? When the proposal for negotiation came from the British Government asking that we should try by negotiation to reconcile Irish national aspirations with the association of nations forming the British Empire, there was no one here as strong as I was to make sure that every human attempt should be made to find whether such reconciliation was possible. I am against this Treaty because it does not reconcile Irish national aspirations with association with the British Government. I am against this Treaty, not because I am a man of war, but a man of peace. I am against this Treaty because it will not end the centuries of conflict between the two nations of Great Britain and Ireland.

We went out to effect such a reconciliation and we have brought back a thing which will not even reconcile our own people much less reconcile Britain and Ireland.

If there was to be reconciliation, it is obvious that the party in Ireland which typifies national aspirations for centuries should be satisfied, and the test of every agreement would be the test of whether the people were satisfied or not. A war-weary people will take things which are not in accordance with their aspirations. You may have a snatch election now, and you may get a vote of the people, but I will tell you that Treaty will renew the contest that is going to begin the same history that the Union began, and Lloyd George is going to have the same fruit for his labours as Pitt had. When in Downing Street the proposals to which we could unanimously assent in the Cabinet were practically turned down at the point of the pistol and immediate war was threatened upon our people. It was only then that this document was signed, and that document has been signed by plenipotentiaries, not perhaps individually under duress, but it has been signed, and would only affect this nation as a document signed under duress, and this nation would not respect it.

I wanted, and the Cabinet wanted, to get a document we could stand by, a document that could enable Irishmen to meet Englishmen and shake hands with them as fellow-citizens of the world. That document makes British authority our masters in Ireland. It was said that they had only an oath to the British King in virtue of common citizenship, but you have an oath to the Irish Constitution, and that Constitution will be a Constitution which will have the King of Great Britain as head of Ireland. You will swear allegiance to that Constitution and to that King; and if the representatives of the Republic should ask the people of Ireland to do that which is inconsistent with the Republic, I say they are subverting the Republic. It would be a surrender which was never heard of in Ireland since the days of Henry II.; and are we in this generation, which has made Irishmen famous throughout the world, to sign our names to the most ignoble document that could be signed...

The Ministers of Ireland will be His Majesty's Ministers, the Army that Commandant MacKeon spoke of will be His Majesty's Army. (Voices: "No."). ..Well, time will tell, and I hope it won't have a chance, because you will throw this out...I hold, and I don't mind my words being on record, that the chief executive authority in Ireland is the British Monarch—the British authority. It is in virtue of that authority the Irish Ministers will function. It is to the Commander-in-Chief of the Irish Army, who will be the English Monarch, they will swear allegiance, these soldiers of Ireland. It is on these grounds as being inconsistent with our position, and with the whole national tradition for 750 years, that it cannot bring peace. Do you think that because you sign documents like this you can change the current of tradition? You cannot. Some of you are relying on that 'cannot' to sign this Treaty. But don't put a barrier in the way of future generations.

Parnell was asked to do something like this—to say it was a final settlement. But he said, "No man has a right to set." No man "can" is a different thing. "No man has a right" —take the context and you know the meaning. Parnell said practically, "You have no right to ask me, because I have no right to say that any man can set boundaries to the march of a nation." As far as you can, if you take this you are (cries of "No" and "Yes") presuming to set bounds to the onward march of a nation (applause).

> Source: Full text available at http://historical-debates.oireachtas.ie/D/
> DT/D.T.192201070002.html [accessed 2 June 2014].
> See also National Archives of Ireland website Treaty exhibition,
> http://treaty.nationalarchives.ie/document-gallery/anglo-irish-treaty-6-
> december-1921 [accessed 2 June 2014].

DOCUMENT 17: The Second Craig-Collins Pact (extracts)

Heads of agreement between the Provisional Government and Government of Northern Ireland:

(1) Peace is today declared.

(2) From today the two Governments undertake to cooperate in every way in their power with a view to the restoration of peaceful conditions in the unsettled areas.

(3) The Police in Belfast to be organised in general in accordance with the following conditions:

   1. Special police in mixed districts to be composed half of Catholics and half of Protestants, special agreements to be made where Catholics or Protestants are living in other

districts. All specials not required for this force to be withdrawn to their homes and their arms handed in.

2. An Advisory Committee, composed of Catholics, to be set up to assist in the selection of Catholic recruits for the special police.

3. All police on duty, except the usual secret service, to be in uniform and officially numbered.

4. All arms and ammunition issued to police to be deposited in barracks in charge of a military or other competent officer when the policeman is not on duty, and an official record to be kept of all arms issued, and of all ammunition issued and used.

5. Any search for arms to be carried out by police forces composed half of Catholics and half of Protestants, the military rendering any necessary assistance . . .

(5) A Committee to be set up in Belfast of equal number Catholics and Protestants with an independent Chairman, preferably Catholic and Protestant alternately in successive weeks, to hear and investigate complaints as to intimidation, outrages, etc., such Committee to have direct access to the heads of the Government . . .

(6) I.R.A. activities to cease in the Six Counties, and thereupon the method of organising the special police in the Six Counties outside Belfast shall proceed as speedily as possible upon lines similar to those agreed for Belfast.

(7) During the month immediately following the passing into law of the Bill confirming the constitution of the Free State (being the month within which the Northern Parliament is to exercise its option) and before any address in accordance with Article 12 of the Treaty is presented, there shall be a further meeting between the signatories to this agreement with a view to ascertaining:

a. Whether means can be devised to secure the unity of Ireland.

b. Failing this, whether agreement can be arrived at on the boundary question otherwise than by recourse to the Boundary Commission outlined in Article 12 of the Treaty.

(8) The return to their homes of persons who have been expelled to be secured by the respective Governments, the advice of the Committee mentioned in Article 5 to be sought in cases of difficulty.

(9) In view of the special conditions consequent on the political situation in Belfast and neighbourhood, the British Government will submit to Parliament a vote not exceeding £500,000 for the Ministry of Labour of Northern Ireland to be expended exclusively on relief work, one-third for the benefit of Roman Catholics and two-thirds for the benefit of Protestants . . .

(10) The two Governments shall in cases agreed upon between the signatories arrange for the release of political prisoners in prison for offences before the date hereof. No offences committed after March 31st, 1922, shall be open to consideration.

(11) The two Governments unite in appealing to all concerned to refrain from inflammatory speeches and to exercise restraint in the interests of peace.

Signed on behalf of the Provisional Government:

Michael O Coileain (Michael Collins)
Caoimhghin O hUigin (Kevin O'Higgins)
E. S. O. Dugain (Eamon Duggan)
Art O Griobhtha (Arthur Griffith)

Signed on behalf of the Government of Northern Ireland:

James Craig
Londonderry
E. M. Archdale

Countersigned on behalf of the British Government:

Winston S. Churchill
L. Worthington-Evans

Source: National Archives of Ireland, Department of the Taoiseach, S1801A.

DOCUMENT 18: Eamon de Valera's speech at Thurles, County Tipperary, 17 March 1922

If they accepted the Treaty, and if the Volunteers of the future tried to complete the work the Volunteers of the last four years had been attempting, they would have to complete it, not over the bodies of foreign soldiers, but over the dead bodies of their own countrymen. They would have to wade through Irish blood, through the blood of the soldiers of the Irish Government, and through perhaps the blood of some of the members of the Government, in order to get freedom. If they were good enough tomorrow to secure freedom, why should they be not good enough to do it today? If Lloyd George could threaten immediate and terrible war today, he could threaten terrible and immediate war tomorrow. If the Republic went down, it would only be because the Irish people let it down. Even the man with the stake in the country would not like the Treaty when they saw the amount of the national debt they would be saddled with.

Source: *Irish Independent*, 19 March 1922.

DOCUMENT 19: Witness to reprisal attack by Loyalists in Belfast April 1922

In April 1922 a Catholic priest, Patrick Gannon, a visitor to Belfast recalled visiting a house where loyalists had taken revenge on a local Catholic family for the shooting of a policeman a few days earlier.

A family named Walsh lived in the house, of whom the two adult men–brothers–were ex-soldiers who had been through the Great War. As the policemen were beating with a sledge-hammer at the door, the old mother thought it best to open it. They then swept past her and up the narrow stairs to the bedroom where Joseph Walsh lay, with his son Michael aged seven on one side and little Brigid aged two on the other. They fired some shots; for three were found in Michael, who died next morning. Whether they shot the father or not no one seemed to know. But the sledgehammer sufficed. The priest who came to the house within half an hour told me what he saw. The skull was open and empty; while the Whole mass of the brains was on the bolster almost a foot away. On descending they found a young lad, Frank Walsh, aged fourteen, crouching in the kitchen. Him they kicked and shot in the thigh, but not fatally. Thus was Constable Turner avenged. I asked to see the room upstairs. The wife shrank from conducting me. She had not ventured to enter it since that night. But the brother, an ex-soldier, had stronger nerves and showed me all–the bolster soaked with blood, and the two straw mattresses deeply stained with it. He even raised them up and pointed out pieces of the skull upon the floor, and fragments of dried brain. How they swung a sledge-hammer in that narrow space I know not. But the blow smashed the skull as it would a cocoanut. The brother presented me with a few small pieces in paper, and I still retain this gruesome trophy of Belfast civilisation.

Source: Patrick J. Gannon, *Studies, An Irish Quarterly Review*, vol. 11, no. 42 (Jun., 1922), pp. 279–95.

DOCUMENT 20: Civil Authorities (Special Powers) Act (Northern Ireland) 1922 (extracts)

An Act to empower certain authorities of the Government of Northern Ireland to take steps for preserving the peace and maintaining order in Northern Ireland, and for purposes connected therewith.

[7th April, 1922.]

BE it enacted by the King's most Excellent Majesty, and the Senate and the House of Commons of Northern Ireland in this present

Parliament assembled, and by the authority of
the same, as follows

General provisions   **2.**   (1) It shall be the duty of every person affected
as to offences   by any order issued by the civil authority or
other person in pursuance of the regulations to
comply with that order, and if he fails to do
so he shall be guilty of an offence against the
regulations.

(2) Any person who attempts to commit, or
solicits or incites or endeavours to persuade
another person to commit, or procures, aids
or abets, or does any act preparatory to, the
commission of, any act prohibited by the
regulations, or any order, rules or other
instrument made thereunder, or harbours any
person whom he knows, or has reasonable
grounds for supposing, to have acted in
contravention of the regulations, or any order,
rules, or other instrument made thereunder,
shall be guilty of an offence against the
regulations.

(3) It shall be the duty of any person who
knows, or has good reason for believing, that
some other person is acting, has acted, or is
about to act, in contravention of any provisions
of the regulations to inform the civil authority
of the fact, and if he fails to do so he shall be
guilty of an offence against the regulations.

(4) If any person does any act of such a nature
as to be calculated to be prejudicial to the
preservation of the peace or maintenance of
order in Northern Ireland and not specifically
provided for in the regulations, he shall be
deemed to be guilty of an offence against the
regulations.

(5) Where the offence against the regulations
is committed by a corporation or company,
every director and officer of the corporation
or company shall be guilty of the like offence,
unless he proves that the act constituting the
offence took place without his knowledge or
consent.

(6) Where under the regulations any act if
done without lawful authority or without
lawful authority or excuse is an offence

against the regulations, the burden of proving that the act was done with lawful authority or with lawful authority or excuse shall rest on the person alleged to be guilty of the offence.

Trial of offences 3. (1) A person alleged to be guilty of an offence against the regulations may be tried by a court of summary jurisdiction constituted in accordance with this section, and not otherwise . . .

(4) A court of summary jurisdiction when trying a person charged with an offence against the regulations shall be constituted of two or more resident magistrates, but one resident magistrate may act alone in doing anything antecedent to the hearing of the charge under this Act, or in adjourning a court or the hearing of a case, or in committing the defendant to prison or admitting him to bail, until the time to which the court or case has been adjourned; and a court of quarter sessions, when hearing and determining an appeal against a conviction of a court of summary jurisdiction for any such offence, shall be constituted of the recorder or county court judge sitting alone.

Punishment of offences against the regulations 4. A person convicted of an offence against the regulations shall be liable to be sentenced to imprisonment with or without hard labour for a term not exceeding two years or to a fine not exceeding one hundred pounds or to both such imprisonment and fine, and the court may, in addition to any other sentence which may be imposed, order that any goods or articles in respect of which the offence has been committed shall be forfeited.

Special punishments for certain offences 5. Where after trial by any court a person is convicted of any crime or offence to which this section applies, the court may, in addition to any other punishment which may lawfully be imposed, order such person, if a male, to be once privately whipped, and the provisions of subsection (6) of section thirty-seven of the Larceny Act, 1916, as to sentences of whipping shall apply accordingly.

The crimes and offences to which this section applies are as follows: –

(1) Any crime under the Explosive Substances Act, 1883, as extended by section eighteen of the Firearms Act, 1920.

(2) Any offence against the Firearms Act, 1920, in relation to the having, keeping or using of firearms.

(3) Any offence against the regulations in relation to the carrying, having or keeping of firearms, military arms, ammunition or explosive substances.

(4) Any offence against section thirty of the Larceny Act, 1916, (which relates to demanding with menaces, with intent to steal).

(5) Arson, whether by common law or by statute, and any offence punishable on indictment under the Malicious Damage Act, 1861.

Provided that this section shall not be deemed to apply to any crime or offence committed before the passing of this Act.

Death penalty   6.   A crime under section two or section three of the Explosive Substances Act, 1883, shall be a crime punishable by death: provided that this section shall not apply to any such crime committed before the passing of this Act.

Where a sentence of death is pronounced by the court upon conviction for a crime to which this section applies, the sentence may be pronounced and carried into execution, and all other proceedings thereupon and in respect thereof may be had and taken, in the same manner as sentence might have been pronounced and carried into execution, and proceedings might have been had and taken, upon a conviction for murder.

Power of arrest   7.   Any person authorised by the civil authority, or any police constable, or any member of any of His Majesty's forces on duty may, where it is necessary for the purpose of effecting an arrest in respect of any crime or any offence against the regulations, exercise the like powers as may at common law be exercised by a police constable in effecting arrest in a case where a felony has been committed . . .

Provisions as to inquests

10. (1) For the purpose of preserving the peace and maintaining order, the Minister of Home Affairs may by order:–

(a) Prohibit the holding of inquests by coroners on dead bodies in any area in Northern Ireland specified in the order, either absolutely or except in such circumstances or on such conditions as may be specified in the order; or,

(b) Prohibit the holding of any particular inquest specified in the order; and

(c) Provide for the duties of a coroner and a coroner's jury (or of either of them) as respects any inquest prohibited by the order being performed by such officer or court as may be determined by the order.

(2) Any such officer or court shall have and may exercise, for the purposes of any inquiry directed to be held in pursuance of such order or any report thereon, all or any of the powers which might have been exercised by the coroner or coroner's jury for the purposes of the inquest which has been prohibited and the finding thereon, whether conferred by statute or at common law . . .

Duration of Act

12. This Act shall continue in force for one year and no longer, unless Parliament otherwise determines.

SCHEDULE.

REGULATIONS FOR PEACE AND ORDER IN NORTHERN IRELAND.

1. The civil authority may by order require every person within any area specified in the order to remain within doors between such hours as may be specified in the order, and in such case, if any person within that area is or remains out between such hours without a permit in writing from the civil authority or some person duly authorised by him, he shall be guilty of an offence against these regulations.

2. The civil authority may by order

   (1) Require all or any licensed premises within any area specified in the order to be closed, either altogether, or subject to such exceptions as to hours and purposes, and to compliance with such directions, as may be specified in the order

   (2) Make such provisions as he thinks necessary for the prevention of the practice of treating in any licensed premises within any area specified in the order . . .

3. (1) The civil authority may make orders prohibiting or restricting in any area

   (a) The holding of or taking part in meetings, assemblies (excluding fairs and markets), or processions in public places;

   (b) The use or wearing or possession of uniforms or badges of a naval, military or police character, or of uniforms or badges indicating membership of any association or body specified in the order;

   (c) The carrying in public places of weapons of offence or articles capable of being used as such;

   (d) The carrying, having or keeping of firearms, military arms, ammunition or explosive substances; and

   (e) The having, keeping, or using of a motor or other cycle, or motor car by any person, other than a member of a police force, without a permit from the civil authority, or from the chief officer of the police in the district in which the person resides . . .

10. No person shall, without lawful authority, collect, record, publish or communicate, or attempt to elicit, any information with respect to the movement, numbers, description, condition, or disposition of any police force . . .

11. No person without lawful authority shall injure, or tamper or interfere with, any wire or other apparatus for transmitting telegraphic or telephonic messages, or any apparatus or contrivance intended for or capable of being used for a signalling apparatus . . .

12. If any person, without lawful authority or excuse, uses or has in his possession or under his control any cipher, code, or other means adapted for secretly communicating information which may be prejudicial to the preservation of peace or the maintenance of order he shall be guilty of an offence against these regulations . . .

13. If any person does any injury to any railway, or is upon any railway, or on, under or near any tunnel, bridge, viaduct, or culvert, or loiters on or in any road or path or other place near a railway

tunnel, bridge, viaduct or culvert, with intent to do injury thereto, he shall be guilty of an offence against these regulations.

Source: National Archives of Ireland, Office of the Attorney General, 2002/15/15.

DOCUMENT 21: Report from Seamus Woods, officer commanding the IRA's 3rd Northern Division, July 1922

After a period of over five weeks the demoralisation has practically completed its work . . . The position in No.2 and 3 Brigades of 3rd Northern Division today is that the Military Organisation is almost destroyed [and the enemy] believe that they have beaten the IRA completely in Antrim and Down . . . The people who supported us feel they have been let down by Dáil Eireann, for our position today is more unbearable than it was in June 1921 . . . Today the people feel that all their suffering has been in vain and cannot see any hope for the future.

Source: Seamus Woods' memorandum, 27 June 1922, Mulcahy Papers, University College Dublin Archives, P7/B/1.

DOCUMENT 22: Notes of a conference with the Irish Boundary Commission held in Stanley Baldwin's Room, House of Commons, 3 December 1925

THE PRIME MINISTER stated that he had just had a short conversation with Mr. Justice Feetham and Mr. Fisher, and had given to them a brief résumé of the happenings of the last few days. He had indicated to them that a settlement was about to be reached which was agreeable to the three Governments, and he had explained that if the Agreement were ratified, it would supersede the Commissioners' Report. A difficult situation had arisen, but he was sure that all would wish to help each other . . .

MR. JUSTICE FEETHAM said that he wished to make the following points on behalf of Mr. Fisher and himself. The terms of the proposed Award had been agreed in October. The Commission had studied the matter carefully, had heard everybody, and while the Award would disappoint many, it would also meet the wishes of many on the Border, and remove difficulties which were severely felt. The present Border was an accident. The grievances found at particular places were serious . . .

MR. COSGRAVE said that it had been his deliberate opinion all through that there was bound to be dissensions whatever the verdict; that it would leave bitterness behind. The Award involved the transfer of a considerable number of people from one area to another . . .

MR. COSGRAVE said that he. . .had made up his mind that if good relations with Ulster were to be secured, they had better come by voluntary growth, and that any cast-iron agreement would be thwarted by the supporters of Sir James and by his own. It was important to avoid providing a rallying ground for agitation . . .

MR. COSGRAVE He did not wish to speak disrespectfully, but he believed that it would be in the interests of Irish peace that the Report should be burned or buried, because another set of circumstances had arrived, and a bigger settlement had been reached beyond any that the Award of the Commission could achieve.

SIR JAMES CRAIG said that the matter divided itself in two. If the settlement succeeded it would be a great dis-service to Ireland, North and South, to have a map produced showing what would have been the position of the persons on the Border had the Award been made. If the settlement came off and nothing was published, no-one would know what would have been its fate . . .

MR. CHURCHILL said he would beg the Commission to leave their reputation in the hands of the three Governments. Let them make their report to the British Government and leave it to their discretion. As a historical document it might some day appear. At present it was absolutely in the public interest to merge it in the happier prospect, although it had been the vehicle and agency by which the miracle of peace had come about.

Source: National Archives of Ireland,
Department of the Taoiseach, S4720A.

NOTES

Introduction

1 See D. Fitzpatrick, *Politics and Irish Life, 1913–21: Provincial Experience of War and Revolution* (Dublin, 1977); C. Townshend, *The British Campaign in Ireland, 1919–1921: The Development of Political and Military Policies* (Oxford, 1975) and P. Hart, *The I.R.A. and its Enemies: Violence and Community in Cork, 1916–1923* (Oxford, 1998).

2 See for example the set of challenging essays from leading authorities in the period in J. Augusteijn (ed.), *The Irish Revolution, 1913–1923* (London, 2002).

3 Regan, J. *The Irish Counter-Revolution, 1921–1936* (Dublin, 1999), p. 378.

Chapter 1

1 Hyde, D. *The Religious Songs of Connacht* (Dublin, 1906), p. 4.

2 Townshend, C. *Easter 1916: The Irish Rebellion* (London, 2006), p. 84.

Chapter 2

1 Lewis, G. *Carson: The Man who Divided Ireland* (London, 2004), p. 163.

Chapter 3

1 Jackson, A. *Home Rule: An Irish History* (Oxford, 2003), p. 145.

2 Jeffery, K. *Ireland and the Great War* (Cambridge, 2000).

3 For detailed descriptions of the Rising outside of Dublin see M. Foy and B. Barton, *The Easter Rising* (Gloucester, 1999).

4 Kiberd, D. (ed.), *1916 Rebellion Handbook* (Savannah, 1998).

5 Dorney, J. *The Story of the Easter Rising 1916* (Green Lamp, 2010).

Chapter 4

1 Kautt, W. H. *The Anglo-Irish War, 1916–21* (New York, 1999), p. 65.

2 Hart, P. *Mick: The Real Michael Collins* (London, 2005), p. 98.

3 Hopkinson, M. A. *The Irish War of Independence* (Dublin, 2002), p. 104.

4 Laffan, M. *The Resurrection of Ireland: The Sinn Fein Party 1916–1923* (Cambridge, 1999).

5 Hopkinson, M. A. *The Irish War of Independence* (Dublin, 2002), p. 104.

6 Rees, R. *Ireland 1905–25. Volume I: Text and Historiography* (Newtownnards, 1998), p. 226.

7 Coogan, T. P. *Michael Collins* (London, 1991), p. 111.

8 English, R. *Armed Struggle: The History of the IRA* (London, 2003), p. 12.

9 'Sinn Fein and Ulster', *Notes from Ireland*, 26, no. 4 (1917), p. 74.

10 *Sligo Champion*, 28 July 1917.

11 *Freeman's Journal*, 28 January 1918.

12 *Irish Times*, 9 February 1918.

Chapter 5

1 Hopkinson, M. A. *The Irish War of Independence* (Dublin, 2002), p. 105.

2 Townshend, C. 'The Irish Republican Army and the development of guerrilla warfare, 1916–1921', *The English Historical Review*, 94, no. 371 (1979), p. 337.

3 Dwyer, T. Ryle, *The Squad: The Intelligence Operations of Michael Collins* (Mercier, 2005).

4 Foy, M. *Michael Collins's Intelligence War: The Struggle between the British and the IRA 1919–1921* (Gloucester, 2006).

5 For a fuller examination of IRA tactics and counter-insurgency tactics see W. H. Kautt, *Ambushes and Armour: The Irish Rebellion 1919–21* (Dublin, 2010).

6 Hart, P. *The I.R.A. and its Enemies: Violence and Community in Cork, 1916–1923* (Oxford, 1998).

7 Hopkinson, M. A. *The Irish War of Independence* (Dublin, 2002), p. 82.

8 Dwyer, T. Ryle *The Squad and the Intelligence Operations of Michael Collins*, (Dublin, 2005), p. 191.

9 Sheehan, W. *British Voices from the Irish War of Independence 1918–1921* (Cork, 2007).

10 Hopkinson, M. A. *The Irish War of Independence* (Dublin, 2002).

Chapter 6

1 Foster, R. F. *Modern Ireland 1600–1972* (London, 1988), p. 505.
2 Hopkinson, M. A. *Green Against Green: The Irish Civil War* (Dublin, 1988), p. 45.
3 *Irish Times*, 20 January 1922.
4 *Evening Herald*, 18 December 1922.

Chapter 7

1 *Sunday Express*, 19 June 1921.
2 *Daily Chronicle*, 22 June 1921.
3 Copy of a letter to 'My Dear Stewart', from Hugh de Fellenberg Montgomery, Fivemiletown, Co. Tyrone, 17 June 1916, Montgomery Papers, PRONI, D627/429/39.
4 Candidates for the election consisted of 40 Unionists, 19 Sinn Fein, 11 UIL and 5 independent nominees.
5 Louis J. Walsh to Harry Boland, 4 Jan. 1919, Count Plunkett Papers, N.L.I., Ms 11,405.
6 *Northern Whig*, 21 May 1921. For a broader view of the nature of Sinn Fein's attempts to appeal to Unionists see Richard Davis, 'Ulster Protestants and the Sinn Fein Press, 1914–22', *Eire Ireland*, XV (Winter 1980).
7 *Irish News*, 18 May 1921.
8 Donnelly to O'Keeffe, 24 May 1921, de Valera Papers, 140.
9 For an analysis of Sinn Fein's propaganda efforts prior to the election, see Keiko Inoue 'Sinn Féin Propaganda and the "Partition Election", 1921', *Studia Hibernica*, no. 30 (1998/1999), pp. 47–61.
10 *Chicago Tribune*, 15 April 1921.
11 See Lynch, R. ' "The People's Protectors?" The I.R.A. and the Belfast Pogrom', *Journal of British Studies*, no. 2 (April 2008).
12 *Nationality*, 9 February 1918.
13 Griffith, A. *The Resurrection of Hungary* (Dublin, 1904), p. 79.
14 *Irish News*, 17 May 1921.
15 Hand, G. J. *Report of the Irish Boundary Commission* (Shannon, 1969), p. xii.
16 Mansergh, N. *Nationalism and Independence: Selected Irish Papers* (Cork, 1997), p. 17.
17 James Craig to Austen Chamberlain, 15 December 1921 quoted in M. A. Hopkinson, *Green Against Green: The Irish Civil War* (Dublin, 1988), p. 147.
18 House of Commons Debates, 14 December 1921, vol. 149, cols. 38–9.
19 Diary of Lady Lillian Spender, 25 June 1923, Spender Papers, PRONI (D/1633/2/26).

20 Letter to Hugh de Fellenberg Montgomery, Fivemiletown, Co. Tyrone, from Charles Frederick D'Arcy, Bishop of Down, 12 May 1917, Montgomery Papers, PRONI (D627/430/8).

21 Herbert Asquith, speech in House of Commons, 30 September 1924, House of Commons Debates, vol. 177, col. 46.

22 Winston Churchill, House of Commons Debates, 16 February 1922, vol. 150, col. 1270.

23 Martin, G. *The Irish Border: History, Politics, Culture* (Liverpool, 1999), p. 148.

24 Cosgrave to MacNeill, 22 December 1925, MacNeill Papers, LA1/H/126.

25 Hansard, *House of Lords*, series 5, vol. 59, cols. 653–4 and 662–3 (8 October 1924).

26 James Craig, Northern Ireland House of Commons, 7 December 1922, vol. 2, cols. 1151–2.

27 See Hand, *Boundary Commission*, pp. 29–41.

28 House of Commons Debates, 14 December 1921, vol. 149, cols. 39–40.

Chapter 8

1 Hopkinson, M. A. *Green Against Green: The Irish Civil War* (Dublin, 1988), p. 46.

2 For a detailed analysis of the political aspects of the Irish Civil War, see Kissane, B. *The Politics of the Irish Civil War* (Oxford, 2005).

3 Hopkinson, M. A. *Green Against Green: The Irish Civil War* (Dublin, 1988), p. 258.

4 Hopkinson, M. A. *Green Against Green: The Irish Civil War* (Dublin, 1988), p. 248.

SELECT BIBLIOGRAPHY

Abbott, R.	*Police Casualties in Ireland, 1919–1922* (Dublin, 2000).
Andrews, C. S.	*Dublin Made Me: An Autobiography* (Dublin, 1979).
Augusteijn, J.	*From Public Defiance to Guerrilla Warfare: The Experience of Ordinary Volunteers in the Irish War of Independence 1916–1921* (Dublin, 1996).
	— (ed.) *The Irish Revolution, 1913–1923* (London, 2002).
Bardon, J.	*A History of Ulster* (Belfast, 1992).
Barry, T.	*Guerrilla Days in Ireland* (Cork, 1955).
Beckett, J. C.	*The Making of Modern Ireland, 1603–1923* (London, 1966).
Bell, J. Bowyer	*The Secret Army: A History of the I.R.A., 1916–70* (London, 1972).
Bew, P.	*Ideology and the Irish Question: Ulster Unionism and Irish Nationalism, 1912–1916* (Oxford, 1994).
	— Gibbon, P. and Patterson, H. *The State in Northern Ireland 1921–72* (Manchester, 1979).
Bowman, J.	*De Valera and the Ulster Question*, 1917–73 (Oxford, 1982).
Boyce, D. G.	*Englishmen and Irish Troubles: British Public Opinion and the Making of Irish Policy, 1918–22* (London, 1972).
	— *Nationalism in Ireland* (London, 1995).
	— (ed.) *The Revolution in Ireland, 1879–1922* (Dublin, 1988).
	— and O'Day. A. (eds.) *The Making of Modern Irish History: Revisionism and the Revisionist Controversy* (London, 1996).
	— *Ireland 1828–1923: From Ascendancy to Democracy* (Oxford, 1992)
Brady, C. (ed.)	*Interpreting Irish History: The Debate on Historical Revisionism* (Dublin, 1994).
Breen, D.	*My Fight for Irish Freedom* (Tralee, 1964).
Brewer, J.	*The Royal Irish Constabulary: An Oral History* (Belfast, 1990).

Buckland, P. *Irish Unionism: The Anglo-Irish and the New Ireland, 1885–1923: A Documentary History* (Belfast, 1973).
— *Ulster Unionism and the Origins of Northern Ireland 1886–1922* (Dublin, 1973)
— *The Factory of Grievances: Devolved Government in Northern Ireland 1921–39* (Dublin, 1979).
— *James Craig* (Dublin, 1980).
— *A History of Northern Ireland* (Dublin, 1981).

Budge, I. and O'Leary, C. *Belfast: Approach to Crisis: A Study of Belfast Politics, 1603–1970* (London, 1973).

Clark, W. *Guns in Ulster: A History of the 'B' Special Constabulary in Part of County Derry* (Belfast, 1967).

Coleman, M. *County Longford and the Irish Revolution, 1910–1923* (Dublin, 2003).

Coogan, T. P. *Michael Collins* (London, 1991).

Dangerfield, G. *The Damnable Question: A Study in Anglo-Irish Relations* (London, 1977).

Denman, T. *Ireland's Unknown Soldiers: The 16th (Irish) Division in the Great War* (Dublin, 1992).

Doak, J. C. 'Rioting and Civil Strife in the City of Londonderry during the 19th and early 20th centuries' (unpublished MA thesis, Queen's University, Belfast, 1978).

Elliott, M. *The Catholics of Ulster* (London, 2000).

Elliott, S. *Northern Ireland Parliamentary Election Results 1921–1972* (Belfast, 1973).

English, R. *Ernie O'Malley: I.R.A. Intellectual* (Oxford, 1998).
— *Armed Struggle: The History of the IRA* (London, 2003).
— and Walker, G. (eds.) *Unionism in Modern Ireland* (Dublin, 1996).

Fanning, R. 'Anglo-Irish Relations: Partition and the British Dimension in Historical Perspective' *Irish Studies in International Affairs*, vol. 2, no. 1 (1982).
— *Independent Ireland* (Dublin, 1983).

Farrell, M. *Northern Ireland: The Orange State* (London, 1980).
— *Arming the Protestants: The Formation of the Ulster Special Constabulary and the Royal Ulster Constabulary 1920–1927* (London, 1983).

Farry, M *The Aftermath of Revolution: Sligo 1921–23* (Dublin, 2000).

Fitzpatrick, D. *Politics and Irish Life, 1913–21: Provincial Experience of War and Revolution* (Dublin, 1977).
— *The Two Irelands, 1912–1939* (Oxford, 1998).

Follis, B.   *A State Under Siege: The Establishment of
                                Northern Ireland 1920–1925* (Oxford, 1995).
Forester, M.   *Michael Collins – The Lost Leader* (London,
                                1972).
Foster, R. F.   *Modern Ireland, 1600–1972* (London, 1988).
Fox, C.   *The Making of a Minority: Political
                                Developments in Derry and the North,
                                1912–1925* (Derry, 1997).
Garvin, T.   *The Evolution of Irish Nationalist Politics*
                                (Dublin, 1981).
                                — *1922: The Birth of Irish Democracy* (Dublin,
                                1996).
Gaughan J. (ed.)   *Memoirs of Senator Joseph Connolly* (Dublin,
                                1996).
Gilbert, M.   *Winston S. Churchill* vol. iv, *1916–22* (London,
                                1975).
Greaves, D. G.   *Liam Mellows and the Irish Revolution* (London,
                                1971).
Griffith, K. and O'Grady, T.   *Curious Journey: An Oral History of Ireland's
                                Unfinished Revolution* (Dublin, 1982).
Gwynn, D.   *The History of Partition, 1912–1925* (London,
                                1950).
Hand, G. (ed.)   *Report of the Irish Boundary Commission*
                                (Shannon, 1969).
                                — 'MacNeill and the Boundary Commission' in
                                F. X. Martin and F. J. Byrne (eds.) *The Scholar
                                Revolutionary: Eoin MacNeill, 1867–1945, and
                                the Making of the New Ireland* (Shannon, 1973).
Harbinson, J. F.   *The Ulster Unionist Party, 1882–1973: Its
                                Development and Organisation* (Belfast,
                                1973).
Harkness, D.   *The Restless Dominion* (London, 1969).
                                — *Northern Ireland since 1920* (Dublin, 1983).
Harris, M.   *The Catholic Church and the Foundation of the
                                Northern Irish State* (Belfast, 1993).
Hart, P   'Michael Collins and the assassination of Sir
                                Henry Wilson', *Irish Historical Studies*, xxviii,
                                no. 110 (November 1992).
                                — *The I.R.A. and its Enemies: Violence and
                                Community in Cork, 1916–1923* (Oxford,
                                1998).
                                — *The I.R.A. at War* (Oxford, 2003).
Hepburn, A. C. (ed.)   *Minorities in History* (London, 1978).
                                — *A Past Apart: Studies in the History of
                                Catholic Belfast, 1850–1950* (Belfast, 1996).
Hezlet, Sir. A.   *The 'B' Specials: A History of the Ulster Special
                                Constabulary* (London, 1973).
Hopkinson, M. A.   *Green Against Green: The Irish Civil War*
                                (Dublin, 1988).

— 'The Craig-Collins Pacts of 1922: two attempted reforms of the Northern Irish government', *Irish Historical Studies,* xxvii, no. 106 (November 1990).

— *The Irish War of Independence* (Dublin, 2004).

Jackson, A.   *Ireland, 1798–1998* (Oxford, 1999).

Johnson, D. J.   'The Belfast Boycott, 1920–22' in J. M. Goldstrom and J. A. Clarkson (eds.) *Irish Population, Economy and Society: Essays in Honour of the Late K.H. Connell* (Oxford, 1981).

Kautt, W. H.   *Ambushes and Armour: The Irish Rebellion 1919–21* (Dublin, 2010).

Kelly, B. (ed.)   *Sworn to be Free: The Complete Book of I.R.A. Jailbreaks 1918–1921* (Tralee, 1971).

Kennedy, D.   *The Widening Gulf: Northern Attitudes to the Independent Irish State, 1919–1945* (Belfast, 1988).

Keogh, D.   *Twentieth-Century Ireland: Nation and State* (Dublin, 1994).

Kiely, B.   *Counties of Contention* (Cork, 1945).

Kleinrichert, D.   *Republican Internment and the Prison Ship Argenta 1922* (Dublin, 2001).

Laffan, M   *The Partition of Ireland 1911–1925* (Dublin, 1983).

— *The Resurrection of Ireland: The Sinn Fein Party 1916–1923* (Cambridge, 1999).

Lee, J.   *The Modernisation of Irish Society, 1848–1918* (Dublin, 1989).

— *Ireland, 1912–1985: Politics and Society* (Cambridge, 1988).

Lyons, F. S. L.   *Ireland since the Famine* (London, 1973).

— *Culture and Anarchy in Ireland, 1890–1939* (Oxford, 1979).

Longford and O'Neill, T. P.   *Eamon de Valera* (London, 1974).

Macardle, D.   *The Irish Republic 1911–1925: A Documented Chronicle* (London, 1937).

MacDonagh, O.   *Ireland: The Union and its Aftermath* (London, 1977).

MacEoin, U.   *Survivors* (Dublin, 1980).

Maguire, G.   'The Political and Military Causes of the Division in the Irish Nationalist Movement, January 1921-August 1922' (Unpublished DPhil thesis, University of Oxford, 1985).

Mansergh, N.   *The Irish Free State* (London, 1934).

— *The Government of Northern Ireland: A Study in Devolution* (London, 1936).

Matthews, K.   *Fatal Influence: The Impact of Ireland on British Politics* (Dublin, 2004).

McColgan, J.   *British Policy and Irish Administration 1920–22* (Dublin, 1983).

McDermott, J.	*Northern Divisions: The Old I.R.A. and the Belfast Pogroms, 1920–22* (Belfast, 2001).
Mercer, E.	'For King, country and a shilling a day: Belfast recruiting patterns in the Great War', *History Ireland*, 11, no. 4 (Winter 2003).
Miller, D.	*Queen's Rebels: Ulster Loyalism in Historical Perspective* (Dublin, 1978).
Mitchell, A.	*Labour in Irish Politics, 1890–1930* (Dublin, 1973).
	— *Revolutionary Government in Ireland: Dáil Eireann, 1919–22* (Dublin, 1995).
Morgan, A.	*Labour and Partition: The Belfast Working Class and the Belfast Labour Movement, 1868–1920* (London, 1991).
Murphy, R.	'Walter Long and the making of the Government of Ireland Act, 1919–20', *Irish Historical Studies*, lxxxvii (1986).
Murray, C.	'The 1918 General Election in the three Derry constituencies' (unpublished thesis, Queen's University Belfast, 1990).
Murray, P.	*The Irish Boundary Commission and its Origins 1886–1925* (Dublin, 2011).
O'Broin, L.	*Michael Collins* (Dublin, 1983).
O'Donnell, P.	*The Gates Flew Open* (London, 1932).
O'Donoghue, F.	*No Other Law* (Dublin, 1954).
O'Drisceoil, D.	*Peadar O'Donnell* (Cork, 2001).
O'Halpin, E.	*The Decline of the Union: British Government in Ireland, 1892–1920* (Dublin, 1987).
O'Mahoney, S.	*Frongoch: University of Revolution* (Dublin, 1987).
O'Malley, E.	*On Another Man's Wound* (London, 1936).
	— *The Singing Flame* (Dublin, 1978).
Patterson, H.	*Class, Conflict and Sectarianism: The Protestant Working Class and the Belfast Labour Movements, 1868–1920* (Belfast, 1980).
Phoenix, E.	'Political violence, Diplomacy and the Catholic Minority in Northern Ireland, 1922' in J. Darby, N. Dodge and A. C. Hepburn (eds.) *Political Violence: Ireland in a Comparative Perspective* (Belfast, 1990).
	— *Northern Nationalism: Nationalist Politics. Partition and the Catholic Minority in Northern Ireland 1890–1940* (Belfast, 1994).
	— 'Michael Collins: The Northern Question 1916–22' in G. Doherty and D. Keogh (eds.) *Michael Collins and the Making of the Irish State* (Cork, 1998).
Quinn, R. J.	*A Rebel Voice: A History of Belfast Republicanism, 1925–1972* (Belfast, 1999).

Regan, J.   *The Irish Counter-Revolution, 1921–1936*
                                   (Dublin, 1999).
Rumpf, E. and Hepburn, A. C.   *Nationalism and Socialism in Twentieth Century*
                                   Ireland (Liverpool, 1977).
Shearman, H.   *Northern Ireland, 1921–1971* (Belfast, 1971).
Simkins, P.   *Kitchener's Armies: The Raising of the New*
                                   Armies, 1914–16 (Manchester, 1988).
Smith, J.   *Britain and Ireland: From Home Rule to*
                                   Independence (London, 1999).
Staunton, E.   *The Nationalists of Northern Ireland 1918–1973*
                                   (New York, 2001).
Stewart, A. T. Q.   *The Narrow Ground: Aspects of Ulster,*
                                   1609–1969 (London, 1977).
                                   — *Edward Carson* (Dublin, 1981).
Sweeney, J.   'Donegal and the War of Independence' in
                                   Capuchin Annual (1970).
Townshend, C.   *The British Campaign in Ireland, 1919–1921:*
                                   The Development of Political and Military
                                   Policies (Oxford, 1975).
                                   — 'The Irish Republican Army and the
                                   development of guerrilla warfare, 1916–1921',
                                   English Historical Review, 94, no. 371 (April
                                   1979).
                                   — *Political Violence in Ireland* (Oxford, 1983).
                                   —*The Republic: The Fight for Irish*
                                   Independence, 1918–1923 (London, 2013).
Towey, T.   'The Reaction of the British Government to the
                                   1922 Collins-De Valera Pact', *Irish Historical*
                                   Studies, xxii, no. 85 (March 1980).
Urquhart, D.   *Women in Ulster Politics, 1890–1940* (Dublin,
                                   2000).
Vaughan, W. E. (ed.)   *A New History of Ireland*, vol. VI: *Ireland Under*
                                   the Union II, 1870–1921 (Oxford, 1996).
Walker, B. M.   *Parliamentary Election Results in Ireland,*
                                   1801–1922 (Dublin, 1978).
Walsh, O.   *Ireland's Independence, 1880–1923* (Abingdon,
                                   2002).
Younger, C.   *Ireland's Civil War* (London, 1982).

Index

www.ingramcontent.com/pod-product-compliance
Lightning Source LLC
Chambersburg PA
CBHW050444280326

41932CB00013BA/2241